AND YOU MAY FIND YOURSELF

A Guided Practice To Never Fearing Death Again

GERRY MURPHY

Paperback ISBN: 978-1-7348376-0-5
Hardcover ISBN: 978-1-7348376-1-2
eBook ISBN: 978-1-7348376-2-9

SEL031000 SELF-HELP / Personal Growth / General
BIO026000 BIOGRAPHY & AUTOBIOGRAPHY / Personal Memoirs

Cover design by Lisa Barbee
Typeset by Kaitlin Barwick

For my children, Kevin, Caitlin, and Frances.
In the days captured here, I saw you all most clearly.
I celebrated what you each bring to the world and grieved
for what I would miss. My love for you took on new
dimensions that I didn't believe possible. I hope this
book helps you see me more clearly, now and later.

For my wife, Jen. Thank you for your love, strength
and support in getting me through this. And for continuing all of them while I wrote about it.

spread your wings
above you
the time has come to fly
away in time
where I can't choose to follow
I was not born to fly
away in time

—"Hellespont in a Storm," Chris Thomson, The Bathers

CONTENTS

CONTENTS

SIDE 1

INTRODUCTION

And You May Find Yourself . . .

INTRO TRACK: ONCE IN A LIFETIME

And you may ask yourself, well
How did I get here?

—Talking Heads

I have been encouraged to write this story by several people whose opinion I respect greatly. When I tell this story in full, the listener's conclusion is always the same—you have to write this down! And as I've thought about it, why *not* write it down? It's kind of incredible really. Fateful, dark, breathtaking, inspiring, and cause for pause. "Something for everyone" as a well-worn phrase from my marketing world would often promise.

Let me also say that I know many people have gone through much worse and not survived. Indeed, many people have gone through much worse and continue to live with the daily impacts of those challenges. I know how lucky I am, and none of this is meant to glorify my survival or to minimize any suffering anyone goes through. I've had that loss in my own family. This is a story of survival, of crazy circumstances, of the realization of what is really important. It's a story about not taking anything for granted.

I am not going to give you the big set up with my backstory and full history. I will say I have lived a full, blessed, and interesting life of forty-nine years prior to the starting point of this story. Sure there is some interesting stuff, but I will use that to color in some of the moments that are pivotal to this part of my story. So I will start at the end, or what could have been the end.

There are two recurring themes that are central to this story that I would like you to be aware of right from the start. They both need some explanation:

1. Practicing Death

As I went through my discovery process to write this book, a certain theme became intrinsic to its construct. It really is what I hope you take away from the book. My gift to you is that by sharing this story, you get a ten-year head start on what I came face to face with. If it was not for the grace and intervention of some higher power, I may not have had the chance to share it with you.

I saw a play on Broadway recently called *Sea Wall/A Life*, written by Simon Stephens and Nick Payne. The production consists of two monologues by two different actors. In the first, the actor (Tom Sturridge) deals with unbearable loss through reliving and recounting the story. In the second, the actor (Jake Gyllenhaal) is dealing with the arrival of his first child juxtaposed against the terminal illness of his father. They are beautifully written pieces that make you feel guilty for laughing and repeatedly expose your most vulnerable emotions. Gyllenhaal's monologue has a line that hits home. His wife is going into labor, and she tells him to "Get the list! Get the list!" In his panic, he rushes off to get the list but then stops abruptly. He looks out to the audience, as if conversing with us, and says, "Here we have a list for someone who isn't even here yet. So why are we so fucking bad at death?"

We are pretty bad at death. My story exposed me to this firsthand. And I think we need some practice.

The theme of "practicing death" is about putting yourself in a situation where you strip back your life to a level that is in tune with what is in your heart and connects with what matters to you the most. I believe that by reenacting a version of this story, you can create an environment that allows you to make that evaluation. My purpose in telling my story is to reveal that you don't have to wait until you face a life-or-death situation before you start the process of evaluating your life. The end goal is that the personal transformation you want for yourself can come to you on your own terms.

What if you had the chance to experience certain elements of death but were given the greatest gift of surviving it? Let's not think of it as a mulligan but more of a reset or reboot! What would you do? If the dead could be our advisors, what would they tell us? What would they tell you, and what would you change?

In each chapter, I will reflect on what it has meant to me and how it has in some way shaped my outlook, if not my actions. (There will be more on the difference between the two later on!)

2. My Soundtrack

The second theme is somewhat quirky but remains true today. I have always had this ability to "hear" life moments with songs. Some emotional connective tissue between what I am feeling and what I have heard. Maybe it's some form of synesthesia or maybe it's just how music talks to me and echoes through my life. The soundtrack for this story will weave its way throughout, sometimes because those songs were protagonists at that time or in some cases because they sum up the feeling and sentiment from each chapter.

There is a song for every chapter, and indeed this view gave me the title right away. Right from that first day in the ER, the song and lyrics that played over and over in my head was "Once in a Lifetime" by Talking Heads. David Byrne, the lead singer, is also Scottish and was born across the River Clyde near Glasgow, close to where I did a large part of my growing up. A little touch of home. Maybe that is what took me there, memories of a simpler time, as I faced a challenge that it was far from clear that I was going to survive.

Music has been my constant companion throughout my life, going back to the days growing up when I only had a cassette recorder. I played those tapes until they needed to be spooled back in with a pencil—that was a valuable skill back in the day. It wasn't an insular passion though. I always wanted to share it with others, and my adolescent years were spent doing just that. The music was also a gateway for me, either in reference or in influences to the performers. It opened me up to the worlds of Warhol, Cocteau, Kerouac, Salinger, Rockwell, Keats, Monroe, Dean, and so many others. These worlds transcended my West of Scotland high school education curriculum and were way

more captivating, enchanting, and influential. It was only logical that this would be my dream too.

I was always a wannabe. I wanted to be in a band my whole
life. And I have been. It started in high school, then I was in
a university band then through the rest of my life—whenever
there was a chance, I took the opportunity to be in a band. Over
the years, it has been a blend of serious "musos," young pretend-
ers, casual, and even corporate. Whatever the circumstances, I
was your man. None of the bands were ever really serious about
making a mark. The uni band and the one immediately after
that were the only bands where we wrote and played our own
songs. I guess the connection between theme 1 and theme 2 is
that as my career choices developed, my dream of being in rock
'n' roll for a living effectively died.

There's a reason for connecting these two themes and bringing
them to the forefront of the story. I wanted to write this story
as if it were the album of this point in my life, with each track
carefully selected to connect and build the story. Sequential
and chronological with a change of sides in the middle. While
technological progress has mostly diminished the art and the
delivery of the concept album, the romantic in me wanted to
recreate the hours spent lovingly putting together a mixtape
and the expectancy of the reaction when your 'target audience'
hears it for the first time. I imagine you reading this for the first
time and what it says to you. In return please imagine for me
the sound of the stylus landing on the black vinyl as you turn
the pages and the silence between each track commanding your
attention before the next bars burst into life. (And thank you for
the indulgence.)

Back to the title track and the song, rewritten within the context of my story:

And you may find yourself
In a New York ICU,
And you may find yourself
With an internal temperature of 107 degrees,
And you may find yourself
Watching some of the best Doctors in the world
With no idea what is wrong with you,
And you may say to yourself, well
How did I get here?

CHAPTER 1

Oh, you know we've got to find a way
To bring some understanding here today

—Marvin Gaye

The story starts on December 17, 2014, and it starts inno-
cently enough. I had been training for a marathon, building my way back to having another crack at an Ironman race.
(There had been a failed attempt at Ironman UK in 2006).

The race was a January marathon, but six weeks into
training, I succumbed to a knee injury. It turned out to be
a torn meniscus and it would need surgery. My schedule was
busy with a lot of travel, but I managed to get my surgery
set for December 17, much to my wife's chagrin. Jen is the
boss, organizer, social secretary, and keeper of the calendar!
This surgery date was infringing on a prearranged deal we
had made while our nanny headed home for Christmas. This
wouldn't be the last time I would challenge the authority of
the family calendar!

I had a cold and a fever running up to the knee surgery.
As per instruction, I called in to the hospital forty-eight hours

before the surgery to report this development. It was left to a game-time decision on the morning of the surgery to see if I would be healthy enough to get it done. I rocked up to Lenox Hospital in Manhattan early on the seventeenth, and all vitals were good enough to proceed.

The surgery itself was uneventful, and the surgeon reported a good cleanup. I was told that after normal recovery times and postsurgical pain, it wouldn't be too long before I was back out there. Off home I went to start the recovery process.

Thursday 18 December a.m.

I woke early from a Percocet sleep. I felt really awful—sweaty, feverish, and with a barnstormer of a headache. I couldn't settle at all. My TV-doctor self-diagnosis decided that it was the US meds that were messing with me. This was the first time I had ever had to take a US prescription since I moved from the UK two years prior. Also, I should point out here that I am not one for pills. I rarely take them for anything. I have never used drugs in my life, so the truth is that there was definitely some deeply held belief there driving that outlook. In addition, it became very clear to me why US pharma ads were really one big disclaimer. Each pill blew my head off! Each time it wore off, I was left feeling worse than before taking it. So those postsurgery twenty-four hours were strange and somewhat disorientating.

Thursday 18 December p.m.

Still no improvement in how I was feeling. We decided to call the surgeon to see what advice or concerns he had and what we should do about my current status.

Predictably, the verdict was "see how you get on in the next twenty-four hours." No one could have predicted what that next twenty-four hours held in store for us.

Friday 19 December Midnight–4 a.m.

I was trying to go to sleep but just couldn't get comfortable or be still. The fevers were even more out of control, and now I had a swinging state—one minute blistering hot followed quickly by tundra-like temperatures and, a new entrant into the fever stakes, violent shivering! I have never suffered from convulsions or epilepsy, or any legitimate condition that caused me to be an unwilling participant in a type of fit that just took over my body. It was frightening and exhausting in equal measure. It felt like I had been possessed by some force. And this wasn't a short-term glitch. Each fit was lasting north of fifteen minutes and building. Also added was an involuntary shuddering breathing noise, like an overdramatic rendition of a teeth chatter. Which is funny because that is exactly what my lovely wife had decided it was! To be fair, I had worn out the little reservoir of patience she has for pretty much anything.

Let me expand on the earlier assault on the family calendar and fairly put Jen's view of things into the situation she was facing:

1. Husband books surgery the week before Christmas—UN agreement on childcare for that week now torn up.
2. Nanny heads home for the holidays, leaving my wife solo with Frances, our one-year-old daughter—this does not need any color commentary for those who have been through that experience.

3. My wife's work blows up—meaning not only is she not in the right place but also the demands on her time are relentless.

It's now 3 a.m. on Friday 19—picture the scene. My wife, an unhappy prisoner of some legal discourse, sits in the living room of our two-bedroom apartment. Frances is now asleep, and the forty-nine-year-old "calendar killer" is in the other bedroom, chittering and chattering like some Euro overactor! (Remember that ability to see situations in song—this is most definitely "Should I Stay or Should I Go" by The Clash. I am sure Jen was considering the latter!) By 4 a.m., her allocated portion of patience had worn out. She stormed into the room and said, "Right, that's it. This is ridiculous. We are going to the emergency room." She is great at many things, but her bedside manner is not her strong suit. So many things happened in the next hour. Some of them are so blurry and yet some others are so vivid. Let me try and get them in order:

After Jen issued her directive, she headed next door to wake up our sleeping child. That is never a great plan, especially for a child who fought sleep right up until two hours before!

I attempted to move and get ready (and I will drop the flippancy here), and for the first time I realized I was in trouble. I couldn't move. I was not in control. I was at the end of the latest convulsion and I was exhausted, scared, and completely unsteady—not to mention in pain from the knee surgery.

Jen bundled Frances up—it was freezing outside and early morning—and got the stroller. Then I realized we had another mixed signal. Jen was fully expecting to take a cab for the ten-block drive south to NYU Langone. I, on the other hand, was not confident of my ability to get to the bedroom door.

This next interplay gave me a reality check and foreshadowed what would happen much later on.

Jen: "Why aren't you ready?"

Me: "I can't move."

Jen: (exasperated) "Oh come on! How do you expect to get to the ER then?"

Me: "Call 911, I guess?"

Jen: "Do you know how much that will cost to go ten blocks?"

Me: "It's the only way I am going to get there."

She wasn't wrong to be concerned—the answer to the pop quiz question was $3K (retroactive discovery). We could have bought a car to take that journey. This was my first eye-opener to the great ball of confusion that is health insurance. There were to be many more.

Can I offer some backstory color here? This was definitely not my normal behavior, as future elements of this story will attest. Giving up is just not in my DNA. And outside of the occasional man-flu episodes, I have really been healthy my whole life. Like I said in the intro, I have been blessed.

To complete the picture, here is some backstory for Jen too: she is definitely one of the least patient people I have ever met. She freely admits it. She is consistently, in every walk of life, in every circumstance, impatient. Nothing gets a pass. Nothing! Yet her life story is laced with elements of such strength of character that it is easy to reconcile that she is quite simply short on patience but long on heart, strength, and resilience. She lost her mom to leukemia when she was eighteen years old, and then helped to raise and support her three younger siblings. She then lost her first husband, Michael, to Sarcoma when he was thirty-six years old. She has bags of character, just a very small bag of patience.

There we were, back at 4 a.m., and emergency services were on their way. I can remember how bad I felt. Like I was outside myself and not really in control. I mustered enough clarity to take three things with me—my phone, ID, and health insurance card. Somewhat ridiculously, I was dressed in shorts due to the bandaging around my knee paired with a heavy sweatshirt. My fever was pitching as I was trying to navigate the apartment to get on the gurney. The whole time, I was fighting to stay upright and conscious, and I weirdly became fixated with those three items that at that point represented my life.

After surviving the ignominy of being "rolled out" of the building, the paramedics got me into the ambulance and immediately gave me oxygen. I was panicking inside. I put my three items into my pocket, but because I was wearing sports shorts, they tipped toward the floor. I remember thinking, "I cannot lose these! How will they know who I am?" Ridiculous, but representative of the fact that I didn't expect to stay conscious. Those three items became vital to me. I was hanging onto them like my life depended on it. I felt so bad, I think in some ways they gave me something to focus on that provided enough of a distraction from my current plight.

As I look back, that was when my personal life clock stopped. Time became so incidental and insignificant. I was now in a void of only moving between where I was in that moment to the next. In a world where we measure so many things in time—our ages, the longevity of our career, how many hours we worked, how many days off we get, how fast we can go, the list goes on and on. However, there at a defining point in my life, time didn't matter.

Breathe!

Stay awake!

Hold on to your things!

These were my immediate priorities. All of them connected but not built around time. The paramedic spoke to me to keep me "with him." And this is how the ten-block journey passed.

The Impact of Time, Particularly When There Is None Left

There is so much talk about quality time over quantity, but why is time even part of the metric? Isn't true freedom boundless, beyond any measurement criteria? If you couldn't use time as a measure, what would you use? Think about how we flippantly use the notion of time as a currency:

"I just don't have the time!"

"I can spare an hour."

"Time is money."

We are so programmed by it that it can dominate our experiences and interactions. Which elements of your time are truly timebound? Yes, I do have to get my daughter to school at a certain time, and some meetings are scheduled at certain times. Perhaps the rest of the restrictions we put on time are because we need the structure. Being freeform is hard for us to comprehend and handle. But how much freedom and balance could it add to your life?

Consider this: If you were faced with the fact that your clock was stopped, that your meter had run out, what would you say then?

"If only I could have . . ."

"If I get out of this, never again will I . . ."

And yet we have that power all along. We can do most anything what we want to do, and wishing for more time is a byproduct of not prioritizing your time to what really matters to you.

Place yourself in my shoes in this moment. How would you complete those two statements? (Visit www.pentalogymarketing .com to get a daily exercise to help you with this.)

The coming days were going to ask me those questions several times. Deep down, I knew my usual answers were not going to cut it!

CHAPTER 2

I've got chills.
They're multiplying.
And I'm losing control.

—John Travolta & Olivia Newton-John

Y ou will afford me the poetic license for using a lyric rather than a song title for this chapter. (Yes, I know I did it in the book title too; I figured "my book, my rules.") I know this choice is kind of cheesy, but it is also kind of appropriate. *Grease* was one of the biggest launches of anything in teen culture when I was in high school. It was released late summer of 1978. I had just turned thirteen, and so it was the perfect adolescent movie for me and my friends. I remember queuing for hours to get tickets to see this in the cinema, a queue the likes of which we only see now when Nike has a new limited-edition sneaker drop, or a new hot spot for brunch in Manhattan has its fifteen minutes. If you hadn't been to see it, then you missed out on the majority of the playground conversations and references. It was that influential.

I don't remember the journey to the hospital. I remained conscious throughout, but I still felt like I wasn't really there.

I also know I still had my items in my hand. Everything was hazy. You know that view they give you in the movies where the foreground is out of focus? That kind of hazy!

We arrived at the ER entrance. I kissed Jen and Frances goodbye. I hoped that was temporary. There was no time to dwell on that for now. I was shuttled into the ward, and the ER team quickly had me in a bed in the far corner of the room.

The usual formalities followed. The nursing team assigned to me came over, and I started the inevitable paperwork with one of them while the others organized me as per house rules. There were so many instances of paperwork that I don't know the numeric adjective. I was sweating profusely, almost violently, which made completing the paperwork quite difficult without drenching it and having to start again. The sweat was appearing in areas normally reserved for heavy exercise. The nurse took my external temperature and it was 99 degrees. It didn't seem possible, but that's what it said. They quickly decided to get me on a saline drip and put in a line to take blood. I was sweating so much, no amount of medical adhesive tape would stick to my skin. My veins had also disappeared from view, so getting blood was like some sort of archaeological dig. They ended up calling on Sheila, who was the resident expert for difficult blood sticking. Why I remember her name, I have no idea. She was a really nice lady and fortunately lived up to her billing.

(Sidenote here: I haven't changed any of the names to protect anyone or anything. Some people I remember their names, some I do not. Maybe it was my distinct lack of clarity, or maybe it was the role they played. Anyway, the account is as accurate as I can remember.)

So there I was. Salined up. Sweating from glands I didn't even know I had. Then some bad luck came into play: In my multiple form fillings, I had to explain that I just had knee surgery and was on Percocet for pain control. This, quite reasonably, led them down a garden path of theorizing around some sort of infection in my knee. The next hour or two was spent on the early theories of that knee infection and concerns about dehydration due to the amount of fluid I was sweating out. As I said previously, the clock had stopped for me, so I was unaware of time passing and how long I had been there.

I calmed down a bit. I think the oxygen, the saline, and the location added up to an eased state of mind. They now knew my immediate medical history, and I felt like I was in the right place should anything untoward happen. The one question that was perplexing everyone though was, how could I be sweating this much and yet only have a mild fever? Time for a closer look. Out comes the rectal thermometer to get the real read. This prompted several retakes (look away now if you are squeamish)—I did say I was sweating from everywhere, and that made it difficult to get a read (I will leave it at that). I think three attempts were made and the final result was around 107 degrees. I am going to admit here that I didn't know what the human body could withstand. (If you are in that camp too—its around 108/109 before really bad stuff starts to happen.)

As if by magic, this prompted the next fever attack—maybe that was some kind of intervention to physically demonstrate that yes, my temperature really is that high. The medical term for the fits/convulsions is *rigors*. Again this is post-applied knowledge. Our family nursing community (Jen's youngest sister, Ali, is a nurse, as is her husband, Drew) would text that one in later! I am glad I didn't know, as my only point of reference would have been rigor mortis—I knew what that meant!

The rigor lasted twenty minutes. This prompted the nursing staff to administer some intravenous Ibuprofen. So many sidebars here but it's all wrapped up in the fabric of the story—that intravenous Ibuprofen is incredible stuff. Not your regular "off the shelf" stuff here. Oh no! Pure rush stuff. This must be how a junkie feels when that needle hits the vein but in a "licensed medicine / you are allowed to have it" sort of a way. In fact, our family nursing community told us that this used to be normal practice, but the pharma companies jacked their prices so severely that a cheaper alternative became drug du jour! Don't get me wrong, I ain't hating or commentating. Just relaying this tidbit as part of the story. You will have your own experiences and views and you are welcome to them.

Anyway, the upshot was that the meds seemed to square me up for a little while. Now I had to deal with the inquisition into the rigor and how often that had been happening. The answers sent the nursing team back into their huddle, and this time they definitely came out in their two-minute offense. Suddenly I had some more white-coat presence at bedside. And of course, like every time you have ever gone to the doctor, when you finally get to see them, you are not quite the mess you were twenty minutes before!

The medical investigation started in earnest to find the source of the fever. Off came the bandage on the knee, which wasn't hard since it was soaked in sweat. Nothing visible to the trained eye—theirs not mine. I have had a few knee surgeries over the years, and this one didn't feel that much different. It is like a toothache pain is the bass line, with a melody of "someone has been digging in my knee with something sharp" overtones and a middle eight that reminded me that the surgery was only forty-eight hours ago. And all these new fun and games weren't ideal for following the "take it easy for a few days" parting shot from my knee surgeon.

As I started to calm down from the rigor, I wondered how much time had marched on. I didn't even know if Jen knew what was going on. As if reading my mind, the nurse looking after me assured me that Jen had called and was on her way up with the now-rested one-year-old. She then mentioned that the admissions person would be over shortly.

Wait, what?

With everything going on, it had never once crossed my mind that I wasn't going home. I asked the nurse to get the admissions guy over, who was already hovering with yet another set of forms. It went something like this:

Me: Am I being admitted?

Him: Yes. We are just waiting on the room in the ICU.

Me: Okay. (you could probably hear the penny drop as the last three letters landed.) ICU? Intensive Care Unit, right?

Him: Yes. The room should be ready in an hour or so.

Me: So what is wrong with me?

Him: We don't know, but you have a significant fever, you are dehydrated, and we don't know the cause. We need you in ICU for observation until we work it out.

Me: Oh.

About ten minutes later, as that bombshell was sinking in, Jen arrived with Frances. I was still sweating but was calmer and a bit more relaxed due to the administered drug. We relived the last twenty-four hours to try and identify where this all started and if there were any other symptoms we could share with the medical team to help with the investigation.

Whatever was happening administratively, it seemed to speed up after the internal temperature discovery. I was told

I was being moved soon. Jen took the opportunity to get out of there. It really isn't an ideal place for a toddler, and Frances was clearly disconcerted with me lying in a hospital bed. In addition, the news of the ICU admission meant no kids allowed, so Jen had to go and get to work on getting babysitting cover organized.

Pretty soon, I was on my way up to the ICU. The environment felt very different right from the start. Instead of being in the corner of the open ER, I was now isolated in a big room with a view of the East River from the bed. If I moved toward the window, I would have the FDR freeway and the Pepsi sign for company. It was now early afternoon, and a heavy winter sky hugged the jagged outline of the buildings on Long Island, making the view below me similar to the haze I had experienced in the ambulance. Now that I was in the unit, I was told to stay in bed until all my vitals were taken again and everything was logged in the ward.

Soon after getting settled in, the effects of the drugs wore off and I was back to sweating and shaping up for another rigor. It was the strangest sensation. I could feel it starting in my body. A sense of almost cartoon-like temperature rose through my body, and the sweating intensity increased immediately. Pretty soon my body was shaking involuntarily.

This prompted some activity from the doctors. For the most part, I think they wanted to witness it happening to see the physical impact on me. But also they wanted to monitor my temperature and vitals, while I curled up into a ball to try to absorb the impact it was delivering. After ten minutes or so, my body must have made the necessary adjustments because everything swung violently to being really cold. My teeth were chattering, and my body moved even more involuntarily. It took my breath away in a way that I imagine panic attacks do. Thirty minutes in total passed and then it was gone, almost as quickly as it came. It left me more scared and disoriented than I already was before it arrived.

The resultant medical action was to put me on a broad-spectrum antibiotic to deal with the presumed infection. This would be the primary action until they had a complete diagnosis. They would also increase my blood sticking to every two hours and move me to complete bowel rest. Ice chips had never tasted so good—and now they were gone too!

I was ordered to stay in bed. They changed the saline drip, and then they decided to put in a catheter to take away the need for me to move to go to the toilet and to monitor the volume of fluids being processed by my body. We were on bag number three of saline, and I still hadn't felt the need to pee. Apparently this was a concern.

The rest of the day followed this routine. Vitals, bloodwork, monitor checks, saline update, and a repeated reminder to rest. I dozed in and out, and outside of the rigors, I actually felt no worse than I had that morning. I was drawing a crowd. There was a stream of medical visitors all checking in to see what was going on and to lend an opinion. This continued until early evening and until the shift changed for the night.

CHAPTER 3

They must know by now I'm in here trembling
In a terror ever growing
Crackin' up

—ABBA

It was dark now and everything looked very different. The medical traffic diminished with only my nurse and the blood sticking process for company. I was left with my thoughts and my fears. I felt bad, but I wasn't sure how bad. I became concerned that my two older children, Kevin and Caitlin (twenty-five and twenty-three respectively at this time), would know what was happening and that I should do something to allay any fears they may have. So I decided to do what every person would do in that situation. I made a valiant attempt to convince the world (and myself, I am sure), that I was fine. I posted to Facebook the most incoherent, rambling nonsense you ever did read as proof of me being "just fine." Of course, I didn't think that it was nonsense at all. I had that inner smugness that can only be achieved by a "top class" social media post!

My eldest daughter, Caitlin, contributes this next paragraph as part of an episode I don't remember at all. As part of my campaign to put everyone's mind at ease, I thought it was a good idea to FaceTime her to assure her I was okay! Here is her memory from that call.

The FaceTime

My memory of a lot of the details isn't great, but what I do remember very clearly was the worry and dread I felt after I hung up the phone. I immediately burst into tears. Until this point, I knew my dad wasn't well. Jen had told us he was in hospital. I was getting ready for bed when a FaceTime came through from my dad's phone. When I answered, the first thing I remember was the color of his face. He was so pale and had a sheen from the sweat on his skin. He was telling me that he felt great, and that he wasn't really sure why he was in hospital. He was laughing and smiling, but the beeping of the machines attached to him by tubes and wires distracted me. I tried to find out what was happening, but he wasn't making much sense and kept repeating how great he felt. The call must have lasted only around five minutes, but I immediately felt an intense panic. I remember trying to call Jen repeatedly and messaging her through every app I had. My mum came into the room and asked if I was okay, and I remember saying "I won't be able to sleep until I've spoken to Jen and know he is okay." It was only once my dad was out of hospital and on the mend that I discovered that he had no memory of this call.

Oblivious to the panic I had just caused in FaceTime and in Facebook world, I put on my music and allowed it to take me away from my reality. It was December, and for some reason my thoughts turned to John Peel's Festive Fifty. If you are of a certain age and a music fan brought up in the UK, you would know the legend of this feature in a nightly radio show. John Peel was different from any standard radio disc jockey stereotype from the late '70s/early '80s. His whole purpose was to listen to demos sent into him by unsigned bands. He played not only the ones he liked but also the ones he thought we would like. This launched many a career, including The Clash, The Undertones, The Smiths—and he also brought Velvet Underground and REM to a UK audience. Imagine a pirate radio station being run within the BBC—that was effectively him. Kids from my age group would all go to sleep listening to Peel at 10 p.m., anticipating hearing the next big thing. I had to smuggle my radio into my bed and hide it so my parents didn't know my plans for the rest of the night. Anyway, at Christmas he recapped the top fifty songs of the year in his Festive Fifty. We always had our tape recorders at the ready to catch as many of the unsigned acts as possible!

The memory comforted me and took me back to that time. Each night's recording became key currency for the inevitable "trading" of the resultant tapes in the playground, as well as the debates about where each song rested in the final fifty. In the ICU that night, I felt less lonely and less scared as I thought about the people I had shared those moments with. I was in contact with very few of them by that point, and I found myself resolving to reach out once this medical episode was over.

Speaking of medical episodes, the next rigor arrived shortly after. This time it was longer and slightly more violent. This gave me a chance to demonstrate the experience to the night staff. The frequency of the rigors was very worrying to the medical staff, and their physical impact was very worrying to me. And since no one could tell me why they were happening, there was no plan for how to stop them.

I was scared and started to anticipate them coming back. I couldn't sleep. I felt like I wasn't in control, and so all the things you take for granted, like waking up when you fall asleep, were now question marks in my head. It was a very restless night with no real sense of time, just trepidation.

Saturday morning started with another rigor. It was half-light outside so probably not quite dawn yet. The rigor pattern continued. Each one grew longer and more demanding than the last, and each one took a slightly bigger bite out of me. There were still no clues as to what was wrong. With the morning came the unit medical rounds and another rigor granted that crew an audience as if it were "on call."

The breaking news was that I was in the medical side of the ICU as opposed to the surgical side. The main belief was that my knee was infected, which was causing the temperature spike that in turn was "shocking" my body with the rigors. However, all tests taken showed no sign of an infection in my knee. The decision was made to take my blood and my temperature during the rigor to see if it gave any clues as to what was happening. Obligingly, another one came along during those processes. So there I was, going through this fit with a thermometer inside me, and a junior doctor trying to get blood out of me, while my body continued to convulse. Each fit was such an intense experience that the two new added elements were immaterial. It wasn't yet midmorning, and I had experienced three rigors so far. I was really struggling physically and emotionally with this phenomenon. The time in between each incident only gave me time to catch my breath before starting to dread the next one.

I got the team to call Jen to update her. She was waiting on a family friend to arrive, and then she would be up to visit. Between those two things happening, I had yet another rigor—number four of the morning. They continued to lengthen, and now I was seeing several temperature swings due to the extended length. The extra length and the new frequency had me on my heels. I was calling out for the intravenous ibuprofen to be administered, but that would need approval, so I had to wait. The staff were reluctant to prescribe anything without a proper diagnosis, and while that seems prudent practice, in that moment I wanted the rigors to end and the specter of another one to be taken away for a while.

Jen arrived, and it was immediately comforting to have her there. When I told her about my morning, she immediately sought out the doctors to find out what was going on. We waited until they were available, and what happened next will be forever etched in my memory.

I got the early warning that another rigor was starting. I immediately started to kick off the sheets to try and stay cool, but the temperature spike pounced, and this time with a vengeance. It kicked hard, making me writhe in reaction, Jen looking on helplessly. It almost made it worse, seeing the panic in her eyes. As per the other fits, the pendulum eventually swung back to me feeling like I was in a cold fever. This time I was so so cold. The impact of the volume of rigors had to be compounding in both the rigor severity and my resilience. My whole body was shaking, so Jen gave me her winter coat to wrap around me to try and stabilize my temperature. It didn't help. Short of any other options, she laid on me to try and (a) pass heat to me and (b) diminish the amount of shaking I was experiencing.

I have no idea how long that one lasted, but for the first time I felt like this one wasn't going to end. Eventually the fever subsided, and I returned to what had become the holding state: shell-shocked and scared and just waiting for the next one to come along. The last one was different though. It hurt more. It was more severe. I felt exhausted after it. Done in. I remember turning to Jen in the aftermath and telling her, "I don't know if I can take another one of those today." I still can't believe I said those words. I can't reenact in my mind how bad I must have felt to be that close to surrendering.

Between the morning I had and the fact that I had been in the ICU for nearly twenty-four hours, the medical staff were starting to rule things out. The "knee theory" was all but gone. And so the thought process switched to other potential issues and that the rigors must be being caused by an infection, but an infection somewhere away from my knee. The next suspect to investigate was the stomach. There is a medical statistic that shows a high percentage of all infections in our bodies are gastrointestinal in nature. They promised both me and Jen that a more definitive diagnosis, and therefore treatment, would be there shortly. The bowel rest was going to help, but they needed to start to treat me for something. In the early evening, a new theory appeared and some initial investigations on my vitals were started.

Despite this theory, and after a few hours of investigations, nothing could be concluded. The missing key ingredient was what was happening in my blood. While they could take a sample every two hours, the one part they couldn't expedite was what happened with my blood over time. The junior doctor came to my bedside to explain that they were going to continue with the broad-spectrum drugs. I told him to call my wife and tell her that they had drawn a blank. Jen is pretty fierce; she is a lawyer and so it kinda comes with the territory. She is also from the Philadelphia area, and fierceness is definitely a trait of that city. She was also being backed by our Family Nursing Community (Drew & Ali), so she was able to check in in real time with them and put together the pieces of the story she wasn't being told. That call didn't go well for the junior doctor. I was hazy and drowsy, but I could hear him on the phone with Jen. He would say something, and then he wouldn't say anything at all for a few minutes. Clearly it wasn't his turn to talk, and he was being invited to listen to her feedback! I knew he was under attack. That at least made me smile.

Another long sleepless night was ahead of me—just me, my fear, and the city below me. Mercifully the rigors had backed off for the remainder of the day. It was like they had taken me to the edge, shown me my weakness and my frailty, and then left me to continue the battle knowing what was at stake.

Doctor's rounds on Sunday morning brought a revelation, and not a particularly comforting one. It transpired that they were so stumped by my condition that they had googled it! Now we all know Google is smart, but I was looking for a bit more from the team. There was a chink of light, however: the blood-work had developed some sort of culture overnight that showed what kind of infection I was dealing with. C. diff, colitis, and E. coli poisoning so far. They started me on a cocktail of medications to try and get that triumvirate of infections under control. This was the progress we had been looking for the night before!

It also brought a new cast to the table. Enter Dr. Greene. He was the Doctor for Infectious Diseases (not a comforting title), but his bedside manner was the opposite of his title. If I described him as a TV doctor from the '80s, it paints a pretty accurate picture. I would say he was in his late fifties/early sixties with white hair, wearing an equally white, immaculate doctor's coat and sharp bow tie that boasted vivid colors over subsequent days. He was an absolute gentleman, soft-spoken but convincing. I could tell right away that his confidence came from his knowledge, not his volume. He had an assistant in tow. So they introduced themselves to me and started quizzing me. His comment will never leave me.

"Remarkable!"

I responded back, "I've been called many things but that is a new one."

He continued, ". . . well, considering how sick you are."

This was the first time anyone had admitted where I was at in the health spectrum. And it shook me. Serendipitously, Jen arrived in time to meet Dr. Greene.

There was no further diagnosis, but with Jen in the room, the team came up with a proposal. They wanted to scan my abdomen and GI. To do that, they would need to give me this mixture that would show up in the scan. In the UK it is called a barium meal. It has another name here, but I don't recall what it was. The main issue was that it had to be taken in two liters of fluid. This was now Sunday afternoon, and I had consumed nothing at all since Friday morning. In the name of progress, that didn't seem like too big a hurdle, so they said they would be back in an hour. An hour after that they could scan me. That was the plan, but my stomach had other ideas.

The mixture came in two-liter bottles, and I had to drink them in fairly short order. I didn't get to the second bottle. That first bottle bounced back almost as quickly as I could drink it.

No way my body was cooperating. Despite this setback, it was decided I would take it intravenously. This would create a delay of a few hours but still would allow the scan to happen later that day.

In addition, the decision was taken to move me to the surgical side of the ICU as talk of surgical intervention had already started. I think the medical side wanted to hand me off as soon as they could after they had resorted to Google and still had no full diagnosis in sight. And since I would be on the move for the scan, it seemed to suit everyone to relocate me after that procedure. That became the plan.

The rejection my bowel had exercised earlier in the day had left me in some significant discomfort. The retching hurt like hell, and the exertion had brought on another rigor, the first in a while.

As a result, I was really woozy when they started to get me ready to go down to the scan. The journey down to the X-ray room was largely uneventful, but I remember the view of the ceiling of the different parts of the hospital. *A unique perspective of my environment*, I thought. I don't know why I remember it so vividly. But I do. In musical terms, it was like a remix or an acoustic version of an old favorite track. It was familiar but different enough to command my attention. And I remember the challenge of getting the bed into the patient elevator without hitting the sides. My senses were now working overtime for sure.

The scan itself went to plan. There were no hiccups to the process of lying still and being rolled into the tube, and then for the radiographers to do their thing. They asked what music I wanted to listen to. It was clearly a reflection of my mindset that I chose negatively, i.e., "Anything but country and reggae!"

AND YOU MAY FIND YOURSELF

With the scan finished, back upstairs I went. As per the plan, this time my new home was in the surgical ICU. Directionally, for those of you who know New York City, I moved north, further uptown to the other end of the block. So I had pretty much the same river view, but this time the on ramp onto FDR at 34th Street sat below me. If I wasn't quite on the corner, I was close.

It was dark outside, late afternoon, early evening. I was exhausted. The blood sticking routine was still in full effect, but I was so used to it now I was almost immune. It could take three or four sticks to get anything, and there had to be three vials after each take. They were in my feet now trying to find a regular, reliable supply. And with me taking up residence in a new spot, there was a whole new staff to get to know the rules of this game.

I knew I had to try and get some rest to be able to battle this illness, as today had demonstrated that nothing was about to be handed to me. Since it was Sunday night, all the medical big guns would be back in the next day, and I was assured I was top of the list for their rounds.

I settled in and must have dozed off. I have no idea how long I slept, but I came to because I was aware of a presence at the side of my bed. In my somnolent state, I figured it was the new nursing crew. It wasn't. The shadowy figure had longish hair and dark features, was dressed casually, and was carrying a book. (I know who you think it is . . .) He leaned his book on the sidebar of the bed. As my blurry vision started to clear, I realized I didn't know who he was. So I asked, "Sorry, who are you?"

He said, "I am your radiographer from earlier. I think I know what is wrong with you and I wanted to meet the person who was living through this!"

What? You know what is wrong with me? I blurted out, "Could you tell them out there please?"

He laughed and said "Already have. It will be THE big discussion topic in the morning." I could have cried with that news. Only later did I find out that this visit from a radiographer was like seeing a unicorn—it just didn't happen. This unicorn had found that I had some of the trackable substance in my bloodstream. It took me a minute to realize that this was not a normal bodily function. He seemed confident that this was medically justifiable, if rare. After explaining it to me in as simple terms as I could handle, like the mythical creature he represented, he left. It left me wondering if the visit was real or a dream.

The nightshift nurse in particular was incredible. She was immediately in tune with how I was feeling and really got to know my case notes so we could chat like she had been there the whole time. She was also someone new that I could try to push the envelope with. Being on total bowel rest was boring. There was no mealtime or wondering what would be for dinner. I wasn't allowed ice chips, so I took the initiative to deal with my dry mouth and oral boredom by brushing my teeth as often as I could find someone to ask permission. The nightshift nurse quickly was on to my game and shut me down. It was and is a real revelation how much we take that kind of habit for granted. Fortunately, she was more forgiving of my desire to move, as long as I didn't overdo it. So I was allowed to sit at the window (and on the ledge) so I could watch the world outside.

My world was illuminated by the Pepsi sign on the other side of the river, and I watched the occasional late-night headlight dance across the freeway. It wouldn't be long before that fleeting dance would turn into an early morning flash mob as the traffic grew on the FDR. As I watched the inevitable traffic jams build up, I remember thinking that if I was ever given the chance to be in that traffic jam, I would never complain again. In fact, I *wanted* to be in that jam so bad, and I wanted to be looking up with curiosity to these windows and wondering who this guy was in the window fifteen floors up! I found myself visualizing the inverted situation I now found myself in.

And this really is where the thought of practicing death comes from. I was in isolation, mostly separated from my loved ones, deprived of food, sleep, and water. I wished that some mundane situation could be my new norm. I would have made that trade. You can only feel helpless in that situation, realizing that all your normal physical connections with the living world are largely cut off. No one can see you, no one knows what you are feeling, physically and emotionally. It was terrifyingly lonely, and the usual measurement metric of time had simply stopped. It struck me that these three days weren't that different from if I had actually died.

This acute awareness of my mortality shook me to my core. I remember crying. Not wailing or anything dramatic, just fearfully crying about Jen and my children. And not *for* them as in "What will they do without me?" but more selfishly, "What will I do without them?" Kevin and Caitlin were older, so I convinced myself that they would work it out. I mourned for their big life moments that I may not be a part of. I just couldn't get my head around Frances. She was twenty-two months old, and this phrase kept playing over and over in my head: "She just got here. I can't be leaving!" And my poor Jen. She had already lost her first husband, Michael, to illness. How would she reconcile this?

I think this was my version of "fighting for my life." I translated what was in front of me into something I could comprehend and distilled that down into a motivation and purpose. I know there have been many who have gone before me, with just as much purpose and just as much resolve to survive, if not more. This isn't any kind of commentary on those less fortunate souls who lost their battle; this is merely me trying to explain how I found some fortitude even though the cracks in my facade were evident and widening.

This will sound flippant, but in that hour of need, there were no thoughts about "Will I ever work again?", "What will work do?", or any fears about missing upcoming deadlines. My only concern about work was to let my close friends and colleagues know how I was doing. Now that may seem very obvious as a conclusion, but without this experience, I probably *would* expect someone to be worried about work! So what does that tell us about what we think is important versus what really matters? How do I reconcile the fact that, when everything was on the line, something I had put so much emphasis on in my life disappeared from view? That isn't a surprise, but what is a surprise is that I never had this view from the other side, back before when everything was "normal." "Why didn't I live my life like this?" was a logical question. Why didn't I see that my career was out of kilter with the rest of my life, at least in terms of balance? I was always one of those "Do whatever it takes" kind of guys. But there I was, and maybe this time there wasn't a way around it. What good did all of that do me now, other than to demonstrate to me very clearly I hadn't got things right?

It was truly humbling and confusing all at the same time. Surely I had enough to deal with without questioning how I had lived my life?

AND YOU MAY FIND YOURSELF

Take Control

Practicing Death has one big advantage over my unexpected situation. It gives you the chance to take control of your situation, of your timeline. Compare that to my experience. All the anxiety and fears I was facing were crashing together in one momentous collision at a time when I was least equipped to cope with it.

CHAPTER 4

Now I know all the wrong turns the stumbles,
And falls brought me here

—Ben Folds

A little bit of a backstory here to help color in the significance of this song. When Frances was born, she was one helluva baby. I mean she screamed the place down and would never go to sleep in a traditional manner. Any sleep she got was in the position of lying on one of our chests and us shushing her until she finally gave in.

I remember two weeks after she was born, my mum, Caitlin, and my youngest sister, Carolyn, came to visit. They came primarily to meet Frances but also to help us while we adjusted to our new family situation. I will never forget my mum's face when she first came face to face with the "Frances Experience"! Now my mother raised four of us and numerous neighborhood kids. We were that house where kids would be dropped off before and after work. There were always kids about. I was the oldest, so when the time came, it was logical that I became the neighborhood's babysitter—my first enterprise! Anyway, this woman, with vast experience of her own and other kids, looked shell-shocked when she heard the screams of our child. It wasn't that they were blood-curdlingly evil, more the fact she could go for four hours straight without losing volume or frequency. Remarkable! When I saw that look on my mum's face, I knew that we were in real trouble.

When no one else was around, our nightly routine was this: Jen would go to bed at 9 or 10 p.m., and I would pace the apartment in full shushing mode until 2 or 3 a.m. Then Jen would take over so I could get some sleep before work. The reason for telling you all of this is that part of our solution was to sing to Frances when there was enough of a gap between screams or some relative calm had come over her. "The Luckiest" was the most frequent song Jen sang to Frances. I guess she needed to remind herself with this soothing song of just how lucky we are. It was comforting to me in the hospital and in my situation that I remembered that too. That little screaming ball of confusion was one of the three greatest things in my life.

I digress, partly because of context but also partly because this was what I was fighting to preserve. Our little family unit, including a now joy-filled child at twenty-two months, was very much at the front of my mind. It had been four days since I had last seen her.

December 22, Monday morning back in the ICU. The previous night had been spent staring out the window at my adopted city and wondering what today would have in store.

Dr. Greene dropped by first. It was a comfort to see him and to hear what he had to say. He checked my charts, and we chatted about how I had been. We talked about the "Radiographer Angel" and what he had found. And while it was not his area of expertise, he was confident that the doctors would be prescribing some action today.

His summary meant that my own clock, which had been stopped for several days now, was able to restart. The second hand could now purposefully move as there was now something for it to move toward. This new clock was running very slow. Nine a.m. passed—still no rounds. I was growing impatient and desperate to hear what the new information had led them to.

Remember at the start when I told you that I remember some people vividly and some I do not remember much at all? In this instance, I can't remember my allocated surgeon's name. That seems weird, right? I think that it is, particularly since he has such a memorable role in the whole story.

The doctor's entourage arrived, and the usual formalities were exchanged. The first piece of news was that my latest bloodwork showed a magnesium deficiency, so they were going to start a course of magnesium injections every four hours. In my mind, it just meant that every other blood stick was going to be accompanied by a new friend. However, as I was soon to learn, those injections are fierce. They were delivered by a large needle, and the immediate sensation was one of fire running through my veins. It wasn't a rush sensation; it just felt like liquid heat had been injected directly into your body. It didn't last long, but it was going to take some getting used to.

The discussion among the gathering turned toward the radiographer's findings and some opinions about what was next. There was genuine concern about my levels of toxicity and any subsequent surgery while this was in full effect. A number of medical terminology-laden sentences were exchanged. I don't know what was said, but I was aware enough about how it was said. There was clearly a division in the camp.

They soon departed and I was told that there was a staff meeting later that morning and my case would be further discussed then. I wasn't happy with that at all, but what can you do? In addition, this was my first weekday in the surgical ICU, so there was another new team to meet and to get to know. This led to a procession of medical staff coming in to see me. Jen would later describe on social media that it was "as if a new baby panda had landed in the ward."

The new medical team were my kind of people. They asked if they could bring a medical class in to visit, straight off of TV stuff, and I agreed. Hell, at this point if a witch doctor could get me closer to a solution, what did I care? It was interesting to see these faces all trying to "crack the case." There was a Q&A around the bed, partly to explain what had for the most part been ruled out already. Smart crew. I never wanted to be a doctor, nor did I think I was smart enough to be. The student doctors were stumped and trudged away with no doubt more reading and revision to be done. I will come back to this later as it played a part in what happened next.

Help had arrived for Jen for a couple of days, so she came up to visit, and we spent an hour just talking about any updates—the radiographer's findings in particular. How this was happening was beyond both our comprehensions, and even though Jen was checking in with her sister and brother-in-law regularly with meds updates, all we really knew was that my case was so rare that finding historical cases for reference was almost impossible. Our family resident experts informed us that the broad-spectrum antibiotics and dosage were the last and heaviest they could give me before putting me on something more specific. Fairly soon, this would force them to decide what was next.

It is also important to say that the diagnosis had been made at this point. I am not teasing you with some big reveal, but I want to include it in some important context as part of the backstory. In fact, the reveal to you is almost exactly how it was revealed to my closest family, and I want to recreate that feeling as part of telling you the story.

I think it is fair to say that the antibiotics had stabilized me, but I was still feeling really lousy, and I felt nauseous enough to know I would have been sick if there was anything in there. It was a strange sensation. I wasn't hungry, but my mouth was definitely bored. It was an interesting experience to mark time with no mealtimes in it. The morning didn't start with breakfast, but rather it kicked off with a head full of thoughts and concerns about my current situation. It really does show the prescriptive nature of our behavior and that when it is forced to be broken, you can see it for the habit that it is.

A new junior doctor appeared to update us and to confirm that the staff meeting was early afternoon. They would/should have more info then. They promised to call Jen once decisions were made.

Once again the clock was stopped, and I started to count things in new units of time. "Only two more blood stickings and a magnesium burn until I find out what is next!" I was restless, so I put some music on and tried to settle down. Somehow there was a comfort in the medical numbers around me during the day, and so I was less afraid of sleep. I must have dozed off and woke, with no recognition of time, to the surgeon with no name standing by my bed. I tried to shake off the funk from my doze but spent the first minute or two trying to focus. As a result, it took me a few minutes to catch on to the fact that he was clearly annoyed. At first, I thought his annoyance was aimed at me, but I gradually came to the realization that he was irked by the situation and was a man who had not gotten his way!

The conversation went something like this:

Him: "Mr. Murphy, I am here to tell you that my colleagues have decided on a course of action for you. I am also here to tell you I don't agree with that course of action. What they say is wrong with you is so rare that it just can't be that."

It took a minute to make sense of that statement.

Me: "Rare doesn't mean never though, right?"

Him: "True, but it makes it so unlikely that I don't believe it is that. I believe your levels of toxicity are so high that we should send you home until we get you out of that state, and then bring you back and deal with whatever is left. Think about it as emergent surgery versus elective surgery. I am firmly in the camp of getting you to a point where the surgery is elective."

Now I know what those two words mean, but in this context, I was somewhat bewildered by the comparison.

Me: "You really think I should go home like this? I don't know what is wrong with me, but that doesn't seem right."

I was having flashbacks to the early hours of Friday morning and the circus of getting me out of the apartment on a gurney. Plus I felt like crap. I couldn't get my head around that my next stage of care was no care at all! So now I was annoyed too. And this annoyed him further.

Him: "It just *isn't* what they say it is. The radiographer's report doesn't have to take you to this conclusion."

Me: "So what's your conclusion?"

Him: (Clearly irked by my sharpness) "That you have some nonthreatening GI condition that would be best dealt with once you are not fighting C. diff, E. coli, and colitis!"

There was a silent pause as we eyeballed each other. I don't know what he was thinking, but I know what I was thinking, and it wasn't pretty. The truth is in that moment I was terrified of going home to wait this out.

And then the story turns:

Him: "However, you will be glad to hear that I am going to Mexico tomorrow on vacation, so I am no longer your surgeon and Dr. Newman will be taking your case in my absence. He believes that you need emergency surgery now to arrest your condition, so they will be in to see you after surgery later today to talk that through."

What do you say to that? He left as abruptly as he arrived, and I was left somewhat bewildered by the whole conversation. Now I was in someone else's hands, and that someone else wanted to take action. I still don't know who was right or wrong in this situation, but I do thank God for that intervention. Going home felt like the last thing I should do.

Sometime later, Dr. Greene returned to share the same news. I felt I could talk to him, and so I shared my fears in being sent home. He told me in the most discreet, polite terms possible that the meeting on my case had been somewhat heated and that he agreed with Dr. Newman's viewpoint. He also agreed that sending me home could have been a big mistake. That was all I needed to hear.

Enter the next nameless protagonist.

He was an attending physician, I think. Even after this experience, I still can't get my head around the surgeon/doctor hierarchy. His constant companion was a textbook that he somehow managed to look at and absorb in every down minute he had. I don't remember his name because I had given him a nickname and that is what stuck in my head.

The first time he walked into my room, I was in the process of changing into a fresh T-shirt. My sweating was still profuse, so I wore some fitness T-shirts to remove the moisture off my body. This particular one was for my favorite college football team, the Ohio State Buckeyes. As he walked in and saw the T-shirt, he did a doubletake. It turns out he went to Michigan. Ohio State and Michigan have arguably the greatest rivalry in college football. Think the Red Sox versus the Yankees, the Maple Leafs versus the Red Wings, or the bitter soccer rivalry I grew up with in Glasgow between Celtic and Rangers. This most fervent of rivalries was alive and well in our immediate connection! Earlier in November, my Buckeyes had put up 62 points in an absolute slaughter against Michigan, so I am sure he was still self-treating the wounds from that loss!

Despite that rivalry, we hit it off right away. He was a tall, handsome Indian man. He was the kind of heartthrob doctor that would have anyone swooning if he was your appointed physician. As he examined me, with particular attention to my abdomen, we talked and got to know each other a bit. Rivalry aside, he was a fascinating guy, and we found out that we both had one-year-old daughters. This gave us a kinship and a joint purpose that put us on the same wavelength. It was that comfort that allowed us to exchange nicknames in the course of several discussions and examinations. I called him "Ichigan" and he called me "State." The origin for my name for him was based in the Ohio State fan's tradition of dropping the M (Michigan logo as well as first letter) from all words in the run up to the Big Game every year. A sign of disrespect, which I considered harmless coming from a rivalrous and divided city like Glasgow. Believe me, this was a term of endearment as far as I was concerned. Moreover, his nickname for me was undoubtedly more accurate on current circumstances.

My experience with him was the polar opposite of the one with the surgeon now headed to Mexico. The fact that I can't remember either of their names is interesting, but it is fair to say that I will never forget either of them.

His boss and my new surgeon, Dr. Newman arrived early evening. We had a diagnosis now based on the radiographer's report, the blood work, and my unstable condition. They told me what they believed to have happened and that surgery was the course of action required. The diagnosis was full of medical words that I can only pretend to understand, but I could visualize the absolute impact on my body.

I will defer to Jen's explanation on social media that night—captured in full below.

Gerry Murphy likes grandstanding. He has really outdone himself now. He is a real-life case for Dr. House. Every doctor who comes in says "Interesting" and either says something different than the last doctor said or says nothing else. Here is how things shook out today: he has a combo of rare conditions, combining to make a unique case study. He has the unusual case where he has C. diff bacterial infection (source has them baffled) + diverticulitis (sort of like a colon infection). Being treated with antibiotics for that. He also has what's called a colovenus fistula that they think was caused by one of the diverticulitis pockets bursting. This is causing E. coli to dump into his bloodstream. The doctors took a while to diagnose the type of fistula because it is so rare—6 cases ever reported—they all keep coming to see him, like a newborn baby panda. He seemed to be getting better yesterday, but today he had a setback. Seems like the doctors don't agree on next steps, but are shocked that he is as (relatively) healthy as he is given how sick he is. Final verdict is surgery to remove the fistula and diverticulitis this week—maybe tomorrow. We will refer to today's episode as "How the Grinch Fistula Stole Christmas." Thanks a million to all who have reached out to help. F has a nasty cough, so I don't want to infect anyone else's kids—she was up all night last night but seems a bit better tonight. Luckily, that meant Young Kate DiLello got a bit of a break today with two naps— she's totally screwed tomorrow.

This was in the days before social media became, in my view, a toxic element in its own right. It was invaluable for us to keep everyone up to speed with what was going on, particularly my kids and family in the UK. I am forever grateful to that platform for that time.

So there it was. In layman's terms, essentially something had ruptured in my stomach and by the rarest of luck, a blood vessel had attached itself to the rupture. As a result, the waste from my stomach was pouring into my bloodstream.

Ichigan swung by after the formal visit to see if I was clear on what was said and to answer any (dumb) questions I had. Like I said, he was a star, and he helped me feel settled even though now I was facing surgery. Surgery was scheduled for Christmas Eve as this was the first slot Dr. Newman had available. He had a significant surgery to perform the next day, the twenty-third, so I was on standby for that, but it was unlikely that would happen.

This also prompted a scurry of activity with some other departments and functions. As part of the diagnosis and due to the blood poisoning, Dr. Newman advised me that he would be fitting a colostomy bag so that he didn't have to close me up after the surgery. The primary concern was the poisoning could complicate any postsurgical state. By fitting a colostomy, they would have a direct route in without opening me up again. Made sense to me. That prompted consultation with a surgical nurse about the use and effects of a colostomy bag. The thought of it was terrifying, and the first consult did little to ease my fears.

Fundamentally, I knew what it meant. I knew that it meant I was going to poop out of a hole in my side and that it would collect in a bag that was attached to said hole. Until confronted with this new reality, however, I hadn't considered that this meant my normal pipework was considered redundant and that my rectum was basically in a furloughed state. What would that feel like? Would I know it was happening? I had so many questions, most of which drifted into oblivion facing the thought of surgery.

It was at this time it was all explained to me that while this was "almost certainly a temporary state," there were two other (probably three actually, but one was left as a silent conclusion) outcomes that I needed to be aware of:

1. That this could be a permanent status dependent on what they found when they opened me up.
2. That, contingent on their findings, if I needed a full colectomy, other arrangements may need to be orchestrated during the surgery.

Be careful what you wish for! I had spent the last few days unclear what was wrong with me. Now I had a POV that meant I was staring at a new reality post surgery. Of course it was a no-brainer. Faced with uncertainty, and in a condition that is threatening your life, you would do any deal that gave you a life with a future tense, even with strings attached.

Jen had been to visit in the aftermath of the diagnosis, and while there wasn't really a decision to be taken, we agreed that this was the right course of action. We never really talked about the other potential scenarios. Neither of us are worriers by nature. "Why worry about what might not happen?" seemed to be our silently agreed approach. It wasn't that we couldn't bring ourselves to communicate about it. With Jen's loss of Michael, this was all too real for her again. And I could sense that. It was to be some time after this whole episode before we opened up about what we were really feeling at this point. It has more value to cover it later in the story.

Dr. Greene came by again. He was a calming figure and we discussed the surgery. He made me aware that because of the toxins in my blood, even post surgery, I would still be isolated and that those immediate days after surgery would be challenging physically and mentally.

As Jen's social media post had warned, it had been a rough day. This was now balanced with a diagnosis, a new situation, and a million thoughts in my head. The prescribed meds had been updated to deal with the infections I was fighting, but this diagnosis really meant there would be no significant improvement until the fistula was removed and the waste in my system stopped pouring into my bloodstream. It is a strange comfort when you know you are not "supposed" to be feeling better. It takes the pressure off a little. The specter of surgery applied a different pressure, and needless to say, I spent the night in a state of restlessness with my city outside for comfort and company.

I think these situations bring you back to who you really are. So many people use phrases like "he is a fighter" and "he won't be beaten," etc. I think what that means is that you will take whatever hits come your way and that you try to find a way to keep going. I believe it takes you to who you are at your core. When you are challenged by adversity, what is your gut response? Go over it? Under it? Through it or around it? Or do you capitulate? What does this situation demand of you? Here I had been shown a path that at first sight looked bumpy and murky, but it was a path. So I focused all my energy on that. That was my way out, however dark or uncertain. I was really trying not to blink and to stay focused on the new horizon in front of me. So far, this experience had shown me my absolute frailty, but it had also connected me to my very essence, my family. It had given me the fuel I needed for the fight—not physical fuel, but emotional energy, sturdiness, and ballast that meant I would face whatever this next step held for me.

It was going to be a long twenty-four hours waiting for the surgery time. I can't imagine how it feels waiting for a transplant or donor because of the open-endedness of that situation. I had a date and time where this part of the story would conclude and the next chapter would show itself.

Keep in mind the title of this chapter. Yes, the vacationing doctor had been a large slice of luck.

And despite current circumstances, I had to feel lucky.

Because I was lucky. Lucky in so many ways.

Lucky to have something and some people to fight this for.

Lucky that I was in the care of skilled professionals who worked out a way forward.

Lucky that I could have a future.

Lucky that, even if this was it, there was a lot to be happy with.

Lucky that I was loved and had loved.

Incredibly, there was still one more piece of luck to come.

CHAPTER 5

And you sang
Sail to me
Sail to me
Let me unfold you

—Tim Buckley

Tuesday morning, December 23, had started early with a change of pretty much everything medical attached to my body. New meds bag, new saline, new catheter, the next blood sample, and another magnesium lightning bolt in my veins. I was just settling into some kind of undisturbed restlessness when Ichigan appeared in the doorway. He had the biggest grin on his face. Ear to ear. I quickly scanned my somewhat limited knowledge of the outside world to find the source:

- Did the Buckeyes lose? Nope. Weren't playing.
- Did Michigan win? Don't be silly.
- From discussion I knew he didn't celebrate Christmas, so it couldn't be some amazing gift he had received or conceived for his wife or child.

- Did he pass his last exam? That wasn't for a few more weeks yet as the omnipresent textbook bore testimony too.

I gave up.

Me: "Okay, what is it? Why are you grinning like a madman?"

Him: "Well, I have some news for you."

Me: "What's up?"

Him: "Dr. Newman's office called the patient for today's surgery this morning to tell her the arrangements for coming in, and she was finishing her breakfast!"

Pause . . . (I wasn't exactly on top of my game) as he waited for me to get the impact of that sentence.

Me: "Wait what? She was eating? Wasn't she having a Whipple procedure?"

Him: "Yes!" He exclaimed this with such energy I couldn't help but be humbled by his care for me.

Me: "So . . ."

Him: "So the nurses are going to prep you for surgery, and I will be back in an hour to take you down."

Me: "Can someone call Jen to tell her?"

Him: "On it."

Incredible right? A woman I never met or knew contributed to my story in an anonymous but most significant way. Now there is nothing to say that I couldn't have waited out the twenty-four hours and had my surgery on Christmas Eve as originally planned. However, ever since the diagnosis, I had this very real sense that I could feel the toxic presence crawling in my blood. I am sure this was an overtired, hallucinatory sensation, but you never know, and maybe that twenty-four hours saved me. Maybe those twenty-four hours were crucial. How much longer could I have battled on? Luckily, I never had to answer that question.

In a strange way, I always used to celebrate the part the vacationing doctor played in my story more than the unknown woman. However, since I started to write this down, my anonymous surgery slot donor's distant but impactful cameo has played on my mind much, much more. The vacationing surgeon, in my experience, was a disagreeable guy, so he was easy to turn that into a somewhat vilified character. My unknown female benefactor though was really sick herself. That Whipple procedure is no joke (Google it!) and may have been caused by cancer. As time has progressed, I find myself thinking about her more and more and hoping she recovered after her procedure. I hope that her unwitting gift to me didn't cost her any more than the day we swapped. It is so bewildering how this world shows itself to us at times.

The next half hour was a blur. There were no questions about me having had anything to eat as that had been moot for five days now. However, all the other processes had to be taken care of.

The colostomy surgical nurse (obviously not her official title) appeared to draw the surgical target areas on me and to talk me through what I should expect to see when I came round from surgery. She assured me that they would fit the bag post surgery and that she would be around once I was back in the ward to "watch you change the bag for yourself."

If that wasn't terrifying enough, the waiver forms appeared and had to be signed. The waiver could be summed up in two sentences:

"I hereby give you permission to do whatever you need to do during surgery, depending on what you find during that process. And of course, should anything untoward happen, you are exonerated from all liability."

Yeah, *that* waiver!

Next up was the anesthetist. I received an explanation of how they were going to put me under and what drugs they were going to use, as well as a double check of any of my allergies. At this point, all historical record of allergies was irrelevant due to the new toxic state I found myself in. With that quick consult, she disappeared and the nurse came back in to get me ready to head down to the OR.

It's a helluva thing to face this life-saving procedure but not know what the other side of it looks like. What I knew with indefatigable certainty was that I couldn't go on like this. So this was it.

Ichigan reappeared and said they were ready. He was carrying his book as usual, and he intimated to the nurse that he would be traveling down with us. And then I was off, almost with no chance to breathe in. Maybe that was for the best! In what seemed like a blink of an eye, I was on the move and facing the next medical move.

When we arrived, the OR wasn't quite ready, so we parked in the hallway for a while. I have no idea how long, but it was long enough that I offered to give Ichigan a pop quiz on his constant companion. And that is what we did for maybe a dozen questions or so and some follow-up questions from this ignoramus. He was money on that stuff, and that probably made us both feel better.

We got the shout and two more masked faces appeared to roll me into the OR. I remember how cold it was in there. Instant chill to the bone, so much that I could immediately feel my body react. This was disconcerting, as being so cold had been a signal for something much worse over the previous days. As they transferred me to the operating table, my gown rode up, making me feel the chill even more. It wasn't even embarrassing really. Jeez, in a few hours I was going to be pooping in a bag, if I was lucky!

They covered me in a quilted blanket as I assumed the position like I was being crucified. A timely reminder of my lapsed relationship with my religion? I remember the table being very narrow—there was no wiggle room, literally.

The anesthetist reintroduced herself with the OR nurse. My accent always causes some reaction, so we spent the next minute or so chatting like we were at some very specific speed dating event ignoring our very real purpose.

Dr. Newman appeared, masked and ready to go. All the important details were cross-checked, and then the anesthesia process started.

It's at this point, I would like to share the significance of this chapter's song. This is a beguiling chant of a siren calling you to your inevitable end. It haunts and teases but promises nothing but the end. And yet it is so alluringly beautiful. I have always found its trancelike qualities so strong that it is hard to think of anything but the beauty and intrigue in your mind's eye while listening. You can see its resonance in this moment. The clock, which had been suspended for five days, suddenly burst back into life like moving from slow motion to some time-delayed view of my life. It afforded me no time to dwell on the potential outcomes of the procedure. There were brief moments of calm in that half hour, like I was in the eye of the storm and was allowed a breath to reflect. But there was no one there. No last "I love you." No last embrace. Just a sense of "I hope they know how much I love them."

I don't want to overdramatize this moment, but it has left a mark. I cried when I wrote this. I didn't expect to. It just crept up on me as I took myself back to that time. It was like I was grieving at some level. Obviously, no one died, but I think I grieved for the moment. That moment where having no choice surpassed my fear, regardless of outcome. I realize when I tell this story, and I have many times, that I always skip the most confrontational parts. These parts demand a response from the listener, but in reality require some emotional exposure from me that, up until now, I haven't been willing to, or able to describe. That was the moment where the question "What if I die here?" was hanging in the air, quickly followed by "What is after this life?" It was like exam day and I hadn't studied, and now I had to cram all this awareness and understanding into the moments before they put me under. In this case, as in most cramming cases in my experience, if you get away with it, it doesn't teach you the lesson that perhaps you need. This would be the ultimate lesson if I didn't wake, or indeed if I did wake and found my reality was very new and not what I had imagined. The exposure that this caused is telling, and based on this experience, I knew some of the changes I would need to make would be significant.

The last five days had deprived me of some human elements we take for granted, such as physical things like food and water and rest. It also deprived me of some emotional elements, like being connected to my loved ones. It was like a precursor to not being here.

My motivation to change my approach to my life comes from these moments. I was shown what it would look like without me. I was forced to face an uncertainty that begged this question:

"When this time comes again, and it surely will, what do I need to do now that means I won't feel so inept, vulnerable, or ashamed about how I lived my life?

That question is the crux of practicing death.

My Immediate Response

Fast forward to a time not long after the surgery—the changes I made immediately after this scare were small. Now this may seem like a whisper as an answer to the sonic boom radiating through my life, but I could do them right away and they were completely in my control. They were little things that seem so insignificant but certainly owed their genesis to this vulnerable moment. For example, I now make a point of texting Jen to tell her that I love her before I get on a flight. In those situations where I cede control to something or someone else, I want to make sure she knows I was thinking about her and that whatever happens next, she was on my mind and in my heart. I am very aware that when that time comes, I want those three little words to be among the last things said, if not the last altogether.

It is an emotional challenge to face the uncertainty of a surgical outcome versus the knowledge that it has to be done. It must have happened millions of times before, but for me, I was acutely aware of the fragility of the situation and my own frailty within it. We make choices every day, some of them difficult. So when you are faced with no choice at all, that in itself is a shock.

In my mind, I could hear the siren calling me. Dark and mysterious but so, so compelling.

As I lay there on the OR table, the masked face leaned in and said, "You will feel a cold sensation now and this will calm you down." It did. I felt at peace. And then the words followed, "I am adding in the anesthesia now, start to count backwards from 10."

"10, 9, 8 . . ."

CHAPTER 6

Oh how I realized how I wanted time
Put into perspective, tried so hard to find

—Joy Division

The next thing I knew was that I was in the recovery room. I was drowsy, but almost immediately I felt the sharpest of pains in my side. The recovery room nurse was talking to me, but I felt like I was underwater and her words didn't make sense. Gradually they became clearer as both audio and visual inputs found a focus.

Everyone there, I don't recall anyone specifically, was quick to assure me everything had gone to plan and that Dr. Newman would be around soon to talk me through what had happened.

As I regained some clarity, I started to wonder—what can I do and what *can't* I do? I waited until no one was watching, and I slowly raised the covers to see my new appendage. Of course I was in a surgical gown and what would normally require pulling something down, now required pulling something up. I mustered up the courage and energy to reach down and pull up the yellow-stained gown.

My abdomen was bloated, so the whole view was of something unrecognizable. Not only did it look bad, it felt bad. The bag just looked like it was set on my stomach, belying how it was connected to my newly reshaped body. Reaching down to check it out was a bit of an endurance test in itself as the middle of my body felt rigid and completely inelastic.

I returned myself to some sort of decency, and my friend Ichigan appeared. He told me they had called Jen and she would be up to visit later once I was back in the unit.

He explained the following: I indeed had a colovesical fistula, which was responsible for the waste in my blood. The rupture was suspected to be diverticulitis, but they were not completely clear if that was the cause or indeed what caused that to be set off. Regardless of its source, the end result of the surgery was that they had performed a partial colectomy, removing the sigmoid colon and part of the descending colon. This action removed the damaged and infected part of my large intestine.

Let me try to describe it in my terms. (This may eliminate the need of going to a search engine while reading this, or it may not help at all.) First, we have two intestines. The small intestine is the "sausage meat links" part of your stomach that is used in bad horror movies to depict when the victim has been gutted. That was left intact. The large intestine is essentially the colon, which starts with the appendix and ends in the anal canal. It is shaped like a soccer goal with an extra piece on the right post (as you look at the front of the goal) leading down to the rectum. That piece plus part of the right post was what was removed. Forgive my rather simplistic view, but when I researched it later, that was what it reminded me of.

I passed all the necessary vital signs and alertness and was ready to go to the postsurgical part of the ICU. Ichigan said he and Dr. Newman would be around once I was back in the unit and that he would see me later.

This time the journey through the corridors was the normal view. The bed back was elevated as I wasn't supposed to lay flat for the next few days to avoid stretching out the surgical area. We arrived at the new spot, and I was introduced to the new staff. They explained I would be there for twenty-four to forty-eight hours before hopefully getting out of the ICU back into a main population ward. I would still be isolated because C. diff is contagious and therefore would require some separation and preparation, and as a result, all visitors would have to wear protective overalls and gloves.

The next few hours were blurry to say the least. But it was busy. As promised, my Fairy Godmother colostomy nurse was one of the first to appear. She pulled back the blankets and talked me through my new anatomical process.

(I will try not to be too graphic with the description, but it is almost unavoidable when you consider the subject matter).

First, she took me through a dummy run of the process. The bag (at least the one I used) came in three parts. Essentially, it consisted of a connector to the skin, a plastic fixing, and the bag itself. The whole change process would be done every three days or so depending on usage. The bag could be emptied any time necessary during those three days through the bottom. All three parts had holes in the middle, as you would expect, as this is what would surround my stoma. A stoma is essentially the open end of your pipework that protrudes from your side, in my case, my left side. She was quick to point out that there are no nerve endings in a stoma, so I wouldn't actually feel anything when working with it. I would just have to get over the thought of it!

The most important element was to make sure the fit was as accurate as possible to avoid any unwanted leakages. I was pretty much fine up until that point of clarity. The introduction of the thought of leakages made me shiver. The next big decision was what kind of bag I would like to use. We aren't talking designer choices here, but more about the practical elements and which would best suit my circumstances. Did I want two piece or three piece? Clear or skin colored? They would need to be ordered so that they would be at home when I got there. Decisions, decisions! Such a bittersweet statement! The thought of getting home was already top of mind for me, but here it was mixed with the reality that, for the short term at least, my daily functions would be different.

The next person to cross the bottom of my bed was the physical therapist. She introduced herself and immediately launched into the plan for the next few days. First and foremost, she wanted me to be able to split time between the chair at my bedside and the bed itself. We did that there and then, so we could see what obstacles it would bring. Freed from all the wires and plug-ins, the PT told me how she wanted me to get to the side of the bed. This was essentially an "all arms" movement to get me up on my elbows, swing my legs over the side of the bed, pull myself into a position where both feet could hit the floor at the same time, and staying bent over, push my legs into the floor and get upright using my arms. I describe this because what seems such a simple movement was really quite difficult and painful. It was also during this movement that I was reminded of the weakness in my postsurgical knee. It wobbled quite visibly and reminded me that the seven days since the surgery had really involved next to no movement for the joint. This concerned my therapist too, and once I had lowered myself into the chair, she was furiously scribbling add-ons to my PT program.

It was good to be in a different position, but it was painful, as being upright compressed the wound. Discovering such physical limitations showed me the path forward would be challenging. My therapist outlined the plan for the next few days and left.

Jen arrived, and that brought more people to the bedside to give her the updates that had been flowing throughout the afternoon. The unit nurse came back and caught Jen up on all the news. One of my rewards for getting into the chair was I was allowed water again. Not to be guzzled but to be sipped on until they were sure there was no postsurgical reaction. I would be able to return to a limited soft diet the next day. The water tasted like top-shelf liquor. Cold and thirst quenching, I could feel it course down my throat. It had taken on a whole new significance and immediately made me feel like I was on my way back.

It was so good to see Jen. The relief between us was palpable, and while we still didn't discuss what had happened in any detail, we had a new focus of getting me recovered and back home. Dr. Newman appeared while she was still there, so we both got the update together. He was happy with how the surgery had gone. He went over the details of what was found in there and assured us he believed this would solve the problem. Crucially, for me at least, he believed the colostomy would be temporary and that in the next few months, once the infection was cleared, he would be able to conduct a reversal surgery. That would essentially reconnect my pipework to its original, if shortened, state. That news immediately lifted my spirits, as there was a deadline in my head now of what had to happen for me to be returned to my previous bodily functions.

The next day was Christmas Eve, and the friends and family who had come to help and support Jen were now returning to their own Christmas celebrations. They were leaving the next morning, so this would be the last visit for a few days. Frances was still not allowed in the ICU and so we had no choice, however difficult it was to come to terms with. Jen helped me back into my bed in a labored reversal of the previous movement, we hugged, and then she headed back to the little one. We would talk on the phone, but we had decided to postpone the Christmas celebration until I was home. Our nearly two-year-old daughter would be none the wiser, so we didn't feel too bad about it.

I was aware it was dark now and the unit was relatively quiet. The approaching holiday meant that there wasn't too much coming and going and so I started to look forward to that commodity that I had been terrified of for the previous five days—sleep!

I tried to find a comfortable position that accommodated both my knee pain and my side pain. I don't sleep on my back normally (full disclosure, I snore if I do), so I had been encouraged away from that position over the years. However, I was now somewhat forced to since I had to accommodate the discomforts on both sides of my body.

Of course in some sort of ironic twist, a good sleep eluded me, and I nodded off and on for what felt like forever. I am not sure if it was the discomfort from the surgery or the cocktail of drugs and exhaustion, but I felt pretty emotional when it was quiet. The severity of the last few days really hit home, and I was left feeling a mixture of relief, embarrassment, and guilt. I had

had way too much time on my own with some heavy thoughts and questions. Seeing Jen leave, with no hope of a visit in the next few days, really hit hard and added to my isolation. Hence the choice of song for this chapter. Joy Division were known as a "dark" band. I prefer the term "real." That view is compounded by the fact that Ian Curtis, the lead singer, committed suicide at a young age, reportedly due to his difficulty dealing with his severe epilepsy. Having experienced the temporary state of rigors, the parallels were acute. I can't imagine how someone would cope with that if it was a permanent condition. I had barely lasted four days. I was still saddened and frustrated by his suicide, but I certainly felt like I understood it more. This caused a welling of emotion in me that I was struggling to cope with and the isolation was compounding it.

I must have slept eventually because I awoke to the nurse changeover. I was promised more water and some breakfast if I got into the chair to have it. I was also greeted with the news that my progress was strong enough that I would be moving to a non-ICU ward.

I called Jen to share the news. We kept the contact to voice calls as I was still on oxygen and didn't want Frances to be wondering what all the tubes and wires were about. She was at that inquisitive stage where only the questions matter. The answers are almost immaterial as they are beyond her comprehension. She could hear my voice, so we settled for that.

The medical team arrived and examined the stoma site by removing the colostomy bag and checking there was nothing untoward there. To my surprise, there was "content" in the bag—surprise because I didn't recall it happening. The days of "unconscious pooping" had arrived! Weird.

Of course, now with an exposed stoma, that could only mean my "bag lady" (as I affectionately called her in my head) would be around shortly. And I thought, *Please, God, please get here before something embarrassing happens!*

She didn't let me down. She started by walking me through a reminder of yesterday's demo and got me in a position to do it myself. Now I was faced with the reality that I was going to have to touch the area around the stoma. I started to apply the first part and immediately the challenge became obvious. The stoma protrudes slightly above the skin surface, so that everything that exits the wound is away from the skin and free to proceed into the awaiting bag. This was a depth perception challenge that did become easier as I became more proficient. The "bag lady" advised me to use a mirror when I was back up and mobile to help until I was more accurate. The key was to fit the bag in as close to the stoma as possible without strangling it. Too close would lead to irritation of the stoma, and too loose would leave a gap between the patch and the stoma, allowing fecal matter to land on my skin. I mean, never did I ever think that would be something I had to worry about. Just to make sure I understood the importance of getting this right, I actually started to poop in that moment. It was entirely involuntary, and I was completely oblivious apart from the obvious physical evidence before my eyes. It was recognizable in color and odor, but apart from that, like nothing I had ever seen before. It was like a slimy, slender snake sliding out the only exit it could find. Although horrified, I was powerless to stop it. Talk about embarrassing moments. What do you say? "I should be done in a minute" or "When you got to go, you got to go"? Neither seemed appropriate, so I said nothing. My nurse had seen this and much much worse, so she barely blinked. She simply used this as a practical opportunity to show me how to clean the stoma when changing the bag. Man are they heroes!

I finished, and we continued with the bag fitting. The incident helped me relax somewhat—what could be worse than what had just happened?

It maybe took a half hour in total to change the bag, and at the end I started to relax, safe in the knowledge that it didn't have to happen for another few days. As if she could read my mind, the nurse revealed that we would do this every morning until I went home, to get the practice in. It made sense, but I wasn't looking for sense in that moment. She left me with the news it would be someone different the next day, Christmas Day, but she would be back the day after.

With the bag changed, I was feeling freer than I had since arriving in the ICU, so I asked the unit nurse to help me into the chair so I could have breakfast. The only snafu was that because I had been nil by mouth for days, that had overridden my breakfast order, meaning there was nothing for me. I wasn't really bothered, but the staff wanted me to try to eat something to see what reaction, if any, there would be. After some hustling and rustling, I was the happy recipient of a vanilla pudding and a ginger ale. The pudding wasn't Ambrosia, but it could well have been.[1] My taste buds started to awaken, and I was back on the wagon with a very easy start.

---

1. That reference is there for my UK peeps—as well as being the food of the Gods in mythology, Ambrosia is also a UK pudding and dessert brand of some fame to a certain age group! When I was growing up, my mum would make us custard for dessert. Apparently that creation was a labor of love, and no lack of skill, to ensure a lump-free goop at the end. Ambrosia tinned custard was the opposite. It could be eaten straight from the tin, was delicious cold, and really very sweet. The only drawback—it was out of our family food budget range on a weekly basis, so it was reserved for birthdays, treats, and on the occasion my mum made trifles.

It was just as well the sugar was running through my system because my physical therapist arrived next. She was thrilled to see me in the chair, with the admission that she usually has to drag her patients out of bed on the day after surgery. She worked and flexed my knee a little to see the range of motion I had. After testing the knee, she broke the news that we were going to do a lap around the unit. I felt lightheaded but was determined to get going. Gingerly, I took the first few steps and instantly became aware of the lack of use of my legs over the past few days. Due to the bloating, there was an overwhelming sense of rigidity throughout my body. I wouldn't say I walked. Instead, I shuffled into the corridor to the encouragement of the staff. In short order, I found a rhythm and was moving fairly smoothly. I was aware I was hunched over. Apparently this was my body's self-defense mechanism. I had a new weakness and pain in my side, so to compensate, my body would instinctively fold over a little to cover up that area. This meant the other focus of the PT was to be as upright as possible. That hurt for sure, but it was one of several milestones I had to pass to get home, so I wouldn't be dissuaded. In fact, at the end of the first lap, I asked if we could go around again. Pure bravado. Halfway around the second lap, I really started to feel it, but I was all in now, so there was only one way back. I gritted my teeth and shuffled my way back to the room.

After a little rest period, it was time for the move to the main ward. The complication was that ICU beds remain in the ICU, so they were waiting on a ward bed and as soon as it was available, I would be on the move. That move felt good to me. I wasn't sure why, but it felt good. It represented some kind of progress. The dropping of the Intensive Care label was definitely something to relish.

The new ward was brighter than the ICU and had the novelty of having other patients too. There were six bed stations
and four of us, including me. Two of the guys were awake and
welcomed me with a wave. The third of my new companions
was behind closed cubicle curtains.

The new staff introduced themselves as they got me stationed. I would only have one nurse because of the C. diff infection. She was great. We instantly connected and talked through
the last week, the surgeries, and all of the other elements she
would be helping me with. Pretty soon we were talking about
our families, and it turned out she had two kids around
Frances's age. When I clumsily asked her if they were excited for
Christmas, she shared that she was Jewish and didn't celebrate
Christmas. From her viewpoint, the immediate benefit was that
she could work Christmas Eve and Christmas Day, and that
someone who did celebrate the holiday could benefit by being
off. She was that kind of person.

It felt good to have company, and I really appreciated getting to chat with the nurse. It was normal, which the past six
days had been far from.

Lunch came, and for the second time that day, I was foiled.
The order I had placed after the breakfast fail was for the ICU,
so now that I was relocated, there was nothing for me again.
Everyone was so apologetic, unnecessarily so. I really didn't
want anything, but I needed to continue the process of returning my bowel to some kind of normality. I asked if there were
any puddings available. As if by magic, two appeared with
another ginger ale. Result!

Truth be told, after a harrowing run in with school dinners
in my youth, I was never fully trusting of what was in institu-
tional meals and how they were prepared. Would hospital food

be of a higher quality? My experience in the UK had led me to believe that it was a level or two below school dinners, unless you were in a private healthcare facility.

Buoyed by double dessert for lunch, I decided to take on an expedition back to the chair. The nurse came around and helped me through this now practiced, if not smooth, movement. I could certainly feel the pain more acutely today. There was a surety that the pain was there. It was a reminder of what had happened and also a prompt to not ignore the severity of the situation just because I felt like I was out of the crosshairs of it.

The rest of the day passed with some periods of rest and others of discomfort. My ward companions had visitors in the afternoon. I was happy for them but sad for me.

For comfort and company, my mind drifted to the Christmas Eves of my childhood and all that came with them. My inability to get to sleep was consistent with years gone by, but for very different reasons. I was melancholic, but thankful, and as the evening turned to night, I found myself thinking about my children and my family and friends five hours ahead in the UK. They would now be in full-on Christmas Eve "toy-building stealth mode" or party mode. I missed them, but tonight I was more thankful that I was still around to miss them at all.

This idea that everything could be the last time is a basic premise of how we can practice death. It had been a long time since I had shared the holidays with some of the people on my mind, but never did it cross my mind that it could have been the last time. If I had known it was going to be the last time, what would I have done or said differently?

I will leave the last words for this chapter to my Facebook post that night:

As this Christmas Eve starts to turn into Christmas Day across my FB world, I just wanted to thank all my family and friends, some people I know and some I don't, for your kind, sincere prayers and wishes during this difficult time for our family. You have no idea how much of a comfort it was to me. Thank you for supporting the most incredible woman I know, and I am very lucky to call my wife Jennifer Nellany. She is a rock but was even stronger for all your help. For Kate DiLello, Elizabeth Walsh, Tina Pedrick-Scott, and all others who jumped in to help—no words can convey my appreciation. So with all that said, I want to wish you all a very merry healthy Christmas! The Nellany Murphys will catch up somewhere down the road!

CHAPTER 7
Christmas Double A Side

TRACK 7: CHRISTMAS AND GLASGOW

... she's thinking of years
At Christmas and Glasgow
When it meant too much

—Deacon Blue

TRACK 8: CHRISTMAS LIGHTS

The Christmas lights
Go all around the world

—Blue Nile

I am going to invoke a break in the track-per-chapter discipline to hark back to years ago when bands would release double A sides at Christmastime. It was supposed to be extra value for the buyer, but I think that it was just a clever marketing trick to get double exposure for the one release. Or maybe it showed indecision or musical differences between band

and label in who wanted to release which track, and this was the compromise.

In my case, it was very much indecision. Both my favorite Christmas songs are by Glasgow bands but with very different sentiment. The Deacon Blue track reignites memories of my childhood and when I was in Glasgow. It references "the sweet smell of the Kelvin Hall Circus," (it was far from sweet, and it is in my nostrils as I write this). This was a family activity of ours most years when I was growing up. If we were lucky, it would be combined with a trip to the adjacent carnival. That song rolled through my head as I tried to go to sleep and was still there when I woke from a fitful night. It was such a rich childhood memory, but the lyric above caught my attention more and more.

While the memories were sharp, it was really the people that I missed and in this situation longed for. Growing up, Christmas Day was probably one of the longest days of the year—in a good way. I was the oldest of four, so our house would stir early as the present-opening frenzy would begin. As we got older, Christmas Eve Vigil Mass became a bigger part of the routine, but in the early days, it would be 10 a.m. or 11 a.m. mass depending on which parish we would be attending. Then we would head to my paternal grandparents' house for Christmas lunch. My dad was the middle child of three. They were spread out in age and in distance, so sometimes my aunts Christine and Marguerite were there, and sometimes not. A few hours would be spent there, and then it was off to my maternal grandparents' house. This was a much bigger cast. There were three brothers and three sisters, my mum being the eldest. Over the years, the boys would come and go. John was in banking and went to Beirut in the '70s when it legitimately earned its "infamous" tag. Willie immigrated to Canada during my teens, but not until he had two children of his own. He stayed there until his untimely death. Charlie had gone to South Africa at a young age but had returned and had settled back in Glasgow. We would always see my aunts Moira and Elizabeth with their respective husbands, Alex and Bryan. I was the oldest of the cousins. Elizabeth and Bryan had a son, Bryan, six months younger than me, and then there was a run of nine girl cousins. And it wasn't just Christmas. Growing up, we would visit my mum's side of the family every Saturday and visit my dad's side of the family every Sunday. So my cousins were a big part of my life. They say that, don't they, that your cousins are your first friends? It is very true in my case.

Over the years, as the family expanded, Christmas Day got crazier and crazier, in the best way. My papa would disappear and dress up as Santa to give out the gifts. Sheer magic! I use this term because "magic" was one of his favorite words. My gran would somehow feed everyone all at the same time.

As I lay in the hospital bed, looking out the window into one of those foggy New York mornings, where fourteen floors up you feel like you have been enveloped in it, like some precursor to Armageddon, my mind and heart were back in those days. The timing wasn't exactly right, but I remember thinking that in a few hours, that was what would be ahead of us. A tear dropped from my eye, maybe in self-pity, but definitely as a reflection of some of the most formative times and indeed, best times of my life. It was still going to be a long day, but for very different reasons.

As if to snap me out of this melancholy and self-absorbed state, my nurse appeared. However, she added to the emotion. My Jewish nurse brought me a Christmas card, from her and her family to me and mine. That pretty much set me off again. We hugged, and I thanked her for her thoughtfulness. She asked what she could get me for Christmas. I gave the most heartfelt answer ever to her in that moment: "If you can find the time, please stop by and chat. I know you are busy, but I would really like to just talk." She promised she would when the opportunity arose. She kept her promise. She took her lunch break with me and even gave me some of her homemade Matzah Ball soup to try. I had never tried it before. Talk about "just what the doctor ordered"!

I can be a chatty person, and I have faced accusations of using ten words, when three would do, but this request to talk surprised me. It came from somewhere deep inside me, I think, that I hadn't experienced before. I had spent so much time alone and awake, that maybe it was understandable. This was going to be a different kind of Christmas.

The morning hospital routine quickly returned with no regard for the calendar, or for the people carrying out that routine. It was time to change my colostomy bag again. This time the replacement "bag lady" destroyed the mental nickname completely by being a man. The "bag man" has very different connotations, depending on where you grew up. Turned out he was a good guy and supported me through another complete bag change. This time there was no extra drama, just the ineptitude of a rookie. I made a few mistakes, but that added value to the process in terms of me learning. We were done in relative short order, and he went on his way, presumably to destroy someone else's nickname game!

It was now a reasonable hour to call Jen and talk to her and Frances. When she answered, it turned out that I could have called even earlier. Not because of the frenzy of gift opening, but because Frances had a cough and was up through the night. We chatted, and I told her about the Christmas card and

my morning so far. I was aware that their Christmas had been
wrecked too, and so I was keen to know what they planned to
do later today. Jen then went on to tell me that Christmas Eve
had been eventful in a good way too. She had been talking to
one of her colleagues, Dave Koetke, who on hearing what had
been going on, insisted that Jen and Frances come to their house
for drinks and food on Christmas Eve in the late afternoon.
They had accepted the invitation and were entertained by Dave,
his wife, Mara, their four-year-old daughter, Alex, and Mara's
parents. They had a great time, and I could hear that this had
helped ease Jen's stress levels. She too had found some adult
conversation and some company that had soothed her. It is a
tradition that continues. We go there every year now. And if we
have visitors over for Christmas, then they come too! My oldest
daughter has been, as has my youngest sister. And every year I
can't help but think about the first one that I missed, and how so
very grateful I was to Dave and Mara for supporting my family.
We have been good friends ever since. We had dinner recently,
in London actually, and I was telling them about this book and
how they would have their own paragraph.

I am going to pass the keys to Jen at this point so she can
tell you about her NYC Christmas Day adventure. The human
power to be able to turn difficult circumstances into a positive
really is extraordinary.

*I have always been a lover of all things Christmas, espe-
cially the aspects that involve prioritizing spending time
with family and friends. It's a special kind of joy that,
if done correctly, can help steel you for the doldrums of
January and February.*

*The Christmas of 2014 was a different experience for
all of us. I had been excited to see the joy through Frances's*

eyes as an almost-two-year-old. I think my expectations the previous year had been too high for a not-even-one-year-old child. But I was convinced that 2014 would hit closer to the mark.

Luckily, since Frances was so young, she wasn't conscious of dates and time, so there was no counting down the number of days until Santa arrives, which is currently her favorite thing to do as an almost-seven-year-old. Because of the nature of Gerry's illness, no children under sixteen were allowed to visit him in the hospital, which meant I needed to find someone to watch Frances when I went to spend time with him. While we have a full-time babysitter, she takes her vacation during the two weeks surrounding Christmas, so she was back home in Trinidad, blissfully unaware of the unfolding crisis in our household.

We are fortunate to have some pretty amazing friends who rallied to assist at a time when they are just as overbooked (with mostly fun things) during the holiday season as everyone else. Our friend Kate and her mother stayed in NYC until Christmas Eve to take Frances so that I could go be with Gerry (and to shake things up with the doctors so that they knew it wasn't my first time at the rodeo).

When they left, it was just me and my sweet girl. All alone. It felt so wrong to be by ourselves on Christmas Eve, especially when I was so used to that night being full of activity and loved ones. Gerry's family was on another continent; my family and close friends were all outside of NYC, and I didn't want to be too far from the hospital—just in case. But again, a couple of local NYC friends who had been following the drama on Facebook (which I found to be the easiest way to update everyone who cared) graciously offered to open their homes to me and Frances. We ended up taking my friend from work, Dave, up on his offer. I had never met his wife and daughter at that point, which initially made me feel a little uncomfortable, but once we arrived, I felt that it was exactly where we should have been. In fact, we now go to their home every year on Christmas Eve and consider them more like family than friends. It is hard to describe to people sometimes how much a simple thing meant to us at such a difficult time.

On Christmas Day, I would not have felt comfortable crashing anyone's party, so Frances and I were tourists in our own city. It was an unseasonably warm day in NYC that Christmas, so we took advantage of the nice weather and went to see the tree at Rockefeller Center and the other holiday decorations around Midtown. While Frances was napping, I went into a quiet bar and had lunch and a festive cocktail. I avoided mentioning Santa and his impending arrival (or lack thereof, in this case). While Frances and I had a lovely day together, it was obviously tainted by the knowledge that Gerry was lying in a hospital bed a few blocks away and we couldn't be with him. But we are a resilient bunch, if nothing else. Once Gerry was home and feeling a little stronger, Santa did arrive, albeit a couple of days later. But Santa's prime beneficiary was none the wiser about his delayed arrival, and the joy I had been hoping for was delivered, both in the delight of our daughter and the fact that our little family was reunited.

I like this other view. I like that they had a day to remember out of the ashes of our Christmas Day. I didn't know it at the time, but in a reflective state, I like to think about them running around the city below where I lay.

Back in the hospital, my therapist arrived, and it was time to get moving again. The movement out of the bed wasn't any better, and the two laps were uneventful but equally uncomfortable as they had been the day before. We returned to my cubicle, and she worked my knee some more to get the joint as flexible as possible. Then it was back to bed. I called Kevin and Caitlin in the UK before they went out for Christmas dinner, and this time I chatted without creating panic!

The surgical pain was manageable for the most part. It would peak around every three and a half hours as the previous dose wore off, but already I was fixated with lengthening each interval. Maybe it was some internal symbolism that indicated to me I was getting better. What was challenging to deal with was my inability to move without difficulty. Getting into the chair was an athletic trial in itself, and staying seated felt like an endurance test. My abdomen and sides just ached and were so inflexible it felt like individual parts of my core muscle group had been shut down and given Christmas off. I found myself gearing up mentally in advance of any planned movement. It was taking a lot out of me, so much so that I just felt drained in between exertions. I was still surrounded by a masked, gowned, and gloved team as they worked to ensure the infection didn't spread. This also meant that my cubicle curtains were mostly closed when my ward companions had visitors. Today, most of the visitors coincided with lunchtime so they could celebrate together in some form or fashion. I was comforted in knowing that they could still share the day with their nearest and dearest.

My lunch as described earlier was off-menu and with my nurse. I don't remember much of anything we talked about. It wasn't about that. It was about companionship and company at a time when all my emotions were running high about times of togetherness. I am sure we talked about Hanukkah, as I was largely ignorant to its traditions and meaning. We talked about our kids, as mine were heavy on my mind. I missed them. I didn't miss the gifts or even the traditions. I just wanted them near. That day showed me that my memories of Christmases past were actually about who I spent them with, not what I got! Thinking about it, I couldn't remember many gifts from through the years, given or received. I remember my record player. Man, I used that until it couldn't be used any more. I must have been eleven or twelve, because we moved when I was ten, and all my memories of it are in the then new house. It is a heavy lesson that what appears to matter the most at the time isn't at all what matters over time. Even the religious significance had lost its meaning to me, particularly since I had lapsed in my attendance and practice. This wasn't the first time it had shown itself over the last seven days, and I knew that a part of any outcome from this experience had to be some form of spiritual reconnection. The accepted loanword here would be "renaissance," but in my Italian studies I always loved the Italian equivalent of "rinascimento." I am not sure why, but it always meant more to me even though its translation is exactly the same. By some accounts, the Renaissance began in Italy—and yet it has a French name. Still makes no sense to me even though there have been many books on the subject.

Until I considered this concept of practicing death, I had really only thought of rebirth as if it were in a different form or a different body. What this experience was telling me was that a rebirth was possible from our existing form and life. The impetus could be created to show the person what matters most to them.

The rest of the day was relatively quiet. Understandably, the ward was running on minimum staff to maximize the numbers taking time with their loved ones. I settled for listening to my iPod, and that was how the significance of the second song for this chapter entered the day.

It is such a dreamy song and felt like Christmas nights from the past when all the commotion had calmed down and you were left to reflect on the day and the people. I also realized that this song is set at a distance. No matter how far you are from your memories or your loved ones, there are certain connections that take you right back there. As a result, I was calmer that night. The emotional arc of the day had been intense, and as my mind had virtually traveled the globe thinking about my friends and family in different parts of the world, I needed to hear the words "I believe in you." It may have been self-belief, it may have been the rekindling of a spiritual belief. It doesn't matter. I talked to Jen to hear all about her day, and then I was determined to get some decent rest.

SIDE 2

CHAPTER 8
Side Two

And every day's like Christmas Day without you
It's cold and there's nothing to do

—Everything but the Girl

It must have been on my mind as I slept, but I woke up with only one thing on my mind. *I need to get out of here and get home.* This song may be about a lost love and a plea for a return, and while that wasn't a perfect match, I sure was determined to get home. It is an interesting dynamic, post surgery in hospital. They want you to go home, and you want to get home. Fairly quickly, once new norms or recovery processes are formalized, then the energy is all geared toward getting you out of there. I thought I would get the ball rolling by getting into the chair myself before any of my morning processes started.

The lack of mobility was still evident, but I was determined to make some progress today. I was waiting in the chair when the nurses did their nightshift-to-dayshift handover. The dayshift nurse was my lunch companion from yesterday. She scolded me for getting into the chair myself, but she could also see I didn't care too much for her rebuking. When she was done lecturing me, I said to her, "I want to go home. What do I need to do today to get to go home?"

There was a list. Instinctively, I'd known there had to be.

- Eat more of the soft diet they were serving me
- Complete another successful bag change
- Get off the catheter
- Show more mobility (this was supported by the above point)
- Satisfy PT that I was steady enough to get home and be safe
- Be supervised at home for the next few days
- Make arrangements at home for C. diff separation (separate bathroom and toilet for me away from Jen and Frances)

None of the above were out of the realms of possibility. I asked her to raise it at the doctor's rounds when they came round later.

Of course when that happened, the first thing Dr. Newman mentioned was "So you want to go home?" I confirmed I did, and he agreed that we would swing a plan into place for the day to allow that to happen, but only on those conditions listed above. Assuming all items were met, I could potentially go home that afternoon. You can imagine my smile!

I called Jen to tell her the news. She was somewhat surprised but happy we would soon be able to get back to some kind of normal. I would need clothes brought to the hospital when we got the green light. It was cold but bright outside, and yesterday's fog had given in to bright winter sunshine. My favorite kind of day! Remember I had traveled in a week prior in shorts and a sweatshirt, and while Jen had brought a few other items in over the subsequent days, none of it was ideal for leaving hospital.

First task on the list was to get the catheter out, and that was done fairly smoothly and without any setbacks. For the record, it doesn't hurt; it just feels really weird. The other condition attached to this was I had to pee before I would be allowed to leave. They gave me a cup so they could see if "number ones" were working! There was no doubt in my mind it contributed to my starting to feel a bit more normal. While one bodily function was on a bypass for the foreseeable future, having the other back somehow made me feel more complete.

The pain was still very real, but that was going to be true whether in hospital or at home, so Ichigan came back around, and we discussed pain control at home and what he would be prescribing for me. None of the names meant anything to me, so I just agreed and the nurse and I formalized which drugstore they would send the prescription to. Ichigan and I said goodbye, he fully intended not to see me again, and while I knew I would never forget him, I was happy with his confidence that he and I were done. We launched some collegiate insults at each other for the last time, and he left my life and no doubt went on his way to make a profound difference in many other lives.

My "bag lady" was back. We exchanged Christmas greetings and got down to business. As uncomfortable as I was with the process, I told her she was just to observe me doing it from start to finish and only jump in if I was making a big mistake. It passed without incident, and I also got to demonstrate my ability to empty the bag, clean the exit seal, and replace it back into its locked-down position. She was satisfied with my ability to take care of the process and reminded me that there would be a home nurse visiting in the next few days to check on the stoma and my care of it. Like I said, I wasn't comfortable with it, but I felt reassured that someone would be around to check my work in short order.

Next up was PT. I was back in the chair after changing my bag and was determined not to get back in the bed if possible. She worked the knee first, and that genuinely felt like it was working. Continued movement was going to be a case for going home, where mobility would be demanded more, so any discomfort here was easy to ignore. We went out to do our laps and, as if to prove a point, we went for three! Look, I wasn't breaking any ambulatory speed records, but I was moving, and being upright kinda helped me feel like everything was in its normal place.

By the time I had worked through all the criteria, the only one left was to eat something for lunch. It duly arrived, and despite my misgivings, it was actually edible and quite tasty. I also concentrated on fluids, so I decided I was going to drink the whole jug of water that arrived with lunch. And for dessert—ah, my delicious little pudding that had seen me through the immediate hours after surgery. I ate what I could and drank everything in sight, then settled back into the chair to wait for the green light.

I had to pee fairly shortly after, and I provided the evidence to the staff. Everything on the list now had a check mark against it. I went back onto the bed primarily because the process of getting in and out of the bed was difficult and, hopefully, in a few short hours that would be my challenge at home. It was the strangest motion and not at all natural. That first movement in the bed was hateful. To go from a semiprone position to an upright position with no strength or confidence in my core took a disproportionate amount of effort. This was also clouded by some level of doubt about how it worked now with the bag sitting on my left side. This was a move I had made thousands of times without ever thinking about it. And now it was a motion that took some planning and a three-part sequence. It is amazing how difficult it is to go back to the start on a process that has become so unconscious. It's amazing how your emotional capacity limits your physical capacity. My athletic ability had shown me this many times over the years, but here was a stark reminder that this limiter wasn't reserved for great athletic feats.

Here the concept of practicing death transcended the emotional into the physical. The idea that simple movements can be taken away and reset in the blink of an eye is something that we should reframe in our lives. The joy and rhythm of movement, when replaced by something more cumbersome is sobering, and if you let it, it can help you reset your boundaries for how you can use your body in your transformation.

I cleared out my bedside locker to make sure everything was together. I was so desperate to get home that it was almost like I was planning a jail break and getting everything organized was all part of the master plan.

I didn't have to wait too much longer before the good word came down that I could go home. I called Jen and told her the good news. Due to the C. diff, Jen and Frances were still not allowed into the ward, so we would have to run a relay with my clothes when she arrived. The next hour took forever, but it was filled with instructions for when I got home about pain control, C. diff restrictions, and preparations. A dietician came by to talk to me about what would be good foods to eat over the next few weeks to deal with postsurgery condition, what could inflame my colon and what foods to avoid to prevent any unnecessary incident with the colostomy bag. For the first time we discussed the fact that my diet would have to change in the mid- to long-term because of my new physiology. Now wasn't the time for that, as I still had to get over the surgical phase, but I was to watch for bad reactions to certain foods and keep some notes. He went through a list of food items that it would be unlikely I would be able to eat or that I shouldn't even consider eating. Spicy food was the one that stood out, and I guess it was the most obvious. A plain diet, mostly white in color, and fiber kept to a minimum for the next few weeks. Good to know!

As I digested that info (sorry), a bag of clothes appeared from the lobby signaling the fact that Jen and Frances were here. The cubicle was closed off, and the last of the medical attachments were removed as I prepared to go home. The process of getting dressed was way more difficult than I had anticipated. With a body held fairly rigid and inflexible by excessive fluid retention, the simplest of tasks—getting dressed—became a bit of a struggle. With help from my nurse, I was able to maneuver into the clothes. Those clothes bore witness to how bloated I was. Even my feet! The sneakers Jen had sent over proved almost impossible to get on, though I eventually managed to squeeze my feet into them. There was no need to tie the laces, as they were snug to say the least. I stood up, and it felt like I was wearing moon boots or something alien. It also felt strange, in a good way, not to have to worry about my ass hanging out of a hospital robe.

I secured everything from the locker and the bag of belongings that I came in with. A week had passed since they had last been used, but it felt like a lifetime, and having relived so many thoughts and memories, in some ways it had been. There was no doubt this changed things, and going home was the next step in that discovery of just how much.

I signed the release paperwork, picked up the brochures and info sheets that would keep me right when I was back home, said my heartfelt goodbyes, and started the shuffle to the elevator. Jen and Frances were in the lobby of the surgical wards a few floors below.

It took a minute or two to get out of the ward and another minute to get the elevator down to where they waited. In my head, I thought that I could pull a Keyser Söze–type stunt and speed up the further I got from the ward. The opposite was true, and this made it clear to me how much work I would have to put in to accomplish some very basic movements.

I walked out of the elevator to the greatest sight. My two loves were sitting waiting for me. None of us knew quite how to greet each other. The time apart had created some emotional uncertainty—not any loss of feeling, just uncertainty of what we had been through very separately. This was also compounded by sensitivity to my surgical sites, my colostomy bag, and the cloud the C. diff infection had created (not physically, I don't think).

We got back in the elevator to get to the main lobby so we could get out of there. As we shuffled across the hospital lobby and out the front doors of the ER, Jen went to hail a cab. It was cold and the air was sharp, but it felt good. I felt alive and I sucked it in deeply, partly for the pleasure of feeling it shift the sterile air of the hospital out of my lungs, and partly for the symbolism of breathing in and out.

The cab arrived, and then the next challenge presented itself. It was a yellow cab car, and for those of you have been to NYC and traveled in one like it, you will know there isn't much legroom in there. Jen had Frances and me to get in there, and I presented the biggest obstacle. Literally.

They got in the far side of the car, leaving me to negotiate the near side. My body was rigid and defiant, and I was terrified of it. I decided the best route was to use my "get back into bed" process from the ward. The struggle this time was the limited headroom that added a head duck to my routine! I got my butt on the seat, head inside the cab and then tried to swing my legs in. Due to the space limitations already mentioned, that wasn't going to work. So I had to twist my torso, allowing me to lift my first leg in, and then taking a deep breath, lift the other leg in. What a carry on just to get in a cab! But I was in, and the driver started the ten-block ride home up First Avenue.

The city looked different from ground level. It was a very different view from the one that had accompanied me over the last week. It turned out, at that time, that First Avenue was not in good shape. I felt every bump of the road and sharp movement of the car. When he hit the brakes hard for a red light, I thought my newly shortened large intestine was coming out to meet me. Man, I couldn't wait to get home.

We arrived at our building, and I reversed the process to get out of the cab. I shuffled into the lobby and thought of my somewhat ignominious exit the week before. Our doorman was thrilled to see us and wished me well as we got to the elevator.

It had been a big adventure getting from the hospital to home, one that taxed me way more than any other of my daily routines. It was a great relief to enter the apartment. Christmas was alive and well with the telltale signs of unopened presents still sitting below the tree. We had decided that I would sleep on the sofa for the next few weeks. Its back and sides would be supportive of me sleeping a bit more upright with no threat of causing discomfort to my left side. This would also allow Jen to get some sleep without worrying about me and my condition.

I shuffled over to where I would continue my recovery for the foreseeable future.

I had been aware of Frances watching me in the cab, but because I was in some discomfort, I didn't want to engage too much in case my expression gave anything away. Now here in the apartment, I got to get close to her a little bit. Her first words to me were "Daddy Boo Boo?" You can guess what that did to me!

CHAPTER 9

My eyes are
A baptism
Oh, I am fuse

—Jeff Buckley & Elizabeth Fraser

It has often been said that the best place to heal is at home. This song captures that sentiment perfectly in that ultimately we gravitate toward that source of nourishment and growth that we all seek. In this case, it was the perfect healing process for me. In deeper thoughts, and true in this case, it can also represent the fact that it can take us quite some time to find "our sun." Our sun is not necessarily a person but maybe more of a purpose and a greater sense of self. That certainly rang true to me.

The backstory to this song is also interesting, so I thought I would share it as it opens up another dimension. Fraser and Buckley's own story is that they were in a relationship at the time they recorded this. You can hear it in Fraser's almost giddy giggle at the start—sound I think we can all recognize, or at least know what it represents. This track was never released, and that is why you need to go to YouTube to find their original version. Apparently, it was never released because they considered it unfinished, but in other writings, I have found it said it was also because it was intensely personal to them. Of course, Buckley died way too young, and Fraser has somewhat turned her back on the music scene, so there is no real hope that it will come out in a format that can be held by anyone else. Maybe that is right. It does feel a bit like eavesdropping when you know this information.

The power of the song, going beyond two mercurial performers at their best, is so compelling that it was at least a once-a-day listen for me when I got out of the hospital. It was also somewhat of an antidote to the emotional funk I found myself in—part anger, part relief, part guilt, and part downer. The balance of power would shift depending on what happened that day or how I was feeling physically. And by "what happened," I really mean how the colostomy process went, how easy it was to get off and onto the sofa, and how I rested.

It was also compounded by Frances being a bit standoffish. I don't blame her, but she was unsure of me in the days after I came home. She really didn't know what to make of the scene, and the fact that home nurses visited regularly only added to her confusion. That hurt, but I was comforted by the hope that her lasting memory of this would be zero. I hoped.

We celebrated the postponed Christmas the day after I got home. It was fun, but on reflection this added to her POV as if questioning, "What the hell is going on around here?" Her world was upside down—it just had more toys in it now! Young children are funny at Christmas when they don't know the gift-opening protocols. So it was late afternoon before she was anywhere near finished opening her presents.

Over the next few days, Jen had to get back to work, our Nanny returned from vacation and New Year came and went with some words of encouragement for 2014 to not let the door hit it on the way out. The days were long as sleep was difficult due to positioning and continued pain. They had prescribed Percocet for me and some antibiotics for the C. diff. The Percocet was crazy. I would go through this four-hour loop:

- After four hours, take the next painkiller
- Then lose an hour or so because it knocked me out
- Then an hour of sluggish, almost drunklike feeling
- Then an hour of normality
- Finishing with an hour's wait for the next pill
- Repeat to fade

When I became aware of this cycle I was in, I resolved to get off them. It was a week after the surgery that I started the process of skipping every other four-hour period. After a few days, I wasn't taking any overnight, and this gave me the strength to stop taking them at all.

This helped my recovery. I am sure of it. Even though it was still painful, I could focus more, rest better, and start to lay down some milestones of what was next. The colostomy bag process was fine and largely uneventful. A stoma is a strange thing to see. It's like some beheaded alien's neck is sticking out of your body. The nerve ending information was huge, because as raw as it was and looked, without that knowledge I would have been more than hesitant to clean it the way it needed to be cleaned. The home nurse was happy with my progress, and my skill using the mirror to position the adhesive patches was slowly improving. The one thing they don't tell you is this initial paranoia that sets in, that you really believe you can smell poop everywhere you go. In some cases, when the adhesive seal didn't hold, there was a very good reason for that!

Things started to fall into place. Progress checkups went well, and the big news was the infection was clear. This gave me a path to get back to work, but the real prize was to be cleared for the reversal surgery. At first, I was allowed only to work in New York, then soon after that, I was cleared to fly and get back to the St. Charles, MO, office. That didn't come in time for me to travel to see the Ohio State Buckeyes win the National Championship, but even I didn't push that one!

I watched that game from my sofa, and my thoughts turned to Ichigan. I wanted to be able to rip him so bad, but conversely, he and this whole episode were largely in the rear-view mirror now, and there was no real reason to go back. I had already started the countdown to six to eight weeks ahead and hoped that this time would pass quickly and without incident.

Two incidents from that time do stand out:

Flying again represented a new challenge. I sought advice on what was the correct procedure to adopt before being scanned. My pockets were empty for sure, but without any warning there was another surprise waiting for the TSA agent if I didn't warn him. So on my first outbound flight, with my luggage on the conveyor belt, I asked to speak to the agent adjacent to the full body scanner. There were two language barriers now: (1) my accent and (2) his understanding of what this bag actually was. He looked at me, puzzled, and I explained it to him in a bit more detail. He got the picture this time and took me through the smaller scanner, which of course went off. So now he told me they would have to search me, and of course I asked for privacy for that to happen. I was escorted to a cubicle and proceeded to strip down to undershirt and underwear at his insistence—a request I feel sure he wished he hadn't made when he saw the bulge in my side underneath the shirt. I raised my shirt and showed him what was happening. He asked me to detach it, to which I refused. In my mind, there was no need, and so a supervisor was called. He joined us and fortunately was more experienced and had seen this before. He instructed his agent to wave the wipe around the outside of the bag and test that. All clear, as expected, and for the second time that morning, I got dressed again. It was still somewhat of a chore and took me a few minutes to put myself back together. On the return leg, the St. Louis TSA agents were much more aware of both the situation I was in and how I may feel about it. They moved me through without incident restoring my confidence to take the one trip a month I had promised to limit my travel to.

As time passes, what seems like a mountain to climb becomes way more of a hill. And this was true about living with and changing the colostomy bag. Everything became more instinctive, and the less it troubled me, the easier it became. This next incident wrecked that improvement. My February travel was scheduled back to St. Louis through La Guardia again. I gave myself more time at the airport to take any time sensitivity out of the situation. I approached an agent before putting my travel bag on the belt. It went without a hitch this time, and again I was on my way. I spent the planned couple of days at the HQ office, and it was soon time to come home again. It was February, so the weather still had its say in most travel plans. I got to the airport, got through security without incident, and waited at the gate. Pretty soon, we were in a significant delay of a few hours, keeping in mind it is only a two-hour(ish) flight. Not ideal but no problem. I became aware that my bag needed emptying, so I went to the restroom to empty it. It was then I discovered that the seal on the adhesive was bubbling. This, I had learned the hard way, was a stage before it opened and wouldn't reattach. I always carried spare bags and cleaning materials, so it felt like no big deal. I would change the bag while I waited for the flight. I walked to the ends of the airport to find the quietest toilet I could so that I could attach it in front of the mirror. To my surprise, I wasn't disturbed as I changed it over.

A few hours later, the flight was finally ready to go. I quickly went to the restroom to check all was well and then made my way onto the flight. The flight was full since a banking conference had taken place in St. Louis that week. Most of the New York contingent were on my flight. It also became clear pretty quickly that they had used the delay to sample the delights of the airport bar and a few of them were in high spirits.

I sat in my seat. I had changed my airline preferences to sit on the left side of the aircraft at the window so my bag was never next to anyone. My row companions arrived. The two women introduced themselves and I could tell they had "had a few." Their colleagues were sitting in the row in front, so there was much jocularity between the two rows as we waited to take off.

Shortly after takeoff, I was aware of some discomfort in my side but wasn't sure what was going on. Almost immediately I thought I could smell poop. I told myself it was the paranoia and that everything was fine. That delusion was shattered by my half-scooped companions loud proclamation: "What is that smell?" Oh no. It was poop. Now I can't attribute the song and dance that followed to be just from the alcohol, she may have been that kind of diva all the time! But she went on and on. I looked out of the window and pretended not to hear (or smell) anything. Pretty soon she was swinging from the call button looking for the steward. He appeared, and she told him her problem in what sounded like a voice assisted by some invisible loud hailer! I wanted to disappear. I recoiled and pretended to be asleep as there was absolutely nothing I could do about the situation. The bag change at the airport was the last one I had with me. The steward's solution was to open a bag of ground coffee and wave it around like a thurible with burning incense in church, trying to chase away the smell of some odorous sin. To his credit, it seemed to work as from my faux-sleeping position I could smell the coffee too. Whoever you are, I am eternally grateful. The coffee smell afforded the alcohol the time it needed to do its work, and pretty soon, they were all sleeping for real. I was scared to move lest it wafted any more of the effluvia from my side. The two-hour flight felt like four, and when we landed, I moved as fast as my rigid body would let me and got a cab home from LGA.

I opened the door to our apartment and was fighting back the tears enough for me to investigate what had happened. For some reason I had pooped again, and this time a lot. That had put undue pressure on the fresh seal of the new bag, and it had opened. I cleaned myself up, replaced the bag again, and went into the living room to recount the embarrassing story to Jen. I have never felt so mortified in my life. At that moment, most of the gratitude I had felt from surviving my illness was lost in a cloud of embarrassment from what had happened on the flight.

I can say here and now, it is so ridiculous how we can get our perspective so messed up. In that moment, I am ashamed to say I hated my circumstance despite what I had just survived. I was humiliated by the flight experience but had lost all perspective of what that represented. Remember my "I would give anything to be in that traffic jam" proclamation a chapter or two ago? Clearly I didn't still think that way. After the humiliation of this incident passed, it was replaced by my shame in losing my perspective of the bigger picture. Living up to all the changes I promised myself (and others) was going to be hard. Deep down I knew that it would take some work, but here was a timely reminder that the changes couldn't be superficial and would need to be way more fundamental.

This realization took the verb of "practicing" to a whole new level. Cosmetic or short-lived changes weren't finite enough to represent the finality of death. There had to be meaningful shift. It didn't have to be instant or a kneejerk reaction—actually, as I was soon to learn, that would be equally inadequate. The benefits or practicing death are that the changes you make in yourself, your life, and your outlook are connected to a purpose. They should be your guide in living the type of life that will leave you fulfilled when your time comes.

This incident sharpened my focus on getting the surgery reversed. My next appointment led to the next noteworthy incident. It started at Dr. Newman's office as I pushed to get on his surgery list. As luck would have it, he popped his head into the examination room, looking for his NP, not me. To my gratification, she raised it with him right away. He stepped into the room and talked me through what the prerequisites would be for that surgery. I would have to have a colonoscopy first. He wanted to ensure there was nothing untoward waiting for him in there and that the fistula had not returned. He referred me to a colleague he clearly he had great trust in, and most probably a friendship with, because he sent me away with his best wishes to his referral.

Like I said, I was motivated, so I called the proctologist's office that afternoon. To my surprise, I got an appointment for two days later. When I arrived at the address, the office was like an apartment—plush, high ceilings, and like a scene from a 1920s Art Deco film set. I felt comforted by my sumptuous surroundings. They smacked of success and confidence, although I remained surprised by what was behind a fairly ordinary door. Manhattan can be like that. Your perceptions from the outside can be completely wrong. Narrow doorways open to vast spaces. Prestigious facias can lead to run-down and unkempt interiors. And then some edifices just blow your mind from front to back. I love that about this city. There is no uniformity, and your first impressions have as much chance to be wrong as right.

This location was consistent throughout—well appointed with the holding area way too vast for what was clearly a slickly run operation. I was in a recognizable medical environment. My proctologist reminded me of Dr. Greene from the previous hospital stay. He was old school, precise in his clothing and manner, exuding the confidence that whatever your issue was, he had probably seen it and fixed it. I shared Dr. Newman's well wishes, and he smiled and gave me a bit of their history. They had trained together many years ago, and while their schedules prohibited them from seeing a lot of each other, they were still connected by memories, patient referrals, and the occasional professional event. This felt good and I felt at ease. He had my files, so he could see the surgical procedure I had been through, and like many others, he was curious as to how all this came to pass. I shared as much information as I knew, and he joined the "Baby Panda Fan Club."

The colonoscopy process would be simple. The only part of the process I had to be mindful of was to move to a clear-liquid diet two days before the procedure and to take a bowel cleanse the night before. The second part is true for anyone going through this. The first part was to make the second part easier in my situation. He explained to me what would happen and how I should cope with it. And with that, the consult was done. His admin promised to be in touch to give me a date for the colonoscopy. She sent me away with a prescription for the preparation so I could be organized for whenever the appointment was planned.

True to her word, she called the next day for an appointment the next Monday. Efficiency was clearly her game. The only element that needed to be arranged was that due to it being conducted under a general anesthetic, Jen would need to pick me up. This was possible, so now it was clear-diet time until prep night. What happened on prep night was quite memorable for all the wrong reasons. It would be accurate to say that a colostomy bag is not built to cope with a bowel cleanse treatment. I had been advised that I should keep the bag on as you don't always get too much warning when the cleanse is taking over, therefore the bag would buy me some time until I got to the bathroom. And true to the advice, that is what happened. Some forty-five minutes after drinking the viscous liquid, and without any warning, my bag started to fill. Quickly. The best idea was to effectively make the bag a funnel between my side and the toilet bowl. However, the flow was fierce and very wet, so the bag detached fairly quickly. Now I was facing reattaching a bag while liquid poured from my side. It was like trying to stay dry under the Niagara Falls. Impossible. Eventually, I gave in and just stood over the toilet for an hour and a half while the cleanse did its job.

My colonoscopy appointment was in the early afternoon. By the time it came around, everything was settled and actually felt pretty good. The procedure was as no-nonsense as the calendar schedule. In, anesthetized, scoped, out. Jen picked me up, and then it was a question of waiting for the results, which would be sent directly to Dr. Newman. I had a checkup on Monday of the following week, and I figured that was when I would hear about any outcomes.

That appointment came around pretty quickly, and soon I was with the nurse practitioner going over the results. The scope had shown that everything was as it should be and that I was good to go for the reversal surgery. Today was Monday, February 23, so it was with some disappointment that I learned the earliest date for surgery was mid-March. I understood the demands on the man, but couldn't help begrudging the delay even as it was scheduled. Luck had another part to play in this story though.

As I was getting ready to leave, the admin's phone rang. The one-sided call ended with, "Let me ask him." The upshot of the call was that there was an opening on Friday, February 27, if I wanted it. This Friday! Four days away. Man, this serendipity stuff just kept coming. I agreed without really thinking about it and went back to his office to wait to see Dr. Newman to hear what the surgical plan would look like and what the prep this week would be. He talked me through the reversal, which was essentially the reconnecting of the pipes. There would also need to be another cleanse and I would need to have blood taken on Wednesday just to make sure there was no infection before the surgery. He also told me that he was leaning toward leaving the stoma site wound open to heal. While I heard and understood the words he was saying, there was no way to understand the impact that this decision would have on me later.

Inside I was elated. The end of this episode was at the end of the week. I could feel the relief swell up in an emotional bubble inside me and as I called Jen on my walk home. This episode was going to be behind us soon.

I remember the bloodwork visit and the endless paperwork in advance of the second surgery. I also remember the second cleanse. This time it wasn't anywhere as near as harrowing as the first one. It happened exactly the same way, but I was so fixated on the outcome of the next day and "getting back to normal" that I wasn't fazed in the slightest. It had only been two months, and I had adapted pretty well, I thought. I had also proven that if this was to be a lifetime situation, it would have been manageable, and the emotional knock would have been surmountable. I also knew about my weak moments, and not just after the flight incident. I had cursed the colostomy bag many times in this short time frame. I had bemoaned my new circumstance and had definitely felt sorry for myself (though it had also afforded me a late Christmas with my family, a return to work, and Frances's second birthday). Deep down, I knew the scars were deeper than just the ones we could see. This was going to take time, but getting the aesthetics back to some kind of normal felt like the important next step. So I approached the next surgery with only hope in my heart and not a second thought on my mind.

CHAPTER 10

Lights will guide you home
And ignite your bones
And I will try to fix you

—Coldplay

My call time on the morning of the reversal surgery was 6:30 a.m. I was going to be first on the table, so they wanted me in early for processing. The surgery unit this time was in a different annex of Langone and was walking distance from the apartment. Armed with my headphones, I decided that is how I would get there. Jen assumed she was going to accompany me, but I didn't see the point. I would get there, take care of the paperwork and admin, and then be in surgery for most of the morning and then back in the ward in the afternoon. That was when I presumed I would really need her, so my logic was "do what you have to do this morning, and I will see you on the ward later." My attitude wasn't blasé, but more focused on getting back to what I deemed normal. In all honesty, I hadn't really considered any other range of outcomes. That is crazy when you consider what I had been through not two months before. Maybe it is the human condition that by focusing on the end game, we can block out all other possibilities.

My confidence was going to be shaken.

I walked into the lobby just before 6:30 a.m. and was told which floor to go to. I took the elevator up to another anteroom, which was effectively an admin office. I waded through the paperwork, and after confirming everything in quadruplicate, sat in the waiting room for my next task. I was summoned by the admin assistant, where she told me without blinking that I would need to pay $6500 before the surgery could happen. Now I knew there was going to be a bill, but that seemed a bit steep for a "part two" surgery. I didn't mention it in the previous chapter, but the financial impact and health insurance paperwork that had arrived over the previous two months had been vast. And not at all accurate. In fact, I would call it more speculative rather than a billing record of what had transpired. That included the now infamous ambulance ride of $3K. It seems to me the system works on some kind of "pay now, fight later" protocol. So I obliged, paid the bill, and returned to my seat. I texted Jen that I was in the waiting room and posted to Facebook to keep the family apprised of what was going on this time since there was way more control than the last time.

I was called by a nurse around 8 a.m., and we walked into the surgery area. The first room was like a gym locker room. She told me to put all my belongings in a locker, including my phone, get undressed, and put the robe on. I remembered for a second that I hadn't updated Jen, but figured she knew where I was, so I followed the instructions to a T and returned to the front of the locker room. I was ushered to a small room filled with armchairs where they would check all my vitals and hook me up ready for the anesthesia.

Dr. Newman came around and explained the process of the surgery. I still had my bag on, and I expressed concern that I should remove it while internally praying for no need to go to the bathroom. After the cleanse the previous night, there shouldn't have been any need, but I had heard that before. He told me they would remove the bag when I was in the operating room, so there was no need to concern myself with that. The surgery should take three hours or so, and he reiterated the decision to leave the wound open post surgery.

Next came the anesthetist who explained how they were going to deal with that aspect today. All seemed routine. A final Q&A to verify all details and an approval form to sign, and we would be going into surgery shortly after. This time I don't remember anything about the journey into the surgery room. I don't think you can be anything but tense when it gets to that moment, but this was my first sense of that tension creeping in.

The OR was bigger this time, which seemed strange. There were several sectioned off cubicles so multiple surgeries could be conducted at the same time, I presume. I was stationed near the back. They helped me slide off the gurney and onto the operating table. I was positioned slightly differently this time and was advised that they would want to get me on my side so this was how I was to lie in readiness. The anesthetist was there and gave me that calming stuff that feels cold in your veins. I was relaxed now, just the right side of consciousness and waiting for the countdown.

The next thing I knew I was in what must have been the recovery room. There were a couple of other beds in there with a few other postsurgical patients. As I came to, it didn't feel anywhere near the same as previous surgeries. I still felt very drowsy and was dipping in and out of consciousness. The pain in my abdomen, not just my side, was sharp. I had this jux-taposition of heavy pain but struggling to maintain alertness. The recovery nurse must have had a day, because evidently she thought I was deliberately rolling from being awake to being out again. I told her I felt very drowsy and I think I dipped back out while saying it. That may be poetic license, but I defi-nitely felt like it was a possibility. She explained to me that I needed to be alert and awake for a sustained period before I would be allowed out of recovery into the ward. The problem with this carrot and stick approach was I wasn't in control. I tried sitting more upright but that only resulted in that neck-breaking involuntary lurch you see (and may have done) on planes. She was raising her voice now, not that it mattered to me. What compounded the situation is she was using my full name—my Sunday name if you will. "Gerard!" Gerard!" But she said it how Americans say my name with the emphasis on the A: "GerAAArd." Unbeknown to her, there were only a few people who called me that. My mother and my grandparents. Both sets of grandparents had passed years before, so it felt like my mother was in the room, but she reserved the use of my full name for when I was in trouble—which wasn't often, to be fair, and it wasn't her parenting style either, but it took me right back there. I guess I should have been focused on staying awake, but I was really struggling. So I tried to appeal to the better side of her nature, only to have the rules reiter-ated! Nothing else for it, I would have to really concentrate on something to keep from dozing again. My mind all of a sudden turned to my wound and I tried to distract myself by gingerly looking under the blankets to see what I could see. My abdo-men was wrapped in what looked like cling film, and hanging out of the cling film were two thick tubes, which were opaque by design but I could see the red of blood through the opacity. I asked how the surgery had gone and she promised that Dr. Newman would be around shortly.

"GerAAArd!"

Oops! Dozed off again. This was like no other experience I have ever had. My head was rolling, and even as I focused on the pain and the wound, I would catch myself nodding off again. It was now about thirty minutes after the surgery. I know this because my nurse told me that fact as she vented once more. I asked for water to again aid my distraction. That seemed to work. I felt a little more alert, so I asked for more. This seemed to get me to a passable stage, and although I was still drowsy, they informed me they were moving me to the ward and that Dr. Newman would see me there.

The motion of the bed moving was all I needed as encouragement, and I must have dozed off again. I woke up again to Dr. Newman and Jen standing at the foot of the bed. I honestly thought I was dreaming. All but for one fact: the look on Jen's face was not that of a bedside welcome. She looked harrowed and tense somehow. I felt like I was stuck in a cotton wool ball. My vision and hearing were distorted, and if this scene were an audio file, the pain in my stomach would have been a white noise drowning most everything else out. I did pick up Jen saying that it was almost 5 p.m. *That can't be right*, I thought to myself. Dr. Newman was standing strong on the party line that everything had gone exactly to plan, to which I could hear my lawyer wife countering with, "Well why did it take twice as long as expected then?" Through this back and forth, I gradually realized that I had been in surgery for more than seven hours.

Jen had been through it today. Again. My relatively relaxed approach earlier in the morning hadn't helped either. When lunchtime came and went at the office, she assumed I had been delayed in going into surgery. Still no call. So she ended up taking the bull by the horns and calling the hospital herself. She was told I was still in surgery but that she could come up as I was expected out soon. That journey, as she tells it, she fully believed would end with her being told that she "had killed another husband." I regret my part in causing that, and I have apologized many times since. I should have been way more sensitive to her past experiences and to our most recent experience together. This explained the look on her face. I am not sure what happened next, but she and Dr. Newman came to a forced peace, and she came to the top of the bed to talk to me. There was no other version of the story than the one being peddled in front of us, so we had to take it at face value. I felt like crap though. Like I had been hit hard by something big and heavy. She had to go and see Frances, but this time there was no ICU to limit or eliminate visiting, so I would see her soon.

Now in the ward, I had a new nurse. She was much kinder and more sympathetic to what I was going through. I asked her about pain control, and she got a junior doctor to come over. There was much checking of files and clock checking, and they decided they would give me morphine in an IV with the same trigger I had previously. They disappeared for a few minutes and then came back with another nurse, I am assuming to cross-check the bag of fluid and my details. They hung the bag and then placed it into the IV in my arm. I felt it immediately. The drug ran hot through my veins, like a double magnesium injection, and my arm started to turn red and also started to swell up. I called them back, and they quickly unhooked it.

Junior Dr: "You told us you weren't allergic to Morphine!"

Me: "I wasn't up until now! I had the same drug after surgery two months ago with no reaction!"

He went away and checked the files and came back satisfied that whatever had just happened was a new phenomenon.

A new drug was chosen, I don't remember which one, but I think it was co-codamol and because of the reaction in my veins, they decided to give me it by mouth. This was easier in that moment for sure but would take away the almost immediate relief of pain by IV and would also mean I couldn't self-medicate when I needed to. That helped, but only really helped me get back to my routine of dozing in and out.

I was stirred from one of those dozes by the news that I was being moved to a different ward and room. When I got there, it was clear that the ICU room was the "Vegas suite" to this NYC budget hotel room equivalent. It was so tight that with my compadre's bed already in position, they had to conduct some elaborate seven-point turn to get me into the location next to the window. They told me Dr. Newman would be around again before the end of the day to see how I was doing. And he was, this time with a hand-off to a postsurgical staff who were going to look after me over the weekend.

For the first time, post surgery, they pulled back the sheets to reveal his handiwork. As previously described, I was wrapped in a clear plastic wrap, and I could see the two drain tubes clearer now from my new vantage point. I could now see that one was in the wound itself and the other appeared to be running through my navel. I could also see that my colostomy bag had been replaced by a drain that I soon learned needed emptying and cleaning. The pulling and positioning of the tubes shot through me like an electric shock. I must have gasped or let out some less brave noise.

Me: "What the hell was that?"

Entourage rep: "The drain is attached to your abdomen and is draining the wound from the bottom, so it must have pulled on you a little."

Jeez. I guess this was how it was going to be with an open wound. And there was a lot of blood-colored fluid sloshing around, so this was going to happen frequently. My stomach was distended from the surgery. I could see the crevice the tubes disappeared into but couldn't see the extent of it. They informed me that the drains would need emptied every four hours and that they would be back in the morning to remove the wrap and let air get to the site. In the meantime, I had to get some rest. I had missed dinner as it was now after 7 p.m., so some crackers and some ginger ale were scared up to get me through the next few hours.

It was then it suddenly dawned on me that the immediate upshot of this surgery was that I would have to be conscious of needing to poop again. The last two months, though they presented different challenges, had taken away that requirement. And now here I was debilitated post surgery (again) and having to get back into the "pooping game." When the nurse was next in, I asked her about that. She assured me that while, yes, I had to be aware of that, there probably wouldn't be anything happening on that front for the next few days. That was something at least.

I settled back in and tried to get some rest. I was exhausted and in pain. I called Jen to say I was settled in and that I would see her in the morning. With it being the weekend, she was on her own again with Frances, so the little marauder would be coming to visit.

I was awakened by the ward nurse coming around to give me my pain meds and to drain the drains. I had to pee, so she helped me up to go to the toilet in the corner of the room. My movement was back to being cumbersome and painful, and instead of antibiotics stands, I had the drains with me. It took a minute, but I was able to negotiate my way through the narrow path to the toilet and back again without incident. That overwhelming sense of the smallest activity being the hardest thing had returned. While they had me up, they wanted me to sit upright in a chair for a while. This was feeling all too familiar. After an uncomfortable ten minutes, which felt like an eternity, I was helped back into bed. I was ready to resume whatever sleep I could get.

I am not sure how much later it was, but I was awakened by my compadre shouting from behind his closed curtains.

Him: "Nurse, Nurse! Milk and cookies!" (getting louder) "MILK AND COOKIES!"

Maybe he didn't know I was there. Maybe he did. Either way, he did what he did. The nurse came running in at the commotion, to which all I could hear him say was "milk and cookies." Whatever had happened behind that curtain was much bigger than the requirement for milk and cookies and a full nightshift squad came in to clean out his area and change his bed. The ward nurse stuck her head around the curtain to see if I was okay. I didn't know what to say other than to inquire if everything was okay out there. She said it was in hand and that she would see me shortly with my meds and for my drains.

When she returned, she explained that my 'roomie' was very sick and that it was unlikely he would get better. Humbled by that news, I felt suitably guilty for my frustration at his outburst.

Morning came, and with it came more meds and the morning rounds. The posse arrived and started to investigate my surgical site. First action was to cut the cling film off and unwrap me from it. It was once that was taken off that I could see the extent of the damage to my stomach. It looked like some sick map of the world, where the continents had been marked by removal of my flesh. And this was away from the wound! It felt as raw as it looked, so I understandably grimaced when they took that wrap off and started to inspect all the open wounds. They called for the nurse and asked for some soothing lotion to try and take the clearly angry wounds down a notch or two. They then pulled the drain up, straining the tube, so they could see what was going on inside the wound. They were going to clean the inside of the wound with one of those extended length Q-tips. To my horror, the whole thing disappeared into the wound. WTF!?! When Dr. Newman said, "I will leave the wound open," I really didn't imagine a full excavation site in my side. For the most part, I couldn't feel anything except for when they hit the bottom of the wound. That sent me through the roof. They wanted to see how much fluid was sitting at the bottom of the opening and to see if the drain was doing a sufficient job. The conclusion was drawn that it was, and they told me that they fully expected a lot of fluid today but that it would gradually wane into tomorrow. There was also no sign of infection, which was good news, but they would be monitoring that over the weekend.

When I asked for an explanation for the other wounds, they were vague and talked about possibly the robot that was used for the surgery being the cause. It was clear it wasn't something they wanted to talk about in any detail.

Jen arrived mid-morning with Frances. Frances was bouncy, in a place where that wasn't a great approach. To the naked eye, I looked like I was just in bed in hospital, so there weren't too many awkward questions winging our way. It was good to see her, and while she was fascinated by her surroundings, Jen and I got a chance to discuss what had happened. The truth is we will never really know. My brother-in-law Drew, part of the previous family medical committee from the ICU, is actually an OR charge nurse specializing in this field of surgery. He shared with Jen his opinion that sometimes the older surgeons can take longer with the robot they use in such reconnective surgeries. It can also happen that in getting the two ends back together again, it can take quite a bit of maneuvering of the patient to be able to free the shortened colon back to the rectal tunnel to be reconnected. This maneuvering could have caused the damage to the rest of the abdomen. What it didn't explain was why they didn't just say that.

This gave us part of the answer but didn't really explain the emotional trauma Jen had endured the day before. There was definitely a tension between the medical team and us, like something wasn't being said. My nurse came in to see Jen and to empty the drains, which gave Jen a chance to see the damage. I could tell by her face that she was also taken aback by it. She quizzed the nurse some more, but the nurse was really the messenger in this case and could only relay what she had been told and what had been recorded. We asked about timing of getting home, etc., and she felt that would be early to the middle of next week. That felt okay, so we left it there.

It was great to see them, but it was really no place for a two-year-old, so Jen and Frances headed off to have some fun in the city.

I had lunch arriving soon, and again it was part of the post-surgical process to prove I could eat and keep it down. My head drifted to some Tom and Jerry cartoon, where in my mind I visualized any passersby being able to see what I had for lunch by looking through my wound! The rest of the day passed with the drains, meds, and chair routines. Time passed slowly there. I couldn't read because the pain was too distracting. My neighbor next door was getting a lot of attention. It wasn't looking good there, based on the freneticism that surrounded him. He would cry out names at times. It was very difficult to hear, and inside I hoped that whoever he was calling on knew they were on his mind.

Sunday morning eventually came, and my medical entourage arrived to check the drains and see how the wound was progressing. I still had so many questions about the surgery and now the aftermath. I was mostly concerned that the wound being open would lengthen my stay, or that even once I was out of hospital I would have so many visitors or appointments that it would be more like a night-release kind of system. From the information they could share, and from the tensions between us, I could glean that there would be an aftercare process, but mostly it would be self-administered.

I was still mad at the situation because my body was sore. All of it. I wanted to know why I was so drowsy in recovery. I wanted to know why my abdomen looked like I had been in a knife fight in Glasgow in its *No Mean City* era. I wanted to know when I could get home. Hospital may be the place to get fixed, but it isn't any place to recover. After Jen's experience on Friday, I didn't think either of us would really settle down until I was home. It feels terribly selfish to say it, but I want to be honest: the man in the next bed was a sharp reminder of what could very well have happened over Christmas. I wasn't ready to face that yet. *We* weren't ready to face that yet. I needed to be on the mend from this experience so that I could evaluate this part of my story. The painkillers were putting me in another four-hour spin cycle, and so my thoughts went from lucid and sharp to blurry and distorted. I was again going to resolve that as soon as I could. I would be weaning myself off of those pills too.

I had dozed off on early Sunday evening and awoke to a commotion next to me. My roommate was in trouble. My curtain was closed as they did whatever they had to do. I closed my eyes and wished him peace and relief from his current situation. They took him away, presumably to another area where they could treat him. And then it was silent. A nurse came by to do my drain drill and she reported, when asked, that he had passed. We hadn't spoken, and I didn't know what was wrong with him, but regardless, I felt sad. He was out of his misery and discomfort, but I wondered whether his cries were ever answered or appeased. I hoped so. Sunday night became like many nights before it, restless and relatively sleepless.

I woke up with the arrival of breakfast and the nurses to check on the drains and give me my meds. I needed to go to the bathroom, so we used that visit to help me do so. They gave me a cup to pee in so they could see that everything was working as it should be. They had been right about my toileting frequency, at both ends. There had been nothing out of the new pipework and very little urine production either. I got into the chair to have breakfast and wait for the rounds. Jen was going to visit later now that it was Monday and she had help again. I texted her to say I was up and was waiting for the doctors.

I didn't have to wait long. Dr. Newman appeared with his medical team to see how things had progressed over the weekend. I had a million questions for him about what had happened, but they really congealed into one big question: "When will I get home?" To my surprise and delight, he answered that there was no reason that I couldn't get home TODAY!

Okay! Tell me what we have to do, and it will be done.

They would be back later to take the drain stitches out and then the drain itself. They would then show Jen and me how the wound should be treated with instructions for further appointments. I texted Jen the news, and she said she would be there as soon as the nanny arrived for Frances and she could get together what I needed. This going-home process was way more controlled, mainly because I had walked in on Friday with everything I would need for the length of my stay. Once they removed the drains, I could move more freely, so I got dressed and waited for Jen to arrive. She was there in next to no time and I was back prone with my sweatshirt pulled up so the nurses could run the demo.

The drains had been out less than an hour and when they cleaned out the wound with the Q-tip, it absorbed quite a lot of fluid. This allowed them to show Jen how to deal with that and how important it would be to get all of that out of the wound every time. This was going to be a twice-a-day process for my wife, the lawyer. That isn't said facetiously at all; this felt like a tough ask and certainly a daunting sight. We got all the instructions and appointments made for the rest of this week, and then I was free to go.

The news of my pending return home had somewhat distracted us from the nagging questions abut what actually happened in the OR that day. What remained true until I left the hospital was that the medical team and I were curt with each other. The nursing team did their best to ensure I was comfortable, but the cloud that hung over the second surgery never really cleared. We would revisit our dissatisfaction with the whole experience in the weeks to come, mostly when the pain was bad or when Jen had to clean out the wound and it visibly hurt. Sometimes you have to move on and focus on getting better. There were going to be more post-op appointments, so at some level, holding on to hostility seemed futile and unnecessarily exhausting. Whatever happened that day, remains there. Ultimately, I remained *here*.

It wasn't quite the same debacle getting in the cab as it had been in December, but it had snowed the day before, and though the skies were clear when I left the unit, my steps were even less confident with the conditions underfoot. We made the short trip home, and pretty soon, I was back on the sofa which was going to double as my bed again while the second phase of healing took place. This was a different kind of pain and movement restriction from the last time. This one needed proper healing due to the wound itself. Remarkably, only seventy-two hours after a seven-hour surgery, I was home and that part of the process could begin.

It was a lot to take in and it was somewhat of a blur. Only seven days had passed from my regular appointment to having had the surgery and being back home. Now recovery and rebuilding parts of my life were the priority. This time I would be focused primarily on three things: healing, diet (due to the partial colectomy), and emotional recovery. There was no better place to be to take on all three.

CHAPTER 11

Blood's running thick
and my blood's running free

—Ben Watt

The challenge of cleaning my wound was significant for Jen, not just because she wasn't a nurse but also because it was pretty grisly, and the process was painful to me. Having to do this knowing both those things meant neither of us really relished those first few days. A nurse visitor came in on Wednesday to check everything was on track. I was due to be back at the surgeon's office the next week, so this was the fill-in until Monday's appointment.

The wound process consisted of unpacking the gauze insert that had been placed in the wound for absorption, adding some saline to the Q-tip and then basically mopping out the wound with the Q-tip, making sure she got to all the surfaces. The surfaces near the top of the wound were numb to me, so I could only feel pressure, nothing specific. The bottom of the wound was a different matter. It was like someone twisting my nerve endings. Our newly created routine was as follows:

We would wake in the morning, and while Jen got ready and showered, I would make my way to our bed from the sofa, get out the wound packaging, then take an inordinate amount of time to lie flat. Jen would then clean the wound and repack it before getting ready for work. We would repeat the process some twelve hours later when she would get in from work. It was tough on both of us—for Jen, because pretty much her first task every day was to dig around a six-inch wound with an oversized Q-tip, and for me, because basically I held onto the side of the bed for grip as the inevitable painful shocks would strike as she cleaned it. We both knew the importance of getting this process right, so it was truly a "tough it out mentality" situation on both sides. There would be a grimace or a sharp intake of air from me, followed quickly by an "I'm sorry" from Jen. It was never her fault, and so we played out this charade of Jen pretending to be confident in what she was doing and me pretending it didn't hurt. I was able to comfort her in the knowledge that when the visiting nurse came and changed it, it hurt me then too. It was a small comfort, but we took it.

The other challenge was what to do about Frances while we went through this ten-minute process. I wasn't allowed to pick her up for six weeks or do anything else with her, so it wasn't like I could carry her or detain her in any effective way. And she was way too mischievous to be left to her own devices for that time. We talked about it and incorporated her into the process. She could see that it was difficult for both of us, so inclusion felt like a better policy. All the bandages and gauze pads were kept in a Duane Reade bag in the apartment. Her job became "tape girl." She had to fish through the bag and find medical tape that would be used to hold the last of the packing structure in place. So at "boo boo" time, she would come into our room, lie next

AND YOU MAY FIND YOURSELF

to me, and hold the recently found tape until Jen needed it. I would look at her, both to distract her and also to save me from the sight of Jen's facial reaction to what she was looking at. This took on a whole new level when we needed to buy a new medical tape after running out one day. The tape we had been supplied with and used since I came home from the hospital was blue. On this occasion, there was no blue tape available, so we bought a white version of the same thing. Supposedly. It turned out that the white tape was substandard, and any time Jen used it, the packing would inevitably move or fall off, leaving me bleeding onto my undershirt. This subpar performance coined the phrase "The white tape is rubbish!" (You can tell these were my words, as rubbish is what we call "garbage" in the UK.) Frances thought this was hysterical and so from that point on, every time she "lucky dipped" into the medical bag, if she pulled out the white tape, she would gleefully proclaim the same phrase! I am happy to report that it may be her only memory of the whole episode. She talks about it today, although we do get confused at times as to which color was defective!

Waiting for the first poop after surgery was a strange thing to track. I didn't feel bloated, but I was concerned about how or if it was going to work. Both the surgical team and the visiting nurses pointed out that it was important to be conscious of this and to report back if there was any discomfort or any blood evident. Graphic I know, but it was the point of the surgery. To this end, I had to eat a careful diet of bland, white, soft food an in attempt to encourage activity without putting stress on the renewed bodily function. For posterity: It happened on day three after getting home, and there were no issues, which was a relief to everyone involved.

Now the wound could really be the focus over the coming weeks. The human body is remarkable. The idea (and actually what happened) was that the wound being left open would gradually close itself over time from the bottom up. Every day there would be some meshing together of the flesh deep in the wound, pulling the wound entry closed over time. This meant the most important part was to avoid infection and any setbacks. Indeed, the benefit of leaving the wound open was that any infection could be treated directly and would not slow down the healing process. I was to attend Dr. Newman's office every week for the first four weeks so that they could monitor progress in the wound and the functioning colon. The first visit was a real boon for Jen as the NP was very complimentary of her work in keeping the wound clean and supporting the natural process.

By the time I was ready for the second visit, we weren't so sure everything was on schedule. Just as the colostomy bag had filled my nose with sensitivity to its contents, the wound now made me paranoid about the smell of an infection. Over the first two weeks, I wasn't allowed to shower, just to wash and do what I could to keep the wound as dry as possible. This was supposed to ensure the first few weeks would be incident free. By the time I was ready for the second visit, we both suspected there was an infection starting to form in the wound. It wasn't an overwhelming stench, but it did have a new odor different from the past two weeks.

Jen came with me to the next appointment, and we greeted the same NP with the news that we thought there was an issue. She checked it out, and while she wasn't completely convinced there was, she wanted Dr. Newman to check it anyway. The setup in these rooms was quite simple. The room was rectangular, maybe fifteen by twenty feet. As we walked into the room, there was one of those dentist-type chairs that could flatten out if required. The sink and medical supplies cupboard were on the left with a chair for a further attendee. The window was at the back of the room and was floor to ceiling. I was sat in the examination chair, with my sweatpants lowered and my under-shirt rolled up to air the wound. Jen was sat on the other chair in front of the sink so she could see some of what was going on. Between Dr. Newman and the NP, I could see her watching. Dr. Newman was immediately suspicious, and they chatted about the possibility of using something called a vac-pac. This device apparently would vacuum the fluid out, and with it would go any existing or threatening infection. The downside would be I would have to go there every day for them to fit it and use it. That idea wasn't appealing. The medical office was eighteen blocks south and two blocks west of our apartment, and though we had walked there for that day's appointment to enjoy the air and each other's company, the thought of walking it every day seemed like a lot. However it would be what it would be.

I could tell by his tone that Dr. Newman wasn't convinced that it was the right, or indeed, the only course of action available to him. It was at that point he looked at me and said, "I am going to put my fingers in the wound and have a feel around. Is that okay?" I really wasn't in a position to argue. I watched as he put two rubber-gloved fingers into the wound, and then the pain told me the rest. He was pushing against all sides of the wound. I gripped the chair tightly and turned my head to the side. As I did that, I saw Jen's terror-filled face. Almost simultaneously he said to me, "This is going to hurt but bear with me." At that point I felt him push down on what must have been newly formed flesh. He pushed and pushed until he broke through that barrier. The pain shot through me like he had connected two starter cables in there. It was accompanied by blood spurting out my wound and by Jen and I making eye contact. Both of us were wide-eyed and shocked by this turn of events. He dug about a bit more and then stepped back and asked the NP to clean out the wound. As he took off the gloves, he explained that there had been a small infection formed behind the new skin and that is what he had broken through. I was still shaking from the experience and he apologized for the discomfort. He said that this could happen and that we should move to cleaning the wound three times a day. He could have said five times a day and I would not have objected. I wanted out of there so badly. The NP repacked the wound, and Jen and I left, both a bit shell-shocked. As we walked out, Jen asked how we wanted to get home. As sure as I had been that I wanted to walk there, I was 100 percent sure I wanted to get a cab home.

This dented Jen's confidence a bit, but as we discussed it, I told her that it was my fault. I needed to be less sensitive to the process and let her do what needed to be done. What we were both sure about was that we didn't want to relive that again. And because I had my little friend to lie next to me through each cleaning, I would focus on that more than anything else.

What also wasn't helping was the fact that I hated that wound. After that visit, I was allowed to shower, and indeed I was encouraged to use the head of the shower to spray warm water directly into the wound to clean it out. It wasn't painful to do that, but it was a weird sensation, and of course what came back out would be blood traced. One of Frances's other games during this time was to see if my undershirt had any blood on it in the morning when she woke me on the sofa. In our bathroom, we have a mirrored toiletry cabinet on the wall next to the door. It is mirrored on both sides, so if the cabinet door was left open (part of Jen's morning regime) it would effectively be directly in line with anyone in the shower. I couldn't stand to look at myself when I was in the shower, so closing the mirrored door became part of my routine. I couldn't take it. I am not sure why. It was probably for the same reason I didn't want to see pictures of it. Jen would routinely take photos of the wound to show how it progressed over time. It would be a year plus before I would look at any of them.

I am not sure what that was. I am not squeamish, so I know it wasn't that. I felt flawed and weak. I was ashamed by it at some level. There were days during this period where I felt very down and depressed. And I was surviving. I couldn't reconcile it at all. There was clearly a lot going on here and I needed to get my head straight before I could tackle the implications of it all.

The challenge you will face if you decide to practice death is that re-creating some of this frailty is difficult without having a similar experience. It is the finality of death that we should use as our urgency and motivation. "Never again" is a bleak phrase to use, but it captures the mood required. In this example, here is my practicing death statement:

"Never again will I let my emotional frailty get in the way of the most important things in my life that are right in front of me."

I think Jen sensed that, so to add some levity to the situation for both of us, she nicknamed the wound. She called it my "side vagina." It made us laugh, and when I finally looked at the photographs a year later, she was also accurate. Ironically, it gave us a way to refer to it with our close family and friends in a lighthearted way that masked the discomfort we both felt about it. Of course as the wound healed and closed up, it became much more like another orifice. It turned out her joke had longevity too! Lifting the mood helped me be a bit more philosophical about it, and I started to make good on some of the promises I made to myself in the ICU. I used the downtime to reach out to people who I missed in my life and started the reconnection process. The sharing of stories from today and days gone by did my heart good as I was able to rekindle some friendship fires that had been left on a low burn for way too long.

Making contact forced me into a realization that in some way, shape, or form, I had retreated from different parts of my life. And that was *before* this illness. I hadn't realized I had fallen into my self-made trap. That trap was largely selfishness. I had been focused on my life and my outcomes and hadn't realized the cost of doing so. In not giving of myself, I could not receive from others. In my darker days after this surgery, I beat myself up for letting my conceit take over. That had to change. There was so much that had to change, and I needed to work out what was the first priority. Retrospectively, this was when I realized I was lost but I didn't really *know* it. So many things in my life were out of whack and needed to be rebalanced. In the months after the surgery, as the treatment became less intense and the wound healed, summer came and gave me a chance to reconnect with friends and family and the outdoors. I still had shaky days. Shaky in energy and shaky in outlook. Work would exhaust me, particularly when it involved traveling. At least without the colostomy bag, my only fear of flying was the TSA process and the wound (which I got stopped for every single time) and sitting on the inside on the left so that no one could get near the wound. I had a new Achilles heel, but it gave me reasonable "aircover" for the true weakness I had discovered in this process.

CHAPTER 12

Race isn't over to the finish line
It's a comeback story of a lifetime

—Kings of Leon

It took a few months, but the wound gradually healed closed without too much further incident. The drain wound healed itself, and the other skin damage gradually faded away, leaving discolored blemishes where once the raw wounds sat. As the main wound closed, I was able to clean it out myself and give Jen a break from this torture.

There is no doubt that we made the most of 2015 after this experience. Some of the highlights were the following:

- Kevin and Caitlin flew in to have a week at the Jersey Shore with us and our extended family. This is a trip that we still talk about today and one we will repeat soon.
- I turned fifty in August, and Jen and I went away to Napa to celebrate.
- Jen had double knee surgery in September. She had chronic knee issues but had postponed her surgery due

to my health detour. So we got that scheduled and got her some much-needed relief.

- With Jen on Injured Reserve, Caitlin and Frances came with me on a work trip to St. Louis—or as Frances called it, "See Louis!" (We never did find that Louis, though.)
- I decided that we would finish the year with a bang and took Jen, Frances, and my youngest sister, Carolyn (who was visiting for Christmas), on a surprise trip to Disneyworld. I told them the afternoon before we went. I loved the drama of the surprise.

It was easy to see that the immediate impact was that we would be more gung ho with our approach to experiences and sharing time with our loved ones. It felt good to put that effort in and be present in those experiences more than I had in the past.

However, it also proved another point. This itch couldn't be scratched by sweeping gestures and plans. It needed more than that. I wanted more than that.

The rest of the year had passed in a blur, almost like the clock that had stopped in late 2014 was now trying to make up for lost time. As the anniversary of my hospital visit came around, I found myself revisiting everything that we had been through. We usually didn't have much reason to be on First Avenue in Midtown, so I took a walk down there just to put myself back in the moment in an attempt to reconnect with the urgency of the feelings from that time. I stood on the corner of 33rd Street near the access to FDR and looked up. I don't know what I expected to see, but I had promised myself this perspective and here I was almost a year later. It is funny how we rely on the calendar for prompts when I could have taken that short walk at any time in the previous year. Maybe this meant I was ready now to take on the changes I knew I had to make.

There was no physical to-do list after being sick, but there was a mental one that helped my focus. The items on it were prioritized by access and ease of change. Maybe that was a cheat; however, I was no longer taking my time here for granted, and deep down, I knew there was no silver bullet and that this would be a building process of putting one piece on top of another to build the life and outlook I desired.

The list is below so you can see how I thought about the progression:

1. Prioritize time with family.
2. Make sure they know how I feel about them.
3. Reconnect with friends that I had lost along the way.
4. Get a better work-life balance, with the emphasis on life!
5. Prepare for being here in the future with a focus on my health.
6. Ask for help and guidance in whatever endeavor I choose to undertake.
7. Balance the love and fear in my life. I subscribe to the idea that fear is omnipresent, and this check and balance is to make sure it doesn't consume the love in my life.

As is our wont, with the New Year upon us, I decided that number five on the list was my next focus since number four was going to take time. I wanted to get myself back in physical shape and find an activity that spurred me on to do that. A big part of that was going to be diet and nutritional understanding based on how my body now worked. While my recovery had been smooth, there were days where my stomach would just turn my world upside down. This was expected and understood, but I hadn't really put in the effort to understand what I needed to do for this to be minimized or eliminated altogether.

That became my focus for the New Year. I did some reading and revisited the advice I had received post surgery. I eliminated caffeine, alcohol, dairy, and simple carbohydrates in a mass change. The first two weeks were brutal. I had withdrawal headaches, and my stomach struggled to come to terms with the new diet even though it was cleaner. I was determined, though, that it was the right path. There were no barriers to exercise anymore either, apart from the ones in my head. In fact, now much of the daily battle was psychological and emotional rather than physical. I have this obsessive streak in me and when I get focused on something, I can be so singleminded that it's annoying. I know it is annoying, but it is how I am wired. It has earned me the nickname of St. Gerard in the past, and my saintly alter ego made his reappearance.

One of my big ah-ha (I told you music follows me everywhere) moments during this whole experience was that I was so stubbornly independent that I would shun help even when it was the best thing for me. But when you have a medical issue like I had, you have no choice but to place yourself in the hands and guidance of others, so not inviting others in showed my weakness. It also exposed a bravado I had always demonstrated and believed to be one of my strengths. I had always viewed my number of close friends as a sign of my own strength—that I valued quality over quantity, which I still do. But it was prohibitive for some other relationships that could have been shared or shared with a deeper connection. It is a tough admission that this badge of honor I gripped so tightly actually was a red flag for something else. That hit me hard, and I knew that I had to change in this regard. I had decided that to support my health goals, I was going to put my foot back on a triathlon starting line. I hadn't raced since coming to the US, and it felt like this was long overdue. I had unfinished business with the Ironman distance and thought that was a good goal to have out there.

In the spirit of looking for help, I went onto the Ironman website and looked through their IM University coaching menu. I looked through a number of bios and found three that I liked the description of as a first stab at it. So I sent off a note to all three coaches detailing my recent experience and what I wanted to achieve. Two of them returned what felt like standard automated responses with a nod to my concerns, but the third coach asked to arrange a call. I decided that this was a logical approach and would help me get a better understanding of being fit. He was a Master Coach, one of the best on the roster and in the world. Scratch that. In my opinion, he is the best. This was where and when I met Coach Lance Watson of Lifesport Coaching. This was going to be a virtual relationship, as he was based on the west coast of Canada, so communication and comprehension were going to be vital. Our connection was instant, and I knew right away that he would be my coach, my guide, and ultimately my friend. It was like some power was rewarding me for my vulnerability in doing something that was alien to me. My relationship with Coach would be integral, not only for my progress in the triathlon discipline, but also in my personal progression. He has more knowledge than my talent will ever use, but his friendship I will keep forever. We agreed on a path forward, one that started to build my fitness regime. He taught me a lot, and not just about triathlon. His first question without fail is always, "How are you feeling?" That set the tone for any discussions about any sessions I had completed or failed to complete. That still means more than anything as we continue this journey together today.

As the sessions' effort level and duration expanded, we started to focus more on my nutrition and how to fuel my body for more demanding workouts. Now I was at a real loss. Building a basic diet had been fine, and "St. Gerard" had seen some positive results since excluding all the items mentioned before. Now I was faced with the challenge of adding nutrition with the purpose of being able to process the intake for energy. I had no idea what to do. Of course Coach Lance did, and he introduced me to a nutritionist who he used as an expert resource to his athletes.[2]

Coach introduced me to Celine Evans on the phone, and we chatted about my circumstances and what I would need to do to find fuel that would help me achieve what I wanted without digestive repercussions. She is fantastic, and with her on my side, we decided that we would strip my diet all the way back and rebuild it through FODMAP (Fermentable Oligo-, Di-, Mono-saccharides And Polyols) principles. This basically put me through days of testing on ten core food groups. Each one would be isolated over three days, growing from a little to a lot of intake and monitoring bowel impact. This would effectively rule in and rule out foods constructed in the same manner. This was a revelation and set me up for a much more controlled diet. For the record, for me, Fructan was my main enemy, and this came through in bread, grains, fruits, and vegetables. By knowing the family of foods, I could check easily what was good and what was not. Celine continues to guide me today, and as

---

2. That term of athlete is used in the mass term not the elite term. Coach Lance coaches and has coached some of the greatest triathletes ever to race, but he uses that term for us all. We just have levels within the term!

our relationship has grown. She puts up with all my "faddy" questions about this method or that supplement. Her patience, understanding, and skill are tremendous additions to my life.

The lesson isn't all the technical knowledge, even though that has been helpful. The real lesson is that by opening myself up to help and support, I had added two key resources in chasing my goals—and, more importantly, two friends in my life. To this day, I have never met Celine in person, but if you eavesdropped on our Skype chats, you wouldn't know it. I was lucky enough to meet Coach Lance in person a year ago when he brought his daughter to NYC. It was great to get to meet and spend time with him and part of his family. It cemented our bond even further. My deeper realization was this:

Triathlon is an individual sport, and I sought help to be the best I could be and get the most from it. And yet in life, which is not an individual sport, I had tried to do that with as little help as possible, and to my chagrin I had prided myself in that approach.

Practicing death taught me a real-life lesson. I was far from alone; however, it showed me so many missed opportunities to share parts of my life and to support and be supported by others. The clarity of this revelation after almost fifty years of "life" was significant.

As I continued to make progress in nutrition and training, we turned our heads to a racing plan for 2017. Coach wanted me to start with an IM 70.3, a half distance. He wanted me to do a few of them as race day can be variable, regardless of your fitness levels. We put together a plan for the year. I was keen to involve the family, and it seemed more than serendipitous when Dubai launched their inaugural 70.3 race in January of 2017. One of my best friends lived there, and so it was decided that we would take a family vacation away from the NY winter. Kevin and Caitlin would meet us there, and we would spend a week in Dubai, culminating in the race. Two other races were chosen, with about thirteen weeks between them. This would give me time to recover, work on the outcomes from the race, and then build toward the next one. After the first race, we would look to put a late-season full IM race on the calendar. When the final plan was made, I chose IM Maryland. Again, a big factor for choosing this race was the proximity of family to the race. Jen's siblings all live in Maryland, a reasonable travel distance from the race site.

Dubai was probably the cleanest race of them all in terms of prep and performance. We had a great week in Dubai. We stayed with our friends Jim and Linda, and although I had some curfews to observe, we had fun between touristy activities and some social activities that they had arranged around our visit.

I won't bore you with the details of race day. They aren't that important, as it happens. I finished the race, although there were some moments of struggle in the desert heat. My time missed the target time Coach had set me, but that was a second-ary goal. First goal was to get around and learn from that part of the experience. It was a thrill to finish the race, and I felt some physical redemption from my experience. It was important for me to realize some physical goals that showed I had recovered. Having the family there with me was really the best part of it. They had all been out cheering me on (also in the desert heat) and though Frances had crashed out in her stroller, these were memories to cherish.

Jen is a lawyer in the hotel real estate industry, and so she couldn't pass up the opportunity to book a room at the Burj Al Arab hotel for that night to celebrate—all in the name of research you understand! We had really gotten the hang of this "creating experiences" thing. In fact, Jen launched her "adventure a month" campaign in January at the same time, and this was the first of those. This was in part her reaction to my illness and the sharp focus it gave on other parts of her life she had gone through. The premise is pretty simple: every month there would be an adventure. Sometimes some of us, sometimes all of us. Sometimes near, sometimes far. The consistent element was that there would always be a focus on being present and opening ourselves up to the wonders experienced with people and places in this life. She is still true to that discipline today. I love that she has this approach. It is a reminder to live today—no one is promised tomorrow.

As the year sped along, it was soon time to get ready for IM Maryland. My races had me ready, and I was in shape both physically and mentally to get it done. We had rented an Airbnb right on the river, and again Kevin and Caitlin would be coming in for the long weekend. In addition, we had a bunch of Jen's family coming for race day and our rented accommodation would be base camp. I went down early in the week to be there and to walk/ride the course and make sure there were no last-minute issues with my bike or my gear. It was going to be unseasonably hot for race day. The forecast said 84 degrees as a high for October 7. Knowing this, I dialed up my hot-weather race preparation and ensured I was ready for anything.

It turned out to be a day to remember but not for the reasons you may suspect. The family at base camp had a blast. I had chosen that house because the run would go past the front yard three times late in the day. I knew I would need that. And when I got to the run, sure enough the transition from the bike to the run was proving to be challenging. I was taking on fuel to help me get a rhythm. My training had taught me that the initial discomfort would pass. It hadn't yet by the time I passed base camp for the first time. I could hear them before I could see them! These Philly girls are like that! As I ran/walked the first mile past them, I remember hearing Jen's sister Ali shout, "Gerd!"—that is what she calls me—"You better be running on the way back!" Clearly a few drinks had been sampled, and as I continued on, I could hear them for quite a while as they cheered on other competitors.

Around mile two of the run, something gave out in my knee and I hit the ground. Something popped and down I went. That early in the run, I was still carrying a few essentials, and they were sprayed all over the tarmac around me. I wasn't really sure what had happened apart from the searing pain in my knee and a new pain in my left arm that had hit the ground first. I figured (hoped) I had just tripped, so with the help from some other racers, I got to my feet. The first step didn't feel good at all. And so I continued to move gingerly as I assessed what I could and couldn't do. I got going and was able to run a little, but that was short-lived before the pain in my knee created some uncertainty in my gait. I created a walk/run/shuffle-type movement so I could cover the ground. I would pass the family at mile five, so I targeted that for the next milestone I could move smoothly through. It wasn't happening, and the pain and panic was etched on my face as I passed them again. They could see the blood coming from my arm, and I told Jen about the knee as I passed her. Almost immediately, my brother-in-law Drew (the nurse) appeared alongside me with my son, Kevin. I was trying to tell them what was going on without me really knowing what that was. I knew the physical limitation without knowing the exact cause. The next few miles went down the pier in a sort of

AND YOU MAY FIND YOURSELF

loop, and they stayed with me as long as they could. They then caught me up once I came out of the "competitors only" area. I was struggling but told them to go back to base camp and I would see them on the next lap. And so they wished me well and headed back.

That was a long lap, and the pain and discomfort only worsened. I wouldn't stop for medical help because deep down I knew my knee was damaged and there wouldn't be anything they could do. Several knee surgeries over the years had taught me this. In addition, my first tilt at an Ironman finish ended in injury after a crash on the bike course back in 2006. I was determined I would make it. I struggled through to mile twenty-one, but in reality, I wasn't moving fast enough now to get to the finish line before the cut-off time passed. I also had the problem that my knee kept on giving way and I would hit the ground time and again.

A medical aid approached me after another fall, and he spoke to me as I lay there. He looked at my knee and called over a colleague. They both knelt down beside me and suggested that my day was done. It was a painful replay of what had happened in 2006 in IM UK. They were right. I was done and in pain, and so they helped me to the medical tent and radioed in that my day was over. Surprisingly, this spawned my most memorable moment of the day. The dream of crossing the finish line wouldn't be the highlight, NOT crossing the finish line perversely created a new high. I sat at the side of the road after leaving the medical tent with painkillers and my damaged knee wrapped and aching. Jen and Caitlin finally tracked me down. We were all in tears. Mine flowed from exhaustion and disappointment of not getting the finish with them there. Their tears I recognized as tears for my disappointment. We talked, and I explained in more detail what had happened. As we dealt with the practicalities of getting my bike and gear back, Jen and I limped our way back to base camp, which was about a mile away. Caitlin was going to find Kevin, and they would pick up my race gear. In that painfully slow walk back, Jen looked at me and said, "I am very proud of you."

To which I answered something like, "But *why?* I didn't make it!"

She then said something that represented some of the change in me: "Because of your attitude. You are not blaming bad luck or circumstance. You know what you have achieved regardless of finishing or not."

And that was true. Up to that point, I had treated failure like a pariah in my life, and when it visited me many times, I had reacted pretty badly. Emotionally. And I only focused on the outcome not what I had learned from the process. This time, deep inside me was a realization that this was way bigger and that I had demonstrated all of the personal traits I value but in a more mature way that I hadn't demonstrated as frequently before. That moment with Jen was a finish line of sorts. This was my medal and new badge of honor.

My physical redemption and mental evaluation weren't complete by any stretch of the imagination, but some vital big steps had been taken. And yet something was still missing. Practicing death had helped me to prioritize many things in my life. The practice had brought me to this point. But what it couldn't do was prioritize something that wasn't there. I had to take stock again, and after coming close to meeting my end, it was clear that it was connected to what was beyond this life.

After some reading and thinking, I concluded that there was a spiritual gap in my life. Maybe this was why I felt lost. While my practices in life could be reorganized and rearranged, the lack of connection to a greater purpose was perhaps the answer. Not religious necessarily, but a higher purpose of what this life is all about. Of course I started with revisiting religion, since that was an obvious place to start. My search was inconclusive, largely because all of my searching took me back to a question about how to find harmony with parts of my religion's beliefs and stances that I just couldn't reconcile. As a result, I found myself exploring learned writers who were far more committed to a religious life than I was and who had also had struggles with their beliefs matching to their churches'.

It was really insightful to see the irreverence of some of those writers on some topics I would have considered sacrosanct. Their investigation and honesty gave me permission to think about these elements in a different way. What once would have been deemed off limits was now more accessible to me. This revelation opened the door to further exploration. I explored what practices and elements mattered the most to me. Praying, beliefs, and interactions with others became heavier-weighted topics than the elements I was frustrated about. And one of the reasons I wanted to be able to answer this for me was that I wanted to be able to help Frances in her spiritual belief choices. She is in Catholic School, so I want her to have a healthy appraisal of what she would be taught, but a belief set nonetheless that would guide her in her daily life.

Clearly that is not something that happens overnight. However, I control the energy and input into creating this and finding the elements that are lacking in me. That journey will continue through my life until my dying day. This is the first time I have mentioned it outside of the help I sought to find some direction in this search. I sought guidance in a virtual group setting. The anonymity gave me the chance to dip my toe in without being over committed or over exposed. The group was called Oath, and it was the new output from Nicole Meline. Nicole delights in not fitting in any prescribed title society would have for her. She is a joyful mix of love, education, spirit, and curiosity. I believe if you asked any of her "beloveds," we would all have a different definition of her. That in itself is something I marvel at.

I first came across Nicole Meline as an instructor on the Peloton bike streaming platform. Her classes were always very challenging physically, but there was always more depth to what she was prompting in her students. She is an Ironman, and she created a class suite as she prepared for her next IM race, which obviously appealed to me and fitted right into my training plan. As I followed more and more of her social media posts and content, I could see there was some spirit in her that shone. It seemed logical to me that now I had reached this stage in my own journey; serendipitously, it coincided with her launching her new platform and practice that was Oath.

Nicole has since augmented this practice further, but in that moment, it created a safe place for spiritual wondering, wandering, and guidance with kindred spirits who remain faceless to this day. In those sessions, I learned that Nicole, among many talents, is a scholar in religious studies and theology. With this background, she proved to be a perfect fit for me. It wasn't the academia that was the real clincher though. The real connection was Nicole's honesty and vulnerability and her willingness to share her own journey. The positive affirmation that came from the incompleteness of her own personal journey gave me confidence I was in the right place. That openness convinced me that I should work with Nicole to find a footing in areas I wanted to explore.

This is intensely personal and is not being trotted out like some zealot's propaganda. I share this with you for you to know that the changes in me are complex and multidimensional, but more than anything, they are my changes.

Truth be told, I didn't see this coming. It wasn't on any of my mental or physical lists created in the ICU. It was the practicing death approach that had brought me here. It was now showing something to me I hadn't perceived but had progressed far enough to know it was missing. And now with help, I was starting to see what it would open up to me.

CHAPTER 13

All your regrets ran rough-shod over me
I'm so glad that we're strangers when we meet

—David Bowie

It was always said this song was about David Bowie's former wife, Angie Bowie. In the context of this experience, I like to think of it as me (and DB) meeting our younger selves and recognizing the change and growth we had made, therefore making us strangers.

The idea that you don't recognize a younger version of yourself and that your outlook, beliefs, and values have changed over time is an interesting concept. In fact, let me lean on David Bowie one more time for a quote from him that resonates deeply with me.

He famously once said:

"Aging is an extraordinary process where you become the person you always should have been."

This idea that all our life experiences add up to make us the person we should have been all along blows my mind. It

141

does explain the fact that some of us find our way there quicker and some of us don't find it at all. This thought also made me come to terms with the thought that I had been shown this path before but hadn't taken it. And looking back, I believe that.

This experience has guided me to reevaluate my life in ways and with others that I just couldn't have imagined. That sense of being saved for another purpose (and sometimes guilt of being saved) is what kept me coming back to dig into what was really behind this story. And that is what this track represents—a lot of what I have learned and why I chose to write about it now.

Here are the three key lessons I learned:

Practicing Death

This is a difficult subject, and probably some of you have winced at the thought of it. I think that maybe it is our refusal to let death in, and certainly our discomfort in talking about it, that keeps us from embracing it. The finality of it, or what may lie beyond it, is such a difficult concept. What if we used its inevitability in our lives? Would it free us up to lead a life more of our design rather than one buffeted by the light and shade of daily life?

When I was in the ICU, I felt like I was practicing being dead. I was, for the most part, cut off from the world, deprived of food and water, scared to sleep, and faced with an uncertain future. I was sitting in a living purgatory while the doctors worked out what was wrong with me. (This was ironic because I have always loved Dante's *La Divina Comedia*, and so the visuals in my mind of purgatory came from him). When so many basic and intrinsic elements are taken out of your hands, what are you left with? Your feelings, what is in your heart, and a head full of memories and woulda-coulda-shouldas! Is that enough?

Think about practices we see regularly: meditation, retreats, missions, vocations. These are all ways for an individual to shut out daily forces, to connect with what lies inside them, and to reflect on what they can do to be more purposeful in what really matters to them.

The ultimate goal is that through practicing death, you are free to live the life that matters most to you. This investment in yourself can take away some of the fear associated with an untimely but nonetheless inevitable end. And when your time comes, you will be calm in the knowledge that you lived *your* life and that you took care of your loved ones by having everything in order at the end. There is so much pressure in this society to bow to the many influences that seep into your life on a daily basis. Practicing death is a way to control all of that noise and still have the life you want.

I Was Lost and I Didn't Know It

One of the biggest revelations to me throughout this process and beyond has been this thought of direction and purpose. I prided myself in my career and the course I had taken. I believed I had taken an unconventional but conscious path to work for and with businesses that I really connected with or was challenged by. And for a lot of it, that was true. However, I now realize I placed too much power in position and status, and that had clouded my idea of where I was in my journey. Yes, I took positions based on opportunity and business challenge, also on necessity a few times. I also took some of them because they would be a better stepping-stone to get to where I wanted to be, only for me to discover that the destination wasn't what I wanted at all. And rather than realize that, I had three different shots at it, because when it didn't fulfill my dreams like I imagined, I blamed the circumstance, not the original goal.

Even after my illness, this imbalance still continued, and I still had a high capacity for making missteps.

Here is an example in the last few years. I commuted to Chicago for work for two years. Sunday night, Monday morning flight, back Friday afternoon or evening. Our family lived separate lives. I was so exhausted at the weekends that I was really just recharging to go do it again the following week. But why? Money? Opportunity? Sure, but the opportunity cost was so high, it was only when I stopped doing it that I truly realized what it was costing me—and us. Actually, it hit me like a sledgehammer. And this came after my illness! So even after everything I had been through, I fell into a well-worn groove despite all my promises and awakening. This shit is hard!

It also made me feel very vulnerable and inadequate. Being made redundant and being removed from corporate life was an extreme but necessary step for me to find an equilibrium, to be able to really evaluate this honestly and candidly. It is liberating but uncomfortable to admit that to yourself, and now by extension to you. As a result, I have started my own business. I want to work on my own terms, and this is part of that determination.

I mentioned earlier that writing the book is part of the transformation too. As part of the process in preparing to write this book, my writing coach, Azul, put me through a number of exercises to explore what was at the core of this experience. One of the real eye-opening outcomes was a life evaluation that showed me that I have always been happiest when material things were not a key input. It showed me that most of my personal happiness was not attached to what I have. My happiness was attached to presence, space, and time. And yet I have always had this drive to push on, to look for the next thing, even immediately after a new level has been reached. I have spent very little time really enjoying the growth afforded by whatever I just achieved. What was I looking for? If you never take time to drink in the view from the summit, what's the point of climbing it in the first place? The next summit? That doesn't end, unless you have an experience like mine that shakes you to your core or you find another way to create some self-evaluation. In my case, it has been my career that I have treated as a porcelain god. My personal shame in not understanding that was a real barrier even after being sick. It is only outside of my career that I am able to breathe and concentrate on what really matters to me.

Now I am not advocating early retirement or career abandonment. I am championing balance. The discipline it takes to say "yes" in your personal life versus saying "no" in your professional life. It's a big change. Think about it though. If you went through my experience, what would you miss or wish for yourself? As I went through this evaluation, my work or career thus far was never the answer for me. Possessions, vacations, experiences were never my answer either. It all came back to one dominant factor. Time. More time doing whatever with the people that matter most. And there will be times where balance is almost impossible. I get it. I have lived that life. However, when those occasions arise, you need to plan the time when balance will return. Make that part of your plans. If you don't then why would it return? You have to make it your priority.

I was lost because I had somehow managed to separate my professional self from my personal self, and as a result I had two compasses spinning me around. The irony is that I talk to businesses all the time about being connected to their purpose. My belief is that once you have that connection cemented in the business, then my role of marketing or running the business has a clear focus to communicate internally and externally.

And here I was not realizing that I had that disconnect in my own life. I was doing more of what I *could* do than what I *should* do.

The Smallest Gifts Are the Greatest

I think the most important takeaway here is not to lose sight of what really matters and what you connect with the most. I have been lucky enough to travel a lot and live in different countries. And while location can be important to your purpose, it can also be overplayed in its significance.

As parents, partners, and professionals, there are many distractions and pressures that mean we don't pay heed to the little things or take time for our most important ones. I think this is where the modern concept of "date night" came from. At its core, it is about clearing time for each other with all the other stuff going on in life. Making space and time and being present are when the little moments creep in. I remember going home after my second surgery and being scared of Frances's reaction to my return since she was clearly affected by the first one. It took a day or two for her to absorb all that was going on, and that is why we engaged her in the "boo boo" process. The most memorable moment though was when one day she saw me struggle to move and wince in pain as I got back on the sofa. Once I settled down, she walked over, didn't say a word, and just placed her sweet little head on my shoulder. Melts me to this day. Those are the gifts that matter. Little shared moments, sometimes stolen, sometimes planned. How many of these did I miss because I wasn't there or wasn't paying attention? Your rewards for being present are these gifts. Seek them out and cherish them.

Compare that with now. My best moments of the day are taking Frances to school, holding her hand and chatting about everything and nothing on the subway ride to the Upper East Side. We make up the dumbest of rhymes, smell bacon from the delis, and chat about whatever is running through her seven-year-old mind.

"Daddy, can I tell you something . . ."

That is the real music to my ears. To be present when she wants me to be present. Then later in the day, I am usually home when she gets in from school. This rewards me with the instant reaction when she comes through the door, and anywhere from a one- to ten-minute download ensues on everything that happened in her day. I stop whatever I am doing for those ten minutes. It is pure gold. I hope she remembers this like I do.

There is, of course, another side to this. It fills me with tremendous guilt that Kevin and Caitlin didn't get the same attention or time. I worked from home for a while when Kevin was two or three and Caitlin was one. They won't remember that time, and I actually find it difficult to remember that time too. I am sure it wouldn't have been as rich as this experience is now. It couldn't have been. I was trying to be a father, a husband, a man, and a professional, and I hadn't learned any of them yet. That bothers me, but I am trying to forgive myself for it. We use throwaway lines like "you live and learn," but never were truer words said. I am determined to continue to learn. During the writing of this part of the book, I went to see David Whyte, the renowned poet philosopher, and he talked about many things that echo through these pages. One thing he said that gave me real energy to power on. He said:

> "Regret gives you a better relationship with the future. Live with them all. Your past, your present, and your future."

This experience is my catalyst to reconnect with these personal discoveries. The only new one was practicing death. There had been other signals and opportunities that I had ignored or bypassed in the past, but this one captured my full attention. And as I sized up the impact and magnitude of this experience, there was always a whisper in my ear that this wasn't just about me or for me. There was a deeper feeling that I was being used to convey the wider message for those looking for it.

There was one nagging question I have returned to time and time again: Why did it take me five years to write this? There are two main reasons, and they lead me to provide some advice for you if this journey is one you want for yourself.

The first reason: Until now, I wasn't ready or equipped to write it. Being made redundant and taking time to evaluate what I was doing opened the door. A chance encounter with Azul Terronez in San Diego, who has coached me through this process, gave me the support I needed to be brave enough to examine what the story was really about. Sharing little snippets with friends and family kept my confidence up and "imposter syndrome" to a minimum and motivated me to keep searching. My natural curiosity peeked on my own experiences, and when they were played back to me, they pulled me in deeper to my own story. All these elements had to come together to find the belief that this story should be told, that it matters, that I had the ability to tell it, and more than anything, that writing it is part of the transformation itself.

The second reason was linked to my embarrassment around how I had lived and valued my life. In fact, it took a break in my normal structure to afford me the head space and capacity to really capture the essence of this story. My career was an essential component in how I valued my life, and I saw that as uniquely different from how I lived my life. I told myself that but never examined it truthfully. Maybe that was just convenient for me, but the truth is that they are parts of the same whole. The real lesson was that all aspects of my life contributed to its overall purpose and value. There is no separate life accounting for "but he was great at his job!" It is all the same.

The badges I wore with pride throughout my career were just that—baubles representing stuff I had achieved and learned and gained, but not learned from. It is true that I met some lifelong friends during my career, but it is also true that the real long-term value of those experiences are those friends and acquaintances, not the titles or the success or the rewards. They are fleeting and feed the ego, not the soul. The people you connect with are the true prize. When you are shoulder to shoulder with someone and you are both learning about yourself and growing individually and collectively, that is the true value. Otherwise the price paid will always be too high. Checks will be cashed and successes long forgotten and proven to be largely immaterial, but the people you do it with, they are priceless. All of them, the good and the bad. Every poor relationship is also a lesson in tolerance, understanding, or celebration of difference. While I valued these experiences and connections through the years, it is only now that they sit atop the achievements in my career.

This story, my story, is a story of human frailty, both physical and emotional. It is still going to be my life's work to realize all the lessons from this experience. Sharing it is my way of committing to it in a different way. As part of the journey in writing this, a friend pointed me toward a psychology model used to understand competence. In a way, using a competence model as a measure for progress in my life may seem cold, but the journey feels very similar.

The competency model has four stages:

1. Unconsciously Incompetent
2. Consciously Incompetent
3. Consciously Competent
4. Unconsciously Competent

There are some key observations and misconceptions that I would like you to consider as part of this journey through these four stages.

1. Only at Stage 2

After five years, it is clear to me I am still in Stage 2. This writing of this book is leading me to Stage 3. This is one of the key points I hope you take away from this story and my experience.

There is no immediate transformation, at least not in my case. I am following the norms in this example of becoming aware of my surroundings and weaknesses and trying to build "life competency" into them.

A large part of that growth is working out what the most important things are to you. That is a part of the journey you can't skip or fast forward through. The self-discovery in this process is the most revealing part. It's a work in progress but a very beautiful work—one I get to enjoy, at times endure, but always feel and be immensely conscious of.

2. The Transformation

I am sure people that know me are scratching their heads and thinking, "I don't see any big change in him." It took me a while to get that too. We are trained and tilted toward the aesthetics of how we look and the optics of what we have. This is reinforced in so many ways, particularly in today's world, that it can be challenging to understand that there may not be any physical manifestation of this change. It isn't necessarily what you see, but more what you feel and how you approach situations in a different light.

Let's take my approach to my career now as a live example. I still want a successful career. That success will be defined by criteria that I place against it, not the benchmarks and norms that have been established in me and in the market over the years.

During this period, I started my own marketing consultancy. It has proved to be difficult to win clients and to be true to my new question set that I use to help me assess any opportunity. I now ask myself three questions when trying to win business:

1. Do I want to do this work? I haven't lost any of my curiosity about why customers do what they do. In fact, that curiosity seems more far reaching now as I focus on that aspect of business.
2. What is the cost to me and my family? Look at the Chicago example. There is no way today that I would take that role. I know I had to go through it to get to that answer, but I have it now and I want to be true to it.

3. Is it worth it? I take the answers to 1 and 2 and decide if this is something I should even be considering. Of course, during the process, new information may be revealed that rescores my answers to questions 1 and 2, but that would still be evaluated in the same order.

In years gone by, I may have had a similar process, but I know the questions were in a different order, if in fact the list was the same length. I don't know what this holds for me, but I do know answering those three questions truthfully and in the right order will bring me more success by my measure.

I had the physical transformation during this process too. I lost a lot of weight through training for my triathlon races. There is no argument from me that being in better shape and living a healthier life will add value to your life; be prepared that the outputs may still disappoint you depending on what burden you put on it. I was never, nor will I be a world-class triathlete. My sport affords us the luxury of age-grouping. That means although I am in with the whole field, my real comps are athletes my age. I am still a long way off being a competitive athlete in those terms. That isn't why I do it and why it matters to me. Testing myself mentally and physically is something I will always value. It is intrinsic to who I am. However, it is not everything, and now that I have proven some things to myself, I can assess and evaluate my effort there too, by a similar question set.

That is what makes this transformation intensely personal and why *your* answer is *your* answer. You can take this experience as literally or as figuratively as you like. What I learned is that it doesn't matter what the answers are. What really matters is the quality of the questions you ask yourself. Everything flows from that.

3. If you are lucky, life goes on

My final observation is that the physical aftershocks of this experience only concluded four years after its uninvited appearance in my life. That was when I had the final surgery to fix the double surgical site and repair a hole in my abdominal wall. The site of the colostomy entry and the surgical reversal points had torn open during my training and had led me to bleed out of it occasionally. While the surgery from my Ironman knee injury was taking some time to heal, I decided to try and end this five-year reign of surgery and recuperation.

This last surgery hurt me more than any of the previous surgeries and in ways that I was ill prepared for. Having that part of your core reopened and repaired cosmetically, while effectively reshaping my chest to allow the abdominal wall to repair, was way more intrusive than I could imagine. After a year I still couldn't feel all of the surfaces of my abdomen. Worse than that was the impact of stretching and physical effort. It felt, and some days, still does feel, like there is a tight band running north to south in my abdomen. Stretching out filled me with doubt and concern for further injury or just straight fear of ripping it apart. It is the strangest thing not to trust your body to do the easiest of movements. And with this being my third major surgery in four years on that site, there were bound to be compounding factors.

There were emotional impacts too. For the first three months after that surgery, I really regretted getting it done. I hadn't actually had much choice, but in my mind, I exercised an option and it didn't work out the way I imagined. It has been over a year since that surgery now, and I have exercised patience and worked hard to get my mind right about it, though admittedly I wasn't happy about it for the longest time. My body is taking longer to respond and repair this time, but I have become more accepting of it. Yes, it is frustrating, but I am able to look beyond that and be happy to be here and going through this growth. So that is where I am in my physical journey today.

I have a ton of work to do to get back on the starting line, but I am determined to find my way through this emotional and physical minefield to do just that! Telling my story is undoubtedly a part of the healing process. So please be prepared for life to get in the way of your journey. This process and clarity will not make you immune to what comes your way, but it should make you better prepared to see it for what it is.

So my conclusion, in the context of Mr. Bowie's words, is that my younger self and I should be strangers when we meet. However, none of this is his fault or blame. He created a path that brought me to this point. And as he reached the goals he had set out for himself, he was changed by the journey. Or in this case—I was shown by my illness that I had many of the rewards that such a rich journey brings, but I was emphasizing the wrong ones. This newfound "stranger" had to discover that for himself.

THE NEXT CHAPTER

I got the key to my heart
I don't need nothing else

—Paul Weller

For Me

So what now? Where does this process invite me to go next?

The competence model in the previous chapter is really a measuring stick of where you would draw your line at any time. It explains the development you will go through but doesn't really help with the "how" to do it.

I mentioned Nicole Meline in a previous chapter and the support and challenge she offered through her Oath group. There were so many layers to the work and study that she introduced the group to that I have been revisiting it. It is interesting that I started the forty days in Oath while I was still in my last corporate position. Deep inside, I must have known that there was something out of kilter and that I was opening up to it revealing itself.

One of the most thought-provoking exercises and elements of the work with Nicole was the writing of a sankalpa near the end of the forty days. *Sankalpa* is a Sanskrit word for a solemn vow, a determination, or an intention formed by the heart and mind. It is a serious word in that you are committing to something bigger than yourself.

I thought it would be good to share my sankalpa here so you can see the output. This was written a year before I started writing the book.

> **I see my life as a soundscape, pure, passionate, warm, inviting, melodious, piano to a cymbal's crash, smooth, staccato, purposeful, meandering, and a playground for dreaming and reflection. A scape for my virtuosos and the orchestra of others, that soothes my rest, pulses my pace, and fuels my opera.**

It looks heavy and verbose, but it actually feels very light to me. I take great comfort in the fact that music plays as heavy an influence in my sankalpa as it does in this book. It genuinely is my heartbeat, and it talks to me in ways that other influences and people can't. Like paint or some other substrate to an artist, like words to a writer, like mountains to a climber, it is how my essence expresses itself. The sankalpa is also clearly a projection of where I see myself with many more strands and elements than the competency model. The key premise is that this vow to myself would be a reflection at some point in the future. This is the desired end state of my life. It was formed and expressed from within the confines of an exercise that allowed me to breathe deeply and envision my future. Not an epitaph, but rather a way to live my life. I believe that practicing death can be a similar experience for you.

In context of this illness, if I found myself in that same situation again, my proximity to my sankalpa would give me comfort that I had lived my life the way I intended and would diminish my fear of death. What I had faced was an absence of that intention, and that is what caused so much fear, anxiety, and pain of an unfulfilled life potentially coming to an end.

This is where I can use the previous competence model to help understand my progress. Not as a checkbox exercise but to honestly evaluate how I feel I am developing and where I should place my energy.

I can tell you I have a lot of work to do, but these lines written over a year ago mean a lot and resonate even more now than they did then. I can see a path to them, and that is what drives my determination and my purpose.

For You

My wishes for you are the following:

- If you recognize the signs I identify here in my story, I hope that you look for help to support your personal transformation. I would love to be that help. The support network I called on all started with the same jumping off point—a chat. When someone experienced, caring, and willing allows you to open up and ask your deep-rooted questions of self, it is an immensely powerful place to start. The sharing of vulnerability I have received back from my network has demonstrated that I am not alone, and by extension, so many more people go through something similar in silence.
- I said at the start that I believe everyone has a story. I hope you tell your story to someone, to everyone. In telling that story, my wish for you is that you experience

the liberation and preparation for transformation that could be yours if you want it.

- Allow my enforced practicing death to shape how you celebrate your life. By acknowledging all that is lost in death, it can be balanced by all that is achieved in life. By accepting this inevitable end, no matter your belief system, you can enrich how you live your life with and through others.

- I wish for you clarity on what your transformation means to you. It isn't open to evaluation by others. It is you, and only you, that can evaluate if this transformation gives you the answers that allow you to be comfortable with the question, "If this were your last day, what would you feel?"

- In your transformative process, I wish you find the understanding that your journey may not be speedy, nor will it necessarily manifest itself in physical ways that you can point to and share, but in your heart, you will know. When it all comes down to it, only you will know.

- I wish for you the understanding that missteps are all part of your journey. They add discovery, understanding, and imperfection to a purpose that was never meant to be perfect. I wish for you the gift to forgive yourself in the context of trying to move yourself forward. This may be one of the hardest lessons for me, and so my hope is that it is easier on you. Remember that the questions you charge yourself with answering are the most important part. The answers you give, right or wrong, are contextualized by being for the right questions in the first place. These aren't exam questions that will allow you to demonstrate intelligence or proficiency. They are more vital than that. I wish you

the time and clarity to define those questions that will shape your life.
- And my final wish for you is that you have your own passion like music is mine, some joy that is so intrinsic to you that you express yourself in it, with it, and through it.

As for me, well, I continue my journey. There is still a lot of work to be done. Still a lot of balance to be achieved, still many paths to be explored. I consider this book one of those paths, and I thank you for taking the time to read it. By doing so, you are contributing to my own transformation and helping me on my way. Let me know if I can be of help to you.

I will leave the last word to the last lines of the track for this chapter.

I've got love all around
I don't need nothing else

WORD FROM THE AUTHOR

THE HIDDEN TRACK

Like many great albums, the last track is hidden. Sometimes it was a reward for the avid listener, others it was a personal add-on to the work laid down in the vinyl grooves before it. Whatever its reason, the discovery was always memorable.

When you finish this book, I want you to think of the song that played to you or was in your head either as you read it or finished it.

Then I would love you to get in touch with me to answer two questions:

1. What curiosity in you or about you brought you to the book?
2. What song did you "play" in your head for the hidden track? Or if you used another medium, what was it? And if there are reasons behind the choice, then I would love to hear them.

I want to learn from you too. Telling me how this book touched you or made you feel will give me a sense of how I could help you and others with your next steps.

In return, I will tell you what my own hidden track was and why.

I look forward to hearing from you and hearing your choice.

I have put all the chapter tracks into a playlist called "And you may find yourself . . ." in both Spotify and Soundcloud if you are curious about hearing the tracks I chose. You can find the links at my website: www.pentalogymarketing.com. Enjoy!

Thank you once again for reading.

ABOUT THE AUTHOR

GERRY MURPHY

Gerry is a fifty-four-year-old Scot, born and raised in Glasgow. He has three children, Kevin 30, Caitlin 28, and Frances 7. He lives with his wife Jennifer and Frances in NYC now, having come to the US seven years ago. In his career, Gerry has led the marketing for some of the biggest retail brands on both sides of the Atlantic, and over his thirty-five-year career, you have probably been his customer.

As a marketer, the art of writing and communication has always been important to him, but it is his love for music that has been his real passion. An avid listener with an eclectic palette, a collector, a singer, and gig-goer, Gerry has had music as his constant companion. It is only fitting that his first book is set to his soundtrack of these events.

The Terrifying Realm of the Possible

of the Possible

Nearly True Stories

DEYST.

An Imprint of WILLIAM MORROW

DEYST.

THE TERRIFYING REALM OF THE POSSIBLE. Copyright © 2024 by Brett Gelman. All rights reserved. Printed in the United States of America. No part of this book may be used or reproduced in any manner whatsoever without written permission except in the case of brief quotations embodied in critical articles and reviews. For information, address HarperCollins Publishers, 195 Broadway, New York, NY 10007.

HarperCollins books may be purchased for educational, business, or sales promotional use. For information, please email the Special Markets Department at SPsales@harpercollins.com.

FIRST EDITION

Illustrations © Brett Gelman
Designed by Alison Bloomer

Library of Congress Cataloging-in-Publication Data has been applied for.

ISBN 978-0-06-331597-6

24 25 26 27 28 LBC 5 4 3 2 1

The
Terrifying
Realm
of the
Possible

BRETT GELMAN

For Ari Dayan,
the love of my life,
and to my angel children,
Janet and Toni

Contents.

Iris Below

Z

dear reader.

Welcome to *The Terrifying Realm of the Possible*. What you are about to read is a series of stories about five people. They are the essence of deep neurosis and barely functioning madness. They are a people deranged. This is not an autobiography, but rather a series of nightmares. Nightmares of who I really am, or who I could become. Please don't judge me. But when you do judge me, ask yourself: *Am I judging Brett Gelman or am I judging myself?* Is that defensive? Maybe. Okay, scratch that. Let's take judgment out of this. Just enjoy. Or don't. You are your own person with your own free will.

Thank you for your time.

Love,

Brett Gelman

The
Terrifying
Realm
of the
Possible

Abraham
Amsterdam

1.

Abraham and the
Demons in His Head

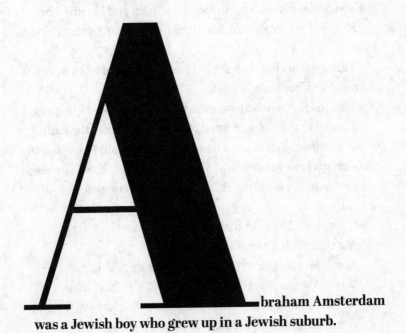

braham Amsterdam
was a Jewish boy who grew up in a Jewish suburb.

Abraham was like any other Jewish boy from a Jewish suburb.

Sometimes he was quiet. Other times he was loud.

Sometimes he was funny. Other times he was serious.

Sometimes he was hungry. Most times he was very hungry.

And he was nervous all the time.

Many things made Abraham nervous.

His dad. He liked to yell.

The bullies at school. They liked to scare him.

The girls at school. They liked to laugh at him.

The teachers at school. Well, not all of them. But some of them liked to yell just like his dad.

His own reflection. It made him want to puke.

That was thanks to his mother's side of the family, who had given him a fat round ass.

That was also thanks to his father's side of the family, who had given him a huge egg-shaped head with stupid curly hair.

He tried to straighten his stupid curly hair by brushing it back.

This gave his hair the shape of something between a pompadour and a motorcycle helmet.

This made his head look even more like a stupid giant egg.

Also a big thanks was owed to cheddar cheese, the eating of which had given Abraham a double chin that would morph into a triple chin whenever he opened his mouth to eat, speak, or laugh.

Let's see . . . What else made Abraham nervous?

Ah, yes.

Gym class. Because that's where Abraham had to run.

Abraham hated running.

Abraham's feet were turned out like a duck's.

When Abraham ran his legs would spin behind him.

His fat ass and helmet hair would bounce clumsily.

His open mouth would pant as his chins drooped.

4.

All the kids would point at, laugh at, and imitate Abraham.

Kickball was the worst.

In kickball the kids were particularly vicious.

Not just in how they skewered Abraham's run.

But also in how they mocked Abraham in his kicking of the ball.

Rather than kicking the ball in the normal way with his toes, because Abraham's foot was turned out, he kicked it with the side of his foot.

Giving all the kids a mini duck-foot preview before the main event of the Duck, Duck, Goose base run. And as he kicked and ran you never heard a group of children laugh harder.

Yes, all of these things made Abraham nervous.

Very nervous.

But the thing that made Abraham the most nervous . . .

The thing that made him more nervous than his dad . . .

or bullies . . .

or girls . . .

or teachers . . .

or even kickball . . .

The thing that made Abraham the most nervous was . . .

the demons in his head.

Abraham didn't know how the demons got there. Or where they came from. Or how long they had been in his head. But they were there.

Their bodies were made of shadows. Thin and muscular.

Their eyes were candy-cane red. Their mouths were orange from the furnaces that burned inside of their skulls.

They had two big horns.

The demons would speak to Abraham. All day, every day. And when the demons spoke, Abraham would be transported to the chamber of his own mind: a giant room at the center of which sat a large throne made of skulls. Surrounding the chair was an inferno. The floor, wall, and ceiling all covered in flames. Burning everywhere. Just like hell. Hell was in his head. And in his head the demons danced.

The demons did not dance out of joy.

The demons danced out of pain.

They danced.

They did not laugh.

They danced.

They did not cry.

They danced.

They danced.

They screamed.

They danced.

And when they danced they spoke. Their voices were the worst voices Abraham had ever heard. They filled his inner ears like an orchestra of broken instruments and goats screaming. Sounds that made him feel as if cactus needles were being pushed under his fingernails.

They danced.

The demons would dance and while they danced they tortured Abraham with words.

"You're going to die young."

"You don't love your parents."

"You're gay."

"When you die you're going to hell."

"You will never know love."

"Your dreams will never come true."

"None of this reality exists. Not your family. Not your dog. Not the kids at school that hate you. You are alone in the world. You are the only person. Everyone else is an illusion being created by a monster that absorbs everything you think you see when you're not looking at it."

"You have AIDS."

Yes.

Words of torture.

Threats of possible truths.

Unwelcome guests knocking on the door of Abraham's potential nightmarish future.

The only way to keep them from becoming reality was to do exactly what the demons said.

The demons had Abraham's full belief that if he did not do exactly what the demons said, nothing good would ever happen for him and everything terrible would happen to him.

Abraham could not step on cracks.

Abraham had to knock on his bedroom door three times before entering.

Abraham could not look at the number thirteen.

Abraham could not put his hat on the bed.

Abraham could not enter or exit the back seat of the car from the right side.

Abraham could not eat a grape without peeling it first.

Abraham could not watch TV with his feet touching the floor.

Abraham could not pet the dog with both hands at the same time.

Abraham could not brush his teeth without first reciting the full Pledge of Allegiance.

The demons' words were a ceaseless infection. Every waking moment was devoid of peace. Upon opening his eyes each morning, his mind was crammed with the demons' voices. Threat upon threat upon empty promises of darkness and doom, which seemed quite far from empty.

They danced and screamed, assuring him it would always be this way. Assuring Abraham he would never be free.

Then came the day.

It's not easy to pinpoint what the difference was from this day than any other day. It's not clear what made this shift in Abraham come about. It's not certain what transformed Abraham's fear to defiance the second he opened his eyes. However, for some reason, on this day, Abraham awoke and decided he had had enough.

On this day, unlike all other days, Abraham did not wait for the demons' invitation to enter the hellish chamber of his mind. Instead, Abraham transported himself to face his tormenters.

As always, the chamber was on fire.

As always, the heat of the fire burned, but it did not burn him.

As always, a large, menacing throne of skulls waited for him in the center of the room.

As always, he sat on the throne, positioning himself as the key audience of his own misery.

As always, the demons danced in a circle around him inside the fire.

As always, their screams made Abraham feel like his ears were bleeding.

As always, from the sea of these screams came an even louder scream.

A scream of a little girl being tortured, as if she was being torn apart. A scream that seemed to hang in the air. A scream that seemed to have its own ghost. A scream so engulfing that Abraham would have given up ever being happy again for the rest of his life if it meant he never had to hear it again.

This scream belonged to the Demon King. The Demon King stepped out of the fire, breaking through the dancing circle of all who served him. He looked like the rest of the demons. Except the Demon King was much taller and had only one horn. A gigantic horn that was larger than any other demon's two horns put together.

As he screamed his scream of all screams, the Demon King glided closer to Abraham. From far away Abraham could already smell the repugnancy of his breath. The foul zephyr from his disgusting mouth wrapped around Abraham's face just as the fire wrapped around the room.

The Demon King looked Abraham up and down. He then gave Abraham a long sniff.

The Demon King then spoke. "Nice of you to visit us, Abraham. But you know you are only to come if you are invited."

Abraham sat up straight. He puffed out his chest. Trying to project that bravery was his best-kept secret.

"I can come in here whenever I want. It's my head," Abraham mumbled, immediately disappointed with himself. He'd hoped his reply would have been more of a battle cry, but the words seemed to stop inches from his face and fall into the fire.

At this the Demon King laughed a laugh worse than his scream.

"No, boy. It's my head. It's my head and it will always be my head."

"You wish!" Abraham squeaked out.

Again, not the most poetically defiant statement ever uttered.

Again, the Demon King let out a blood-stopping laugh.

"No, you wish, boy. I don't wish. I never wish. I do. I do and I say. And I rule. I rule you, boy. I will rule you till the day you die. Which will be very soon, at a very young age. For as I have said many times before, you will die young from AIDS, even though you've never had sex, used intravenous drugs, or had a blood transfusion. And at the time you die, you will never have known love. And everyone will be laughing at you at your funeral, because you're gay. And then they will all disappear, because none of them exist. Not even your mother. You are alone in the world, Abraham."

Abraham tried to push out his chest a little more to seem braver but all he could come up with to say was, "Why? Why say these things to me? Why can't you all just leave me alone?"

Something had to be done. His comebacks, frankly, sucked. They weren't even comebacks. They were whines. The same cowardly whimpers he'd meet any bully at school with. Abraham could only try to remain calm as he figured out a different path of operation. But, as always, Abraham's mind was in a spin. He could hardly see a next step to take, a next word to say. Let alone strategize a whole other tactic.

To be honest there never was any tactic to begin with.

To be honest Abraham had never devised a tactic in his life.

To be honest the only tactic Abraham had was to repeat the flaccid question he had only seconds ago uttered.

"Why? Why say these things to me? Why can't you all just leave me alone?"

The Demon King leapt and howled with malicious glee.

"Why? Because it's fun, boy. It is so much fun. Well, not for you. But it certainly is fun for us. And no one will ever be able to stop our fun. Not you. Not your mother. Not even Dr. Heshel."

Dr. Heshel. Ah, yes, Dr. Heshel. It's funny. Abraham hadn't even thought about Dr. Heshel yet today. Usually not a day would go by that Abraham wouldn't wonder what Dr. Heshel would tell him to do.

Dr. Heshel was Abraham's psychiatrist. Abraham had been seeing him for about a year and a half. Abraham's mother heard Dr. Heshel speak one night at Abraham's school about the signs of obsessive-compulsive disorder in children, and she liked him. She thought he could be someone to help Abraham. She wasn't sure if Abraham had obsessive-compulsive disorder, but he might. And if he didn't have that, he probably had something worse.

"I think you'll really like him, Abey. I think he can really make you feel better. He's got a real way about him. An energy. A healing way and energy."

Abraham felt ashamed at first at the thought of going to a shrink. That was something that crazy people did. He wasn't crazy, was he? He wasn't someone who needed a Dr. Heshel, was he?

The demons certainly thought so. They constantly told him he'd wind up in a booby hatch just like his grandpa Mel, who had been in and out of mental institutions since Abraham's mother was a teenager. Grandpa Mel thought he was a giraffe. One day Abraham's mother came home to find him trying to eat a light bulb from the floor lamp, like it was leaves on a tree.

"I don't want you to end up like Grandpa Mel, Abey."

Neither did Abraham, and so he went to see Dr. Heshel.

Dr. Heshel was kind and made Abraham feel comfortable. He would never push Abraham to say anything or feel anything. He'd talk about anything Abraham wanted to talk about.

Dr. Heshel was warm.

Dr. Heshel smiled a lot.

Nothing seemed to shock Dr. Heshel.

Dr. Heshel had an ease to him that felt contagious.

Dr. Heshel liked to laugh and was also funny.

Nothing seemed to shake Dr. Heshel.

Everything about Dr. Heshel was absolutely top-notch in the shrink department. The only downside was that, more times than one, Dr. Heshel would fall asleep while Abraham was talking.

Make no mistake, Dr. Heshel liked Abraham. He did. But the fact was, Abraham bored Dr. Heshel at times.

The pathetic way he'd talk about the popular kids in school with reverence. These children who would not even come close to making any sort of mark in his life. Their names bled into each other in Dr. Heshel's mind.

The pathetic way Abraham would go on and on about how much he loved macaroni and cheese, but he was also scared to eat it because of a family history of heart disease, but he still refused to stop eating it, and, even more annoyingly, refused to stop worrying about eating it.

Dr. Heshel had grown tired of "sort of screwed-up boys" like Abraham. These boys with petty, small neuroses. These were really the only kinds of patients he had. He wanted someone who was really crazy. A child off the deep end. Often, upon arriving at his office, Dr. Heshel would stay parked outside where he would sit in his car and pray, even though he was an atheist.

"Please, God! Bring me a whack job! A kid to really sink my teeth into. A kid who might very well be a future junkie or serial killer. Someone who I can save."

Abraham was no such child.

There was nothing really that wrong with Abraham.

Sure, there were the demons.

Yet when Abraham talked to Dr. Heshel about the demons, it only bored Dr. Heshel more. The demons were obviously obsessive-compulsive thought patterns. So obvious that, deep down, Dr. Heshel knew Abraham even knew it. Dr. Heshel would have been much more excited if Abraham thought there were actual demons in his head. Now that would have been something to really get into. Alas, it was all just a big laborious verbal trip to Obvious Metaphor City. All Abraham had to do was ignore them. After all, they were just thoughts.

Thoughts can't hurt anyone.

Abraham didn't seem to take this in, though. He didn't want to, yet he also worried about not taking Dr. Heshel's advice. He worried that he might go crazy from the demons but at the same time knew they were just harmless thoughts, but at the same time felt bad about himself that he couldn't just ignore him. The whole dance made Dr. Heshel wonder if he should find something else to do with his life. All this fear of AIDS on Abraham's part made him wonder if he should work with AIDS patients. But that was too much. Dr. Heshel was prone to depression himself, and knew exposure to so much suffering would, in reality, be far too much for him.

So he'd stick with mostly normal and boring kids like Abraham and try to get them to see how silly their little problems were. Plus, it's not like he disliked his patients. He liked Abraham very much. However, he would have liked Abraham even more if the little shit would listen to him for a change. He wished Abraham would listen to him when he told him to think of all his thoughts as subway trains that were passing through the station of his mind. Trains that he didn't need to get on. He'd often say . . .

"Just don't get on the train, Abraham. Just let it pass through the station."

Dr. Heshel knew this hardly registered with Abraham. Dr. Heshel knew that Abraham only understood this intellectually. He knew that in order for it to be ingrained in Abraham, in order for it to have real meaning, he'd have to repeat it and repeat it often. You had to do that with Abraham. And so Dr. Heshel repeated it and repeated it.

"Just don't get on the train, Abraham. Just let it pass through the station."

In the last two sessions it seemed like the phrase was starting to get through. Abraham's eyes started to brighten in that way that comes with a deep registering. They were almost there. Almost there for Abraham having a real tool to fight against the onslaught of compulsion. Their last session had been three days ago. In the following week, in their next session, Dr. Heshel was confident that Abraham would really hear him. Hear him in a way he had never heard him before when Dr. Heshel, once again, simply told him . . .

"Just don't get on the train, Abraham. Just let it pass through the station."

"Just don't get on the train, Abraham. Just let it pass through the station."

"Just don't get on the train, Abraham. Just let it pass through the station."

Abraham sat up with a start as Dr. Heshel's voice echoed from the fire-laced walls of his mind.

"Just don't get on the train, Abraham. Just let it pass through the station."

The demons were laughing and screaming so loudly they couldn't hear it over their own voices. The Demon King jumped up and down ecstatically, continuing his verbal attack. No knowledge of the weapon his victim had just been handed.

"I see the fantasies you have, Abraham. The fantasies of your death day. Of everyone at your funeral crying. Wishing they had treated you better. Missing you. Oh, Abraham, how delusional you are. There will be no one at your funeral. Not even a rabbi. No one will want to waste their time mourning such a pathetic person, and when your ugly body quits, one of two things will happen. You will burn in hell with us forever . . . or there will be nothing. A dreamless sleep for eternity. Dark emptiness."

The Demon King laughed with such ferocity that, again, he did not hear the echo of Dr. Heshel.

"Just don't get on the train, Abraham. Just let it pass through the station."

For the first time Abraham really took these words in.

For the first time Abraham had clarity.

For the first time Abraham had a plan.

Abraham would not get on the train.

Abraham would just let it pass.

Abraham yawned and his head started to nod off just like Dr. Heshel's did when Abraham talked too much about the demons, or the popular kids, or macaroni and cheese.

The Demon King noticed.

"What are you doing, Abraham?"

"Nothing," Abraham mumbled, exhausted. "I'm real tired all of a sudden."

"Tired?!" The Demon King had never heard such a word be blurted from Abraham's mouth before. "Tired, huh?! Hmm-mmm, maybe it's AIDS?"

Abraham now was feeling the beginnings of something from the Demon King that he had never felt before. Something Abraham was sure he had felt himself many times. Just this one little decision to not get on the Heshel train allowed Abraham to take the focus off his own fear and take in who exactly was standing right in front of him. Normally, the threat of the demons' words would drive Abraham to fight back or plead and run away and cry. But not having done any of that, he was really able to take in everything around him for what it was.

"Did you hear me, boy?! Answer me now!"

Something felt different about the Demon King. Something very different. He had changed in some way. Or maybe Abraham had changed. Or maybe nothing had changed and this was as it had always been and Abraham had just not seen it. Whatever the exact situation was, the Demon King felt different. There was a pause to him. There was a shakiness. There was a . . . "OH MY GOD!" Abraham realized. "THE DEMON KING IS ME! I AM THE DEMON KING!"

It was now clear what Abraham must do to defeat his foe. To defeat himself. And from the walls of his mind Abraham heard his own voice vibrate:

"Don't talk to the Demon King. Talk to myself. Talk to me."

A smile swept across Abraham's face. A smile that almost knocked the Demon King down. He had never seen Abraham smile before. He didn't even know he could. The smile felt like his own.

"What . . . ? What are you smiling at, boy? You think it's funny what I'm saying?! Well, it's not! You are very very sick, Abraham Amsterdam!"

"Maybe," muttered Abraham.

The Demon King's eyes widened almost to the size of his horn. "What?! What did you say?"

"It's possible, I guess. Anything's possible." Abraham's grin stretched even wider. "But not likely."

"Not likely? How do you know it's not likely?" The Demon King gripped his skull in what seemed to be an attempt to keep it from exploding in shock.

Abraham leaned forward. "How do you know it *is* likely? You're not a doctor. Are you?"

"No . . . no, I'm not a doctor, but I can tell these things."

"So you're just guessing here?"

The Demon King was at a loss. "Maybe . . . Okay, maybe about this I am, but I'll tell you one thing—you might not have AIDS, but you're definitely gay."

"Oh boy, I hope so."

With this Abraham stood up. Looking taller than he had ever come close to looking before. And the higher he stood, the more the Demon King seemed to sink. Never had the ruler of the Dark Ones been in such a desperate spot.

"What?! But everyone will hate you!"

"I don't know if that's true. My uncle Richard is gay and everyone loves him. Sure, he's got it hard sometimes, 'cause he meets a lot of horrible people like you, but other than that, he's really one of the happiest people I know."

The Demon King blinked as if this was all putting him in some sort of trance. "I . . . I don't know Uncle Richard."

"Oh, you'd love him."

"Yes . . . yes, I'm sure I would . . . Wait! No! No, I wouldn't. I don't like gay people."

"Why not?"

"Because . . . because they're disgusting. They're evil!"

"Evil? A demon is calling someone evil? That's kind of rich. I mean . . . do you have a girlfriend?"

"Of course I don't. Demons can't experience love. Everyone knows that."

"I bet you wish you could know what love is. Even just a little bit. But you can't because nobody loves you. Nobody actually cares about you at all or wants to know anything about you. You think people hate gay people? Sure, I'm sure some do. But I'll tell you what everyone hates much much more than gays . . . Demons. Everyone hates you. No one loves you."

The Demon King froze.

"No, that's not true. Why? Why do you say such things? Why can't you all just leave me alone?"

Then the Demon King started to shake. Like an earthquake was going off underneath his skin. He tried to scream the quakes out of him but they were clenched. His screams could not escape his throat. Then, ever so slowly, the demon-dance circle began to close in on their ruler. This, as it turned out, was not to help him. This was to do something quite the opposite. They smelled his

17.

weakness and they were starved for it. With their shadow claws and teeth they tore into their sovereign's vile flesh. However, as they did so, a strange thing started to happen. As they tore away, they themselves started to be dismembered as well.

Then they all turned to the one next to them, assuming the blame for their injuries lay with the other. They ripped into each other, and after mere minutes, there was nothing left of them but black bubbling goo messily spreading across the floor. And as the goo evaporated, the fire on the walls of Abraham's mind died away.

Abraham sat there.

He sat alone in the room in his mind.

He listened to the silence.

He savored the emptiness.

He then laughed.

It was a laugh of many things.

It was a laugh of pride.

It was a laugh of relief.

It was a laugh of knowing.

Knowing that he had won.

Knowing that win was just for the day, or maybe the hour, or maybe the minute.

Knowing that tomorrow the demons would be back.

Knowing that he would have to do this all over again.

Knowing that he would have to do this all over again every day.

Knowing that he would have to do this all over again every day for the rest of his life.

Knowing that it was him.

Knowing that it was all him.

2 .

Popular

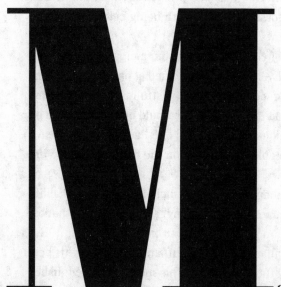ore than anything,
Abraham Amsterdam wanted to be famous.

More specifically, he wanted to be famously funny. Not the famously funny man who wore a leather jacket and shouted profanely about "how it all really is." Not the famously funny man who boasted a Hawaiian shirt and a guitar and sang parody songs about pizza and boogers. Not the famously funny man who wore a toilet as a hat and declared himself a "shithead." Abraham wanted to be the kind of famously funny man who smoked a cigar the size of a Cadillac and who spoke in a language of machine-gun-like acrobatic quips, puns, and jabs. The kind who was friends with gangsters. The kind who had always been old even when he was eight. The kind you pictured welcoming you at the gates of Las Vegas. That is, if Las Vegas had gates, and was at all like a heaven, which was definitely not the case, but Abraham knew nothing about the real Las Vegas. However, what Abraham did know was that all he wanted was to be the emperor of every room he graced with his hilarious presence. An urban oracle, who, at their very worst, was stuck with being celebrated as the very best. Whose flaws were gifts.

Abraham had, of course, never tasted a cigar. But he loved to eat pretzel rods. Every time he chomped at one, he'd visualize exhaling a billowing cloud of smoke, wistfully flowing from his mouth and nose. That imaginary cigar would be accompanied by an imaginary ingeniously constructed one-liner that would leave all the imaginary people in the room on the floor, gasping in the midst of their guffaws.

In real life Abraham didn't know such one-liners. In real life Abraham wasn't funny. If there was any talent for humor that existed in him, he had not yet figured out how to summon it. But that didn't stop Abraham. He would puff and bite, trying his best to embody his ideal future self while his mother cleaned dishes and cried and his father stared at the wall.

Abraham's deep desire for fame grew every day. He'd absolutely lose himself in a never-ending fantastical parade of self-celebration and inspired performances from stage, to screen, to talk show. No one ever not laughing at what he said and did. Rounds of applause as he entered and exited restaurants, grocery stores, and amusement park rides. Feverish adoration from beautiful girlfriends, wives, and ex-wives. Children who worshipped him, yet also understood that he didn't belong to them. He belonged to the world. He'd be able to leave behind everything he didn't like. He'd never have to look at everything he hated looking at. He'd never have to listen to the clanking of dishes drowning out his mother's sobs. He'd never have to look at his father staring at the wall.

The bright lights of his big-city future blinded him to his deadened repetitive present. His father insulting his mother's cooking. His mother obsessively taking his temperature. His father cursing their bills like they were people. His mother talking so loud on the phone he couldn't hear the TV, about relatives he had never heard of before. His father's pathetic pride in finding a ladder that had been hiding in plain sight for two weeks. His mother taking forever to apply her makeup while he and his father waited in the car. The swell of his father's silent rage. His father running back into the house. His father calling his mother a fucking bitch. His mother demanding a divorce. His father granting the request. The silent ride to the dinner, or the party, or the horrible function right after. Then, once at the dinner, or party, or horrible function, pretending that none of it had happened. Pretending their destructive emotional responsibility not only didn't exist, but also pretending that it wasn't the only interesting thing about them.

Someday Abraham would live in a spotlight. Outside of that spotlight would be the darkness he left behind. The mediocrity that invaded every minute of his life. He would choose anything and everything that would be allowed to walk into his light and be seen. His parents would not be invited. Nor any other member of his family. Not even Uncle Richard. Nor his teachers. Nor his friends, for Abraham had none to speak of. But his fans would be. Yes, his fans would be, and Abraham expected a lot of them. Fans: far better than friends. Fans asked no questions and gave no answers. All they did was worship. All they saw was what you let them see. And they knew better than to want to see more. What would that be like? To be adored? To be liked at all? He was sure it would be glorious.

Abraham had just learned about Jesus Christ. How he started Christianity, and Christians believed he was the Son of God even though he was also a Jew, and that the Romans executed him. They executed Jesus by nailing him to a cross, and then left him hanging to die for all to see. Abraham thought of Jesus Christ hanging from that cross. He wondered how Jesus really felt. Surely some pain. Probably some sadness. Maybe even fear. But as the people cried at his feet, Jesus must have felt popular. That's when you know people like you. When they show up to see you die. On the other hand, the Romans were there, too, and they hated him. So maybe he didn't feel so liked. But if he really was the Son of God and God talked to him, that probably made him feel the most famous he could possibly feel.

Abraham didn't know much more about the Jesus story. Except that he made some Jews mad. And they told the Romans and they killed him and that made Christians hate Jews. But what about the Romans? You'd think Christians would hate Romans more. Funny, huh? Christians hate Jews but lots of Christians live in Rome, so how do they not hate themselves even more than they hate Jews? And why don't other Christians who don't live in Rome hate Romans more than Jews? *People must really just want to hate Jews*, Abraham thought.

But not if they're funny. If a Jew is funny, people forget they're a Jew and they could be loved. If a Jew is funny, he or she could become famous. He or she could become quite popular. 'Cause that's what fame really is. Popularity. Popularity on a grand scale. And that's the second thing Abraham wanted the most. To be popular.

Abraham wondered if he even had it in him. Did he even have what it took to be liked by everyone? Was popularity in his genes? Was his mother popular? She dismissed his question with a smirk. "How do I know? I didn't care. I just was who I was. I had friends. I went to the parties. Boys beat each other up to impress me. One of the boys even followed me around and then started leaving me death threats that said if I didn't go steady with him he'd kill me. But these are the things that happened back then. We were innocent. We were wholesome. I knew I was a pretty girl and the handsome boys knew they were handsome boys who were desperately in love with me. But I didn't care. I could care less about their feelings, and they could care less about mine. They just wanted to lose their virginity to me, and sure, some of them did. But I never embarrassed myself, and neither did they. We knew who we were. If that's popular, then yes, I was popular. Very popular. Probably the most popular person in my school. But I didn't pay attention to that sort of thing."

Abraham asked his dad. He had to repeat the question several times before his father even realized he was there. "Dad, were you popular?" His father's bloodshot eyes came to life. They turned into his young eyes. Eyes that saw joyful things. He smiled for the first time in years upon years. Sure, there were smiles in public. But they weren't real smiles. They were just put on so people wouldn't ask him what was wrong. He knew if anyone asked him that, he'd soon be asking himself that, and that might be it. But this smile he was smiling was real. "Popular? Hell yes, I was.

I was the most popular boy in school. Everyone wanted to be my friend. Everyone. I used to hold interviews to see who deserved to be my friend and I'd get the pick of the litter of kids. The coolest kids. And we did the coolest things. And back then, cool was fun. Not dangerous like it is today. Nowadays all the 'cool' kids have guns, and they do heroin, and lose their virginity at eleven. When I was young, the cool kids held each other's hands, and skipped through fields. I can't remember the last time I've seen a field. Let alone skipped through one. Let alone skipped at all. I don't know if I'd even remember how to skip. So don't ask me, Abe. Please, promise me. Never ask me to skip. It'll only remind me of what was and what will never be again."

Wow. Abraham was ecstatic. Both of his parents had been popular. It was in them and that meant it was in him. He had popular genes. There was hope. Childhood might not be one giant shit pie after all.

It was perfect timing to learn about his popular genetics. No better time, actually, to put his genes into practice. It was the first day back from Christmas vacation. It was a new day. A new year. The actual New Year. Not Rosh Hashanah or the school year, but the actual brand-new year. The New Year everyone knew and everyone loved. And this New Year was not just the New Year—it was going to be *the* New Year. The New Year of the new Abraham. This was the first New Year that Abraham made his first New Year's resolution.

He had just learned, for the first time, what New Year's resolutions were, the week before, from his grandpa Mel. Grandpa Mel had been released some months before from the mental hospital and came to visit with Grandma Mimi. At one point Grandma Mimi went to go use the bathroom and, upon her exit, Grandpa Mel quietly informed Abraham and his parents that his New Year's resolution was to murder Grandma Mimi and take her money and spend that money on a "set of hot tits, ass, and pussy, who only knows the word yes." He then proceeded to punctuate his resolution with taking a shit on their kitchen floor. And as Grandpa Mel was being dragged away in a straitjacket, Abraham asked his mother what he had meant by "New Year's resolution." Abraham's mother told him that it was something people promised themselves they'd do or not do, or give up, or start doing in the New Year that usually they ended up not accomplishing, but, once in a great while, they did. Abraham had decided that his first New Year's resolution that he would ever make would be to be popular, and, unlike Grandpa Mel, he'd see it through.

The next day Abraham's dad drove him to school. Just like he did every day. Right before Abraham got out of the car, his father would say the same thing: "Don't kill yourself. No matter how good of an idea it seems." Abraham bounced out of the car. He was beyond excited. This was a new day. A whole new world. A world with a resolution. This was the day. This was the day everything was going to change.

He walked through the door. Everyone was rushing to and from their lockers. It didn't seem like there was one person who wasn't thrilled to be back. New boots were shown off. Fake fighting ensued. Aggressive flirtations enraptured new hearts. Joyful voices and laughter rattled his ears. Yet none of this noise was for him. Not one eye of any of the many present even mistakenly wandered in his direction. Invisibility smacked Abraham like a two-ton plate of steel in the whole of his body. He wondered if he had suddenly died. Was he a ghost? He felt a hollowness so intense that he looked for his own body dead on the ground. In fact: part of him wished he had dropped dead and his soul had exited his body. That way he could walk the halls unnoticed and hear what people said about him. But his corpse wasn't on the ground. Abraham was not a ghost and he was relieved. Not just because he was still alive, but because he knew deep down that if he was a ghost, and walked the halls to hear what people said about him, what Abraham would hear would be nothing at all.

Classes were boring but easy. You didn't have to worry about anyone not paying attention to you because no one was paying attention to anything. There was the one time that Mr. Kaminsky, the math teacher and soccer coach, had a mental breakdown. He took an empty Pepsi can and split it open and then sliced his hand with it and proceeded to write his grocery list in blood on the chalkboard. None of the kids noticed until he was halfway through, and blood had soaked his arm and the right side of his shirt.

The hardest time was lunch. Lunch was a true demonstration of your identity. It's where everyone learned where they belonged. It's where great decisions were made of who you were, not so much by you, but by who surrounded you. Each table was packed with people who knew what people they were and who they could and should sit with. Lunch was an oasis of friendship, no matter how unstable those friendships were. All the jockeying for position never could fully corrupt unadulterated togetherness. However, there were those few who were alone. Rogues with no belonging. Bodies of sadness faced with the cold hard facts of aloneness. Abraham was no one, with no place to go, and nobody wanted him. Not one table welcomed him.

But Abraham was ready to show everyone the new him. "Today's a new day," Abraham said to himself. "A new year. A new year with a New Year's resolution."

And with this, newfound purpose. With this new knowledge of his superior genetics, Abraham stepped to the holy mountain. The table no one dared to sit at unless they received that oh-so-sought-after invite. The table of all tables. The popular boys' table.

Abraham sat down. No one of his social stature had ever dared, and surely there would be harsh consequences. But Abraham was unwelcome at every lunch table. And if Abraham was going to be unwelcome at every lunch table, Abraham figured he might as well be unwelcome at the best table. Abraham sat at the end. A tension filled the room. Everyone looked at Abraham. Watching without noticeably looking in anticipation of what could only be the biggest disaster ever witnessed within the walls of the school. The weight of all the popular boys shifted. Yet, much like the rest of the student body, the only looks they gave to Abraham were barely in his direction. The closer the popular boys' eyes came to gazing upon him, the harder their eyes would become. Abraham knew that they knew how badly he wanted them to look at him. Today they would. Today they would look at him more than they had the whole year.

As the boys sat there, they laughed. Two, three, four at a time. And their laughs were mean. Abraham wanted in on that meanness. He wanted to feel meanness in his body. Meanness was power. Power that would be felt from classroom to classroom, extending through the whole school. It's what would make the girls like him. It's what would make the teachers fear him. It's what would make his parents be proud that their son was not some lonely loser, lost in his dreams, weird and strange, waiting by the phone to hear about weekend sleepover plans that would never come.

Today would be the day. Today would be the day that the boys would see him. Really look at him and invite him into their meanness. They would because he was funny. They would because deep down they would sense that one day Abraham would be famous and the funniest person in the world.

Abraham just needed them to look at him. Really look at him. He stared at the boys and thought, *Look at me. Look at me. LOOK*

AT ME. He repeated it in his head so loud that the thoughts would scream out in his gaze. *LOOK AT ME, GODDAMMIT!* And then:

"Look at Amsterdam. He's staring at us like a fucking psycho."

Prayers answered. The head of the clan, Greg Gillstein, had seen him. And not only that! He was talking about him! Abraham was noticed. The first step to his resolution had been achieved.

The second notice came from the second-in-command, Josh Goldman: "Yeah. He does look like he wants to eat us."

"Maybe he wants to eat us?" asked Rory Wolf, identical twin brother to Brian Wolf, who promptly replied:

"Yeah, or fuck us."

The table laughed in cruel unison. Greg Gillstein's eyes narrowed in on Abraham. Abraham imagined Greg taking aim at him with his eyes and zapping him with lasers that would melt him into the floor in a pool of hilarity. Abraham wouldn't be hurt. He'd relish his melted state. He would be fine. And everyone in the cafeteria would somehow know, and they'd laugh like they were laughing at Elmer Fudd or Yosemite Sam melting. Then Abraham would heal and go back to normal and everyone would applaud and Abraham would bow and take the throne as the funniest person alive.

But no lasers were zapped. Just a knife of a question:

"So which is it, Amsterdam? You gonna eat us or fuck us?" As luck would have it, as this question was being asked of him, Abraham was in the midst of the first chews of his kosher bologna sandwich. And if Greg's crew thought their leader's question was funny, they were gonna LOVE the answer. But the answer would not come in words. It would come in the form of one of the greatest physical-comedy routines ever performed in a school cafeteria. It would come in the form of a fake, flawlessly acted, choking tour de force. Abraham grabbed his throat. He began to writhe. He smacked at his own chest. Pushing on it in a self-Heimlich.

Abraham pretended to plead for help. As his gasps and convulsions grew, so did the laughter, all culminating with Abraham collapsing onto the floor. His face purposefully purple. Nothing moving except his left leg, twitching.

The popular tribe stood up, and applauded like they had just seen themselves dunk a basketball, which they all dreamed of doing, but would never do. Abraham swallowed the mashed-up sandwich, rose to his feet, and took a bow.

"Holy shit, that was funny, Amsterdam," screamed Josh Goldman.

"Yeah, you're funny when you die, Amsterdam," quipped Greg Gillstein through his sly chuckles.

Abraham had done it. He had gotten the praise he so badly wanted. He had gotten the only eyes he wanted on him. He had captured their undivided attention. Today was a success. No matter what else happened, today Abraham Amsterdam had won. But what happened next was beyond Abraham's wildest imagination. It was good right now. Real good. But it was about to get even better:

"Come and play with us outside, Amsterdam," Greg Gillstein said. "It's muddy as fuck out in the field today. You like mud, don't you, Amsterdam?"

Abraham put his hands on his waist. "Do I like mud? Why, that's my middle name."

The smiles left his audience's faces. They clearly were more into physical comedy and weren't so much for wit. But that was okay. The invitation to play was still in play.

Mrs. Metzger blew the whistle, signaling everyone's exodus to the playground, and, more importantly, the field. The muddy field that awaited its new king's arrival.

All the popular boys walked with enthusiasm. Abraham trailed behind them. They all whispered to each other, glancing back at their new star member. *Obviously they're so excited that they just got such a funny friend they can hardly contain themselves*, thought Abraham. *This is probably some kind of initiation. Who knows, maybe I'll even get a tattoo with a safety pin before the day is out.* As they reached the field, the boys took off their Air Jordans. Made sense. The field was so muddy they would surely be ruined. Abraham chose to keep his shoes on. His shoes were just old Adidas. Maybe if his shoes got muddy enough, his mother would finally take him for some Air Jordans.

The mud gripped his feet like a new desperate friend that knew who Abraham had just become. Maybe the mud wanted Abraham to teach it a thing or two about being liked.

The boys surrounded him. They started patting him on the back. They were laughing. The harder the laughter got, the harder the pats got, until the laughter almost became screaming and the pats almost became hitting. Abraham laughed with them. Trying to pass off that he knew what they found so funny. But he didn't know. But the mud knew. And the mud was ready to embrace him as the screams turned into a battle cry and the hitting became a gripping and a pushing and pulling. Abraham sank. It felt soft and warm as the boys piled on top of him, one after the other, pushing him down further. He sank and sank. And as he sank he swore that he heard the mud whisper to him.

"Stay here. Please stay here. You're soft like me. It's good to be soft. Soft like me. We belong together. You're soft like me. Please don't leave. Be warm. Be soft with me. Stay, pretty please."

But he couldn't stay. His audience was waiting. As the boys leapt off him, Abraham continued to toss around in the mud. He did a showstopping routine where he would stand up and then slip like the mud was a giant banana peel. Simple, classic. Every time he slipped, the amount of mud on his body doubled.

As Abraham slipped again and again and again, the boys ap-

plauded more and more and more. Their applause then came in
the form of their feet stomping against the mud as they kicked
more dirt onto Abraham. Brown clumps of approval splattered
against every inch of his body. It was like a grand theatre of old,
when the crowds would throw gold. This was Abraham's brown
gold. He was overjoyed.

Now it was time for the routine to end. A great comedian
knows when to leave them wanting more. Abraham stood up.
He looked at those popular faces, salivating in anticipation. He
took a deep breath and with that did one final half-back-flip slip,
pile driving his head down into the wet earth. As he landed he
felt a crack in his neck. Yikes! That would hurt in the morning.
But it was all worth it. A cracked neck was worth spreading this
much joy and gaining this much popularity. His head was totally
submerged. *I must look like a real ostrich right now.* He giggled.
Finally, with one great yank, he freed himself. He spit dirt from
his mouth in an exaggerated way. A brilliant muddy spit-take to
end all spit-takes. He then cleared his eyes. Ready to take his
bow. Ready for his standing ovation . . . but . . . there was none.
No one was there.

Abraham was confused. Why had his new best friends left?
Did they miss the grand finale? Surely not. That would be crazy.
How could they not see through that which had brought them
such intense joy? *Lunch must be over,* he thought. He must not
have heard Mrs. Metzger's whistle because his ears were clogged
with soil. He started to walk in the direction of the school, and as
he walked away, he swore he could hear the mud whisper again.

"You should have stayed with me."

And as he walked further, he swore he heard the mud crying.

The rest of the day passed. It seemed to dart by in a flash.
Abraham floated from class to class in a bubble of bliss. As the
bell rang, Abraham walked out of school and saw Greg Gillstein,

Josh Goldman, and the Wolf twins giving each other a series of heartfelt farewells. Abraham felt so grateful that he could now look at these boys with new eyes. New eyes for his new friends that he for so long had felt so separate from. Here was his new gang. His new family. How lucky he was. But he wasn't just lucky. He was funny. He was the funniest. He was popular. Finally he had achieved his long-deserved popularity. This popularity would be his dress rehearsal for his all-too-overwhelming fame. And by the time that fame would come around, Abraham would be all too ready for it. As his new family got in the cars of their families, Abraham called to them:

"That was really fun, guys."

The boys all looked at him. Then they looked at each other. Then they laughed. Then they left.

Abraham's father was waiting for him. Abraham got in the car. Abraham's father asked a question that he had never asked before. Abraham thought it a coincidence his dad should choose this day to ask. Maybe his father sensed something. Maybe his father could feel that his son had changed. That he was now a whole new person who now should be talked to in a completely different way. Abraham's father even looked at him.

"How was school today?"

Abraham smiled so hard he felt like his mouth might break his face.

"Dad . . . today was the greatest day of my life."

3.

The Abraham Amsterdam Show: A Play

braham's bedroom has been made to look like a television studio.

INT. ABRAHAM'S BEDROOM

Don't get confused—it's not one of those
television studios trying to pass itself off
as a bedroom. You know the kind: where the
set is made to look even more like a bedroom
than an actual bedroom, and it's real cute,
and it tries to pass itself off as intimate,
but really it's the least intimate thing that
could possibly exist. It's actually a complete
mockery of intimacy. For what's more intimate
than a bedroom and what's less intimate than
a television studio, am I right? A television
studio is a public place of business. A bedroom
is a fortress of solitude, where both your power
and your unmaking lie. It is your place to
become something truly ugly, or truly beautiful.
A "beautiful" no one else will ever see. For
part of the reason for that beauty's existence
is due to its privacy. Within that privacy lies
purity. No, this bedroom has been made to look
like an actual studio set. Well . . . as much
as it possibly can with a modest budget and
no real, actual, working equipment. Cardboard
lines the perimeters. Four sides. Blocking all
furniture from the camera, if there were a
camera, which there isn't. The desk has been
cleared of the things that usually live on it.
Behind the desk and next to the desk sit two
chairs, which are flanked by cardboard cutouts
of palm trees. Seated in one of these chairs
and facing a nonexistent studio audience is our
host, ABRAHAM AMSTERDAN (nine, Jewish). Abraham
looks into the camera that is, along with the
studio audience, very much not there.

ABRAHAM
Hello, Chicago. Hello, America. Hello, world.
Welcome to the *Abraham Amsterdam Show*. I am, of
course, your host, Abraham Amsterdam, and boy,
do we have a show for you today. Oh boy, what
a show. I mean there are shows and there are
shows. And this show is probably the best show
that's on television right now—at least that's
what my first guest tells me. What can I say
about this woman. Well, she gave birth to me.
She also raised me. She was a teacher before
she met my father, who she's been married to
for thirteen years. Always a real hoot to have
her on. Please give a round of applause to the
one, the only . . . Carol Bernstein Amsterdam,
who just also happens to be . . . MY MOTHER!
Carol, come on out!

*Through a beaded curtain walks Carol Amsterdam
(thirty-five, Jewish). She's in a nightgown
that has "President Mom" written diagonally
across it. She kisses Abraham, very softly and
tenderly, on the cheek. He's embarrassed by it.
Normally he would say something, but she is his
guest and he has a show to do.*

ABRAHAM
Hello, Carol, good to see you.

CAROL
Oh, please, Abraham, call me Mom.

She laughs.

ABRAHAM
Okay . . . Mom. It's good to see you.

CAROL
It's good to see you, too, Abey. It's always good to see my baby boy.

She strokes his cheek affectionately. Actually, it's not just affectionate, it's oddly sexual. Not that she's sexually getting off on it. It's more that she's not registering that this action and the way she's doing it and the moment she's deciding to do it could possibly come off as sexual. It's something really only Jewish boys understand. There is a thing there. Of course anti-Semites will use this point as another example of the Jews' inferiority, but this is not the case. It's just a fact that deep down Jewish mothers kind of want their sons to be their husbands. A husband who is truly devoted to them in the way a son is. All of that aside, it's also totally fucked up.

CAROL
Remember when I used to do this to you to help you fall asleep?

Abraham moves his face away. He would very much like to scream at her.

ABRAHAM
Come on, Mom.

CAROL
What? I can't caress my son's face? I can't show my son love?

ABRAHAM
It's just, we are on TV, Mom. America is watching.

CAROL
America is not going to judge a mother for
loving her son.

ABRAHAM
They won't judge you, Mom. You're the guest.
They never judge the guest. They judge the
host.

CAROL
But there isn't an audience. America isn't
really watching, Abraham.

ABRAHAM
MOM!!! You're going to make me get depressed.
Is that what you want?

CAROL
What? No, of course not.

ABRAHAM
I can feel myself sinking right now.

CAROL
Okay. Okay. Please let's just pretend I didn't
touch your face, and let's move on . . .

She looks into the "camera."

CAROL
. . . with this amazing show. Hosted by my son,
who is just so creative.

Abraham looks at the "camera."

ABRAHAM
Sorry about that, folks. Mom, I guess the first
question I have—I'm not going to waste time—
I'm just going to go ahead and ask it because

it's really the thing America and the world are
wondering about, and that question is . . . Am
I going to go to hell when I die?

CAROL
Of course not, Abey.

ABRAHAM
Do you think I'm going to die young?

CAROL
No, Abraham. God forbid. Don't say things like
that.

ABRAHAM
Do you think I'm gay?

CAROL
Gay? Of course you're not gay.

ABRAHAM
But what about how I told you my camp counselor
Gary made me feel weird. Warm weird. Buzzy in
my body.

CAROL
He's just someone you admire, Abraham. And it's
okay to have gay feelings. It doesn't mean
you're gay. When I was young, I kissed girls.
I even had a girlfriend for a while. I tried
it. It was fun, but then I realized that I was
supposed to like boys more. And eventually I
met your father. And he was my favorite boy
I'd ever met. And then I had you, and then you
became my favorite boy I'd ever met.

ABRAHAM
Sometimes I get thoughts that maybe I don't
love you. That I wish someone else was my mom.
Do you think I really don't love you?

CAROL
Those are just thoughts, Abraham. My brain
thinks all kinds of thoughts all the time. Not
all thoughts are how you really feel. Abraham,
you know that I love your grandma. But,
sometimes, when I was a girl I'd just pray for
bad things to happen to her. Like that she'd
fall down the stairs, or get electrocuted while
turning off a broken light switch. That doesn't
mean I wanted those things to happen just
because I prayed for them several times a day.

ABRAHAM
Mom, do you really think I'm not going to go to
hell?

CAROL
Abraham, you already asked me this.

ABRAHAM
Well, I'm asking again.

CAROL
Well, like I said, of course not.

ABRAHAM
Is there a hell?

CAROL
There is, but we Jews call it something
different.

ABRAHAM
What do we call it?

Carol looks into the nonexistent camera.

CAROL
Life.

Carol laughs way too hard at this. It's almost manic.

ABRAHAM
Why did you just laugh like that?

CAROL
I don't know.

ABRAHAM
I've never seen you laugh like that.

CAROL
Really? Oh, you must have.

ABRAHAM
Do you think your life is hell?

CAROL
No, of course not, I have a beautiful life. Is it perfect? Far from it. Do I get sick of it and want it to end fairly often? Of course! Am I surprised that the windows of our house don't have bars on them and that the toilet isn't located in my bedroom, like a jail cell, because my life is a prison? Can't deny it. No, sir. I'd deny the Holocaust before I denied that. But a hell? Please! I'm blessed! I mean, look who my cellmate is. The most wonderful boy who was ever born. The light of my whole life, my greatest accomplishment. You, Abraham. You're all I ever want to be around, anyway, so who cares if the rest of my life feels like it should be the life of someone else who deserves constant unhappiness.

Abraham stares off into space, mentally leaving the interview.

CAROL
Abraham? What's wrong?

ABRAHAM
I don't want to say.

CAROL
Abraham, please! I'm worried. Are you sinking?

ABRAHAM
When you were talking right now, I had that thought again. That I really do hate you. I don't hate you, right?

CAROL
Of course you don't. You love me the most, Abraham. You don't love anyone as much as you love me.

ABRAHAM
Mom, is there something wrong with me?

CAROL
Honey, nothing is wrong with you.

ABRAHAM
Then why do I have these thoughts?

CAROL
Everyone has these thoughts.

ABRAHAM
Not Dad. I've told him about these thoughts and he just looks at me like I'm crazy.

CAROL
Abraham, your father is a coward. He can't look at himself, so how can he understand anyone else? Your dad isn't like us. He might even be against us. Nothing is wrong with you. You're just like everyone else.

ABRAHAM
Then why don't I have friends? Why don't any of
the other kids like me? Why do they all treat
me like I'm different?

CAROL
You're not different, Abraham. You're
special, and these stupid kids don't know
the difference. You remember what I told you
about Steven Spielberg? When he was a child,
everyone hated him. He'd get bullied and beat
on constantly. Every single day the other kids
would strip off little Steven Spielberg's
clothes the second he stepped foot on the
school bus. As soon as he got on, off would
go his shirt, then the pants, then the shoes,
next the socks, and as soon as little Stevie
Spielberg was down to his panties, all of the
kids would take out their least-favorite item
from their lunch bags and throw it at him. He'd
be a mess. Peanut butter on his neck. Jelly
on his arms. Slices of bologna all over his
face. He didn't even shower in the morning. Why
bother? He knew he'd just have to do it again
in the locker room. And now look at him. He's
basically the president of show business.

ABRAHAM
Where did you hear this Spielberg story?

CAROL
It's just one of those stories you hear around.
The thing is, you're just like him, Abraham.
You're a genius who no one liked as a kid. But
you still are a kid, so you still have to deal
with it. Just be who you are and love who you
are. Only, maybe don't be too strange. If you

act too strange then you actually might push
the good people away. You don't want to push
everyone away. Spielberg pushed the bad people
away. He wasn't *too* weird. He knew when to
cut the weirdness off, so even though he was
not liked as a kid, he was liked as an adult.
Besides, Abraham, you're not as weird as you
think you are. To be honest, I think you force
it a bit sometimes.

ABRAHAM
I don't know. I don't think I force it.

CAROL
You do. Trust me. You force the weirdness.

ABRAHAM
Maybe I *am* that weird. Maybe that's just how
people are always going to think about me.

CAROL
Stop it. You know, you really should talk to
Dr. Heshel about this. Why don't you talk to
him about these things? What am I paying the
money for?

ABRAHAM
I do.

CAROL
No, you don't. You just talk about movies.
Every time I pick you up, you tell me that you
talked about movies the whole time. You want
to be a film critic? Go and do that. Please.
That'll pay money rather than cost money. Okay,
I only have time for one more question. I gotta
go make dinner.

ABRAHAM
What are we having?

CAROL
Baked chicken.

ABRAHAM
Baked chicken?! No! Why?

CAROL
It's been marinating all day. Since when don't you like my baked chicken?

ABRAHAM
Since always. I hate it. Every time you make it I ask you not to make it anymore. You don't remember things I tell you. Why don't you listen to me?

CAROL
Not listen to you? All I do is listen. My second job is listening to you, Abraham.

ABRAHAM
Well, is something wrong with your memory, then?

CAROL
Nothing is wrong with my memory, Abraham. I'm probably just stuck in a fantasy world where I have a son and a husband who don't completely take me for granted. Who appreciate me. Whose love and affection doesn't come at a price of a chain around my neck. I can't believe this. I come on this fake show. I pretend to be a guest and that there's an audience and it's being filmed, and what thanks do I get, besides being reminded that no one gives TWO SHITS ABOUT ME!!!

Carol starts crying. It's a hard cry.

44.

CAROL

Oh, how I wish I could be free. Free like the
freest bird flying south for the winter to
something much warmer. Much brighter. Where the
sun will warm my wings, and I can do anything.
Whenever, wherever, and whatever. Free. Free
like a bird! How dare you, Abraham?! How dare
you suffocate me like this! You're a pillow
over my face, Abraham! I'm going to make
dinner. Eat it if you want! Or don't. Starve to
death for all I care!

ABRAHAM

Mom, I'm sorry. I'm sorry, okay?

CAROL

I give you nothing but love. I waste my time
being a guest on your fake stupid show, and
this is what I get? A son who insults my
cooking, and tells me he thinks he hates me,
and makes me worried.

ABRAHAM

Why are you worried?

CAROL

I'm worried that you're going insane. It's in
our blood, Abey. Madness is in our blood!

*She puts her wet face in her hands. Abraham puts
his hand on her shoulder.*

ABRAHAM

Mom, I'm okay. I promise. I love you.

*Carol hears this. She takes six deep breaths to
compose herself. She looks up at her son.*

CAROL
I love you, too, Abey. And I want you to really think about something. That maybe you should go on medication. Think about it. It could really help you. We could even go on it together.

ABRAHAM
I don't know, Mom.

CAROL
Please, Abey!!! Promise me you'll at least think about it. I think it could be good for you. For us.

ABRAHAM
Okay, Mom, I'll think about it.

CAROL
Okay. Good. Well, let's wrap this up. I have to go finish cooking my food that you hate.

ABRAHAM
I don't hate your food. I'm sorry I said that.

CAROL
It's okay. Let's just wrap this up, honey.

Abraham looks into the camera that isn't there.

ABRAHAM
Carol Amsterdam, everyone. Well, that's our show. Thanks for tuning in. This is Abraham Amsterdam saying good night, Chicago!

Carol stands up. Walks to the beaded curtain. Before she walks through the beaded curtain she stops and looks at Abraham.

CAROL
Maybe there is a hell.

Carol exits.

Abraham sits in his chair, silent. He starts to cry.

4.

Dear Diary

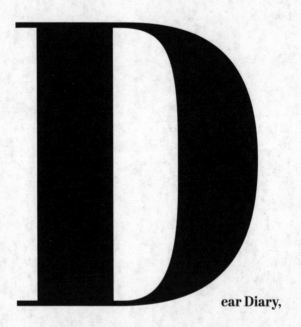

ear Diary,

This is my first entry. I've wanted to write in a diary for a couple years now. I think there's been a part of myself that's been missing because I haven't done it yet. It's what someone like me is supposed to do if I really want to be what I want to be, right? I want when I die (hopefully I'm at least 110) for people to be able to read my diaries, and finally know all my secrets. And then write books about my secrets and argue about them. And then people will write books about those books. And that way no one will ever forget me. So here we go, diary. May no one ever read you but me. That is until I'm dead at the very youngest age of 110. Then may everyone read you, forever and ever.

Let's see . . . What's new in my life? Oh yeah. Finally got Ben Bernstein to say yes to sleepover plans with me. Boy oh boy, that took forever. I thought he'd never be able to. He always had a reason and even though I choose to think the best of people, and not be paranoid, I did wonder if maybe he was lying. He only managed to say yes when he and his family came over for dinner and I asked him in front of everybody. I wondered if he was just saying yes because he felt that everyone else there, his parents and my parents, was pressuring him. I wonder if he would have said no again if they weren't there.

Lots of people are very different when they're around people and when they're alone. Sometimes they're better with other people, and sometimes they're better alone. Me, I'm the same no matter what. If I like someone, I like them no matter where we are or who else is there. I don't change into a different person in different situations and I don't lie.

But maybe Ben did just say yes because he wanted to, and it had nothing to do with his parents being there. And maybe all those reasons he gave for not being able to have plans with me before were real.

Maybe Ben really did have pneumonia, even though he came to school two days later and won a push-up contest in the hall against none other than Jordan Feldman, aka "The Push-up King." Maybe he really was brought in for questioning by the CIA because they found out he lost his virginity to a Russian spy. Maybe his grandmother did die in a tragic inner-tubing accident, even though when my mom offered his mom condolences, his mom didn't know what my mom was talking about. She didn't even know what inner tubing was. Maybe Ben's mom was in denial, though?

But the point is, Ben Bernstein did say yes. And last night we had our first sleepover plans. And it was just great.

Ben isn't the most popular guy in the popular group, but I would say he's the most respected. He gets the best grades and he hangs out with a lot of kids that are not in the popular group. Kids like me. Even though his other friends that are not in the popular group are much more popular than I am. He's always talking these other friends up. Usually that kind of "talking up" is enough to get them in the popular group. That was one of the reasons I chose him to become friends with first. I was realistic, though. I knew it would probably take more than just one sleepover to become close enough friends with him that he would speak up for me. At least two more sleepovers would have to be had. But you had to start somewhere. Besides, maybe we'd hit it off so much that this one sleepover would be all that I needed.

Leading up to the night was a little rough. Ben avoided me all week at school, so much so I thought he was going to cancel on me. Every time the phone rang, my heart would sink, thinking it was him or his mother with the bad news. But he didn't, and last night I slept over at his house and we had an amazing time.

When I first got to his house he acted like we were old friends. There was no hallway weirdness. His mom had already put out snacks. Chips and popcorn. We played video games. We watched some really funny movies. We were up really really late. Really all of that is a blur, though, because the part of the sleepover that was my favorite was us just lying in bed and talking. It was really the part of the night I was excited for most. My thoughts are always the clearest when I'm in bed, and I wanted my head to be clear and focused when I talked to Ben.

I lay there wide awake. We had been downing M&M's and Diet Coke for hours. I was wired. Ben wasn't wired, though. All the sugar we had must not have affected him. I could tell he was dozing. So I felt I had better get right to the point before he fell asleep and I missed my chance to make my case.

I started straight out of the gate asking Ben if he could vouch for me with the other boys that I was cool. Ben mumbled that, actually, he had already brought me up to the group. This made me so excited, I wanted to bounce off the walls. I was also a bit surprised, since he had been ignoring me so much lately. I asked him when he had talked to them about me. He said the other day. I asked what they said. He said that they said I was cool, but they had to be careful who they let into the group because they already had almost too many people and there were others who had been asking to be a part of it way longer than me. Sure, I'd get let in, but it would be a while. At least a few months.

I asked Ben if he liked being popular. He said he never gave it much thought. I told him he should thank his lucky stars. He had no idea how good he had it. He had no idea how hard it was for me. To have no one. To go days without anyone saying hi. I reminded him about the time, a couple days before, when I said hi to him and asked him about our plans and he just walked right by me. He said it was because he was late to class. I reminded him that it was during lunch. He said that he was probably so hungry he was out of it. I told him it was at the end of lunch, and I remember him throwing away an empty lunch bag. He said, in that case, he was out of it because he was so full. I told him I believed him, but I also asked him if he could please try not to be out of it when I said hi to him in the future, and to promise never to ignore me again. He said sure, and that made me happy.

I then started to beg him to mention me to the boys again that Monday, because things for me were getting too difficult to bear. I started crying. I asked Ben if he ever cried. He said no. I reminded him that he didn't know how good he had it. That he didn't know what it was like to be someone like me. He told me he heard me the first time. He said he'd see what he could do. I asked him if the Russian spy was his girlfriend. He said yes and that they broke up because she was mad he had talked to the CIA, but they were now talking about getting back together. I told him that one of the reasons I needed to be popular was to make sure I had a cool girlfriend like him, when I was ready to like girls.

Ben asked me if he could be honest with me. I said of course. Ben said that he didn't think that I'd ever get a girlfriend. I asked why he thought that. Then he asked if he could be even more honest with me. Again I said yes. And then Ben said:

"Abraham, you just have to face the facts. You have a giant egg head."

Then he fell asleep.

When I woke up, Ben was gone. His mother said that he forgot to tell me that he had to go do charity work.

I called him today when I got home to tell him I had a great time and asked when he wanted to have sleepover plans again. His mother went to get him. When she came back to the phone, she told me that he had moved.

5.

Abraham Amsterdam's Nightly Prayers

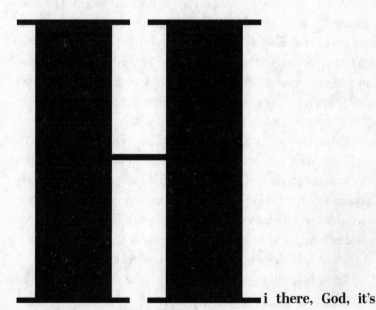i there, God, it's
me, Abraham Amsterdam.

I hope you've had a wonderful day running the universe. Doing all that you do. I should ask . . . is God your real name? Is God the name that you like to be called by? If it's not, I'm very sorry. I did not mean to be insensitive to your feelings. If there is a name you would rather be called by, please tell me. On second thought, maybe you shouldn't tell me. Because even if you tell me, I still might call you God. No offense. Let me explain. Me still calling you God wouldn't be out of disrespect. It would be out of fear that I'm going crazy, because crazy people are the only people who think that you talk to them. But maybe if you give me some proof to show myself and other people to prove that I'm not crazy, then I could call you what you want me to. I don't know why I'm even saying this, though. God's a perfectly good name. Why wouldn't you be happy with it? But if you're not happy with it, please give me a sign that I'm not crazy. I know that might be annoying. I'm sure it is annoying. You know what? Forget it. Forget everything I said. If you didn't like being called God, I'm sure you'd let me know in some way. You're God. You can do anything you want. But you don't need me to tell you that. Or do you? Sorry, I'm babbling here. Anyway, speaking of things you know how to do, I hope you don't mind listening to my prayers tonight again. I'm sorry that they are the same prayers every night. But I figure it's best to remind you, because of how busy you are. So if it's okay, here I go:

Please have me, my mother, my father, my sister, my grandmas and grandpas and uncles and aunts and cousins, my dog Cosmic, my friends, the teachers I like, and Raymond the bus driver have very very very long, happy, healthy, successful lives and afterlives for all of eternity and everlasting.

Please help there be such a thing as eternity.

Please help time go on after we die, and make it not just be the end.

Please help me get used to eternity and the afterlife fast.

Please help there still be delicious food and great TV and movies to watch in the afterlife.

Please help there be world peace one day with no wars and no famine and no suffering.

Please help there be no diseases, and if there are, please have them be far far far away.

Please help me to not ever get addicted to drugs.

Please help me lose my virginity at an age that isn't embarrassing.

Please help the girl I lose my virginity to be surprised that it's just my first time.

Please help me achieve all my dreams.

Please help me become a famous comedian and actor.

Please help me become popular in school.

Please help me never be paralyzed, or blind, or deaf, or any other handicap. Not that I look down on people like that, just please don't have me ever be like them, and please have there be a cure for all disabilities one day so nobody needs to suffer from these horrible diseases and handicaps we have. But until all of that is cured please keep all that stuff away from me.

Please when I have children have them all be normal.

Please when I have children have their eyes go where their eyes go, their noses go where their noses go, and their mouths go where their mouths go.

Please have nothing on my children's bodies look at all like a flipper.

Please have me smile more in my life than frown.

Please have me laugh more in my life than cry.

Please help me not fear death so much.

Please help me not have nightmares tonight, especially the one where a giant orangutan breaks into the house, kills my parents, then sucks my penis off my body like it was hardly even attached, with a big goofy smile on his face, or the other one where my socks come alive and then start eating my legs, and I go and try to return them from where I bought them, but the guy who sold them to me has a sock for a head and tells me that there's nothing wrong with them even though they are chewing away at me and laughing while they do it and their laugh sounds like Eddie Murphy's. Or the one where my toilet comes alive and convinces me to let it switch jobs with my bed.

Please help me not embarrass myself in gym class, baseball practice, or mini-golf ever again.

Please help me never fall down again.

Please help me not cut myself again.

Please help me never burn myself again.

Please help me never break any bones.

I know I already asked to not go blind, but I want to make it extra clear that I really don't want to be blind. You might think that I'd be willing to be blind if you made me a musical genius. Maybe that's a thing you're planning. To make me blind and, so I don't hate you or kill myself, make me a musical genius like Ray Charles or Stevie Wonder. That's okay. I'll keep my eyes, thank you. You can give that gift of musical genius to someone else.

Please help me be a comedy genius. To be clear, I'm not willing to go blind to make this happen, either.

Please help my parents never divorce.

Please help my parents like each other again.

Please help me look in the mirror and think I'm handsome.

Please help me feel like I'm handsome when I talk to girls.

Please help me stop getting made fun of.

Please make everyone who has ever bullied me get cancer and die . . . I'm sorry, I don't mean that.

Please don't let me or anyone I care about get cancer and die as punishment for me wishing cancer and death on people.

To repeat: please have me, my mother, my father, my sister, my grandmas and grandpas and uncles and aunts and cousins, my dog Cosmic, my friends, the teachers I like, and Raymond the bus driver all have very very very long, happy, healthy, successful lives and afterlives for all of eternity and everlasting.

Please help me be rich.

Please help me have a mansion.

Please help me have a swimming pool.

Please help me have four pinball machines, and six arcades, and every video game system and every video game ever made.

Please help me never have to go in the army.

Please help me do what's right.

Please don't punish me if I do wrong.

Please help me stand up for myself or anyone else who needs it and not get hurt or killed while doing it.

Please help me not be scared and depressed when I move out of the house when I'm older.

Please help me welcome adulthood and not miss childhood.

Please have my kids love me as much as my wife.

Please have my wife love me as much as my kids.

Please help me listen to my gut.

Please help me not look to others to see what I think or feel.

Please help me never be racist.

Please destroy racism.

Please help me with a thought I had the other night. The other night during dinner I had a thought. I thought that I have never really seen myself with my own eyes, and that I never will. Sure, I can look in the mirror or at a photograph, but how do I know that reflection or that photograph is how I really look. That maybe the way my eyes see the reflection or photo is not how other people's eyes see the same reflection or photograph of me. I could look completely different. I could be uglier. I could be more handsome. I don't know. I guess there's no way to know and no way to change it. It's not like I can turn my eyes around, and even if I could they would just be inside my head and all I'd see is the inside of my brain. I guess the other option would be to make it so my eyes come out of my head and then turn around. But that wouldn't be good either because my eyes would be looking at my face without eyes. And then it doesn't matter how pretty or handsome I am. A face with no eyes? That's disgusting. I guess it could work if when my eyes came out of my head, they were replaced with another set of eyes. But that's not going to happen, is it? So I guess what I'm praying for is: don't ever let me have that thought ever again.

Please help me channel you through me every day, and let you guide me to do what you would do—not that I could do what you do, but if you were me, please help me do what you would do. And don't worry, I don't expect to fully understand what I'm being guided to do. I know I could never really know what you think or do. I know I'm not you and could never be you. I admit it. Sometimes I wish I were you. But I also admit that sometimes I'm glad I'm not you. I mean, what a job you have. How many people are praying to you right now? How can you listen to all of us at once? You must have real patience. Or maybe you don't. Is that why there's all of this killing and war and hate? Because you're frustrated and annoyed with us all talking your ear off day and night and you're taking it out on us? If so, I don't blame you. Or are all of the bad things in the world the Devil? Is he real? And is he getting away with doing all these bad things because you're too distracted by our prayers to catch him before he does it? Are we making you too busy? These are things I know I can never understand, so please, at least help me feel like you're taking care of me and help me trust in your care and never get in the way of that and always make sure that what I do would be done by you if you were me, not that you would ever be me or want to be me. Not that you ever wouldn't want to be me. Not that you look down on me—I know that you respect me. But please have me be as much like you as a human being can be like you.

Please respect me.

Please hear my prayers.

Please exist, God.

I love you.

Thank you for listening.

Amen.

6.

The Agency

he room was the coldest room
the Amsterdam family had ever been in.

It was a stagnant cold. A cold that wasn't freezing but crept under the skin and into the bones. The kind of cold that got you sick. The Amsterdams stood there shivering as the cold filled them with anxiety on top of the already existing greater anxiety resulting from them not knowing where they were, how they got there, and the fact that Abraham was not with them.

All the other Amsterdams were there, though. Well . . . all except Grandpa Mel, who was still institutionalized. There was Grandma Golda, Grandpa Moshe, Grandma Mimi, step-Grandpa Leonard, Uncle Sid and Aunt Felicia, and their sons, Dustin, Justin, and Sid Jr. Also of course Uncle Jerry and Aunt Gerry, and their daughters, Lily, Jenny, Jori, and Nikki. Surprisingly Uncle Richard was also there, who was known to usually avoid whole family gatherings. Lastly there was Carol and Irv, Abraham's mother and father. Abraham, Carol and Irv's only son, was nowhere to be found.

"Anyone remember how we got here?" asked Aunt Gerry.

"Anyone know where the hell we are?!" asked Grandma Golda.

"Where's Abraham?! Did anyone see Abraham?!" asked Carol.

"Maybe he's in the bathroom?" Irv Amsterdam hypothesized.

Uncle Richard stayed silent in the corner. He knew better than to interject.

Uncle Sid scratched his head. "The last thing I remember was I was eating some chopped liver. I took a bite. It was delicious, then I blinked and now I'm here."

Aunt Felicia was far from pleased with the reveal of this useless information by her husband. "Sid! What did I tell you?! Lay off the chopped liver! You had your fill yesterday, and I made it to last till the weekend."

Uncle Sid smacked his thigh. "What's the use of food if you can't eat it? I deserve that liver after the week I had," and with this Uncle Sid pointed to his foot.

Aunt Felicia's tone changed from frustration to pity. She put her hand on her husband's shoulder and announced, "Sid had three toes removed."

Everyone gasped. Everyone except Uncle Jerry, who shrugged his shoulders.

Upon seeing his brother-in-law dismiss him, Uncle Sid clenched his fists. "What? You shrug your shoulders? I tell you I had appendages removed from my body and all I get is a shrug?"

Uncle Jerry answered with another shrug. "You're lucky it's just toes."

Uncle Sid took a step forward. "Just toes, huh? Let me ask you a question, Jerry—do you have all of your toes?"

Uncle Jerry placed his hands on his waist like Superman. "Of course I do. I take excellent care of my body."

Uncle Sid gave Uncle Jerry a bow. "Well, congratulations, Mr. Olympics, why don't you write a book so we can all read it and learn to not only be just as healthy as you, but just as bad with money, too."

Uncle Jerry raised a fist. "Don't insult me in front of my children!"

Uncle Sid began inching even closer toward Uncle Jerry, his face diabetic red. "Let me explain to you what looking at your foot and only seeing two toes feels like, Jerry. Let's say you're having a great day. Great sleep the night before. No traffic all day. The weather's not too hot, not too cool. Loads of intelligent conversation, both with people you know and with strangers. You come home and you get a kiss from your wife like you haven't had in a while. She's actually happy to see you. What's on the menu? Your favorite dinner. Your favorite program's on TV that night. The kids don't fight. They seem grateful for the life you've provided them. Everything is sublime. Then the day comes to a close. You're getting ready for another soothing night of slumber.

You take off your shirt, your pants, your socks, and OH THAT'S
RIGHT YOU HAVE FEWER TOES THAN A GODDAMN BIRD!"

Just then the door to the room opened. Silence filled the
space. A silence so silent you could hear the beads of sweat that
were rolling down Uncle Sid's forehead. The silence was accompanied by a man. A classically handsome man, in the Gentile
sense. A man who seemed to be from another time. A time when
cigarettes were healthy. The type of man who made people like
the Amsterdams very nervous. A man who hid his hatred for the
sake of propriety. A true all-American.

The man sat down in a chair across the room. He flashed a
smile all of the Amsterdams wished they themselves could flash.
A smile no Jew could smile. A smile that assured everyone everything would be all right. A smile like apple pie. "Hello, everyone. Thank you for joining us this afternoon. I hope this all hasn't
been too much for you. Allow me to introduce myself. My name
is Harry. Welcome to The Agency."

The Amsterdams looked at each other, puzzled.

"Agency? What kind of an agency?" asked Grandma Mimi.

The smile stayed plastered on Harry's face. "Oh, we deal in
various matters of a confidential nature."

"You don't look much like a Harry," pointed out Grandma
Golda.

Harry chuckled. "Yes, I know. I look more like a Randolph or
even a James, but those aren't my names, and as a matter of fact,
neither is Harry. But, you see, my name hardly matters, because
in an hour you won't remember any of this."

"What the hell kind of mishigas is this?" asked Grandpa
Moshe. "Not remember? How would we not remember? Especially me. I got one of the best memories around. I never forget a
face, a name, or a phone number. I know every phone number by
heart of everyone I know. Tell me that ain't a good memory."

Harry gave another chuckle. "I'm sure your memory is as sharp as a Ginsu. It's just we have technology designed to erase certain memories from the conscious mind. This technology was employed moments ago, which is why you don't remember how you arrived at our offices. Don't worry, our methods of memory erasure are absolutely safe. Only pinpointed memories are removed. There is no collateral memory loss or brain damage. You will only forget that you were here and that we had this meeting. However, at the same time, the contents of our discussion will be implanted into your subconscious so that you can carry out what I will now ask of you. That is, if you agree to the proposal. Make sense?"

Carol Amsterdam stomped her foot. "Okay, Mr. Mind Twist. I've had about enough of this bullshit. Not all of us are here. My son, Abraham. Where is he?"

Irv Amsterdam echoed his wife. "Yeah, where is Abraham, you shyster! You're lucky I'm a pacifist or I'd knock your teeth from here to Wyoming!"

The rest of the family joined in on the protest. All except Uncle Richard, who remained silent in the corner, and the cousins who for some time now had collectively buried their faces in their hands in utter humiliation. But everyone else was up in arms. Uncle Jerry stepped up onto a chair. Then Uncle Sid also stepped up onto a chair. Uncle Jerry then accused Uncle Sid of always copying him. Aunt Felicia and Aunt Gerry screamed at them to get down. The grandpas and grandmas grabbed their chests.

Harry clapped his hands for their attention, and then caressed the air like a conductor. "Mr. and Mrs. Amsterdam, we do not have your son. I promise you he is safe at home, fast asleep. He will not wake until your return, and none of you will remember that you ever left."

Carol Amsterdam grabbed the sides of her head. She pulled at her hair, hoping it might shake her from this nightmare. Irv put his hand on her shoulder. He realized it had been some time since he had comforted his wife in any way. He wondered why that was. Did he not love her anymore? Or was he just used to her being self-sufficient?

"Why was Abraham not brought here with us?" Carol muttered through clenched teeth.

Harry leaned forward. His dark eyebrows raised up his handsome forehead as his inviting eyes widened. "Well, Mrs. Amsterdam, your son is the reason I brought you all here. I want to talk to the whole family about Abraham. We think he's special."

Uncle Sid had had enough. "Special, huh? You sound like a grade-A pedophile to me. That's probably what this place is. One of those pedophile safe havens for the rich and powerful."

Harry gave another chuckle. "I assure you, sir, that is not the case. Our organization has been studying Abraham and we have concluded that he has great potential. We think Abraham is a boy who can do great things. He has the makings of a great comedian. A great entertainer. Someone who can bring the world joy in these horribly troubled times."

Irv Amsterdam was now intrigued. "Well, what is this? Are you going to give him some sort of scholarship?"

Harry leaned back. He could relax now that he was no longer being accused of being a child molester. "No, Mr. Amsterdam. Given Abraham's predisposition for genius we don't think that will be necessary. We operate in more of an . . . overseeing type of capacity."

"Overseeing?" step-Grandpa Leonard asked.

Harry looked away, hiding whatever true expression was in his eyes. "Allow me to explain, and I warn you this is going to sound quite strange. The reason we have brought you all here is that we would like you to help Abraham become the special person we know he can be. The special man who will entertain the world. Who will lift people out of their misery and mundanity. Who will become a great, famous man. However, this is not something that just happens on its own. Abraham will have to be . . . pushed."

Carol Amsterdam scratched her head. "Well, I've been thinking of enrolling him in some children's acting classes."

Harry bowed his head in reverence. "That's not exactly what I mean, Mrs. Amsterdam. Although by all means enroll him. No, what I'm asking is that you all give Abraham the *opposite* of any sort of support, from time to time. We've found that children are more likely to lead extraordinary lives if they experience unpleasant childhoods."

Carol Amsterdam gasped. "Are you asking me to abuse my son?!"

Uncle Sid slapped his knee. "See? I told you this goy was a pedophile!"

Harry gave another uncomfortable chuckle. "I'm not talking about any abuse. Of course not. That would be going too far. We don't want Abraham to become a serial killer or a domestic terrorist. By all means show the boy love occasionally. But some good old-fashioned mistreatment, peppered throughout the day, will put Abraham on the road to greatness, Mrs. Amsterdam. And this of course goes for all of you. This is a family effort."

"So let me get this straight," said Carol Amsterdam. "When we leave here you're going to erase our memories, but you'll make sure in the back of our minds we all remember you telling us to treat Abraham like shit, so he becomes a famous comedian?"

Harry politely nodded. "Basically, yes."

"Why would we agree to this?" asked Irv Amsterdam.

Harry rang a bell. The door again opened, and again a man walked into the room. However, this man was not all-American. Nor was he a stranger. This was a man known to every member of the Amsterdam family. A man they unanimously respected. A man who the men of the Amsterdam family secretly wanted to be, and someone all the women of the family secretly wanted to fuck. This man was none other than the manager of the Goldenwide First National Bank: Mr. Fishel Braverman.

Fishel Braverman looked as elegant as ever. No less elegant than when he routinely greeted and "congratulated" any member of the Amsterdam family upon depositing a check. His silken suit draped his statuesque physique. His hair was combed back in luscious waves that made bald men want to commit suicide. His diamond-studded cuff links reflected the fluorescent lights of the room, giving the effect of sunlight.

Mr. Braverman gave a smile and a wink as he reached out his manicured hands and embraced the Amsterdams like the rabbi of finance he was. "My favorite people! All in one place together! How lucky can one happy bank manager get, and how happy can one lucky bank manager be?"

Fishel Braverman's glee filled the room as much as the light from his cuff links. For all of the shocking things the Amsterdams only moments ago had been faced with, it was impossible to resist Mr. Braverman's otherworldly charm.

"Yes, everyone is here! Well, everyone except Abraham, of course. Oh, Abraham. What a boy, huh? Well, you know better than me."

Fishel let out a blast of laughter. "Yes, the man of the hour, who ironically isn't here to celebrate his recent turn of very good fortune. Carol and Irv, your boy is going to give the world more joy than it deserves, but, like my friend Harry right here just said, in order for this to occur, Abraham's got to be pushed in the right direction, and sometimes being pushed doesn't feel comfortable. Sometimes it can even hurt. But it's not how much the pushing hurts. It's about what you get pushed into. And with just the right amount of pushing, Abraham will be pushed into greatness. And make no mistake, that 'greatness' includes not only fame . . . but fortune. And not only fortune for Abraham. Fortune for everyone. My fine friends, if you help us make your son the star he deserves to be so he can do his very important part of keeping humanity sane with the gift of laughter, we at the Goldenwide First National Bank will deposit twenty million dollars into each of your accounts."

The Amsterdams gasped. Twenty million dollars?! Was this real? How could it be? No such sum of money was ever thought possible by any of them. If anyone else would have proposed this to them, they would have been laughed out of the room. But this was Fishel Braverman. One of the most respected men of their community. Again, if it had been anyone else, the Amsterdams would surely have passed it off as a ridiculous joke. But Fishel Braverman was not one to joke. He was a gregarious man, but he was also a serious man, and more than anyone else they knew, he was an honest man.

"Twenty million dollars, Fishel?" asked Irv Amsterdam.

"That's right, Irv." And with this he again flashed his heartwarming smile. "Twenty million dollars. Not too shabby, huh, guys?"

Uncle Sid put his hand up. "Well, even if we each get this twenty million dollars . . . as soon as we agree, this goyim here said he's going to erase our memories. So how will we remember that you owe us that twenty million dollars? Aren't we all going to think it's strange that we all suddenly each get this magical money out of nowhere?"

Fishel Braverman was happy. His favorite customers had not let him down. They were, as always, smart as hell. "Well, Sid, that's an excellent point. In two years you will all have a strong impulse to play the lottery, and after doing so you will experience a family miracle—the first family in history to win three hundred and eighty million dollars. Which divided amongst the nineteen of you is twenty million dollars each. Of course this money will have been in your accounts all along. And just like everything else that has been discussed today, all of this information will be stored in your subconscious. You will remember without knowing you remember."

The Amsterdams checked in with each other. This was beginning to sound like not such a bad idea. "So how exactly are we to 'mistreat' the boy?" Grandpa Moshe softly inquired.

"Nothing too severe. Dismissing major achievements. Calling him stupid and lazy more often. Carol and Irv, you should certainly not get along at all. There should be minor arguments constantly, and huge, screaming arguments once or twice a week. Do your best, without being obvious, to make Abraham feel like the only reason both of you are still together is because of him. Irv, make sure to be resentful of Abraham for this. Think of him as competition. But at the same time: detach. Drift off into the memories of who you were before. And Carol, really cling to him. Almost make him feel like he's your husband. Make him carry your emotional baggage. And this next tactic is for everyone: make sure to put down Abraham's hopes and dreams. Adults, you can do this by reminding him of how slim his chances are of making it in such a difficult field, and strongly encourage him to have a plan B. Now to all of you cousins, you just need to make him think that he doesn't have enough talent. Make fun of him. Rope his friends into it, and one of you could even spread a rumor or two about him at school. Tell everyone that he lets the dog lick him 'down there.' Something like that. Again, nothing too extreme. Just enough to push him in the right direction."

The Amsterdams were dubious, even though it was Fishel Braverman who was presenting them with the offer. However, most of all, the Amsterdams were in shock. In shock that they were considering any of this at all. The family stepped aside to talk amongst themselves.

"Well, what do you think? Do we believe any of this?" asked Carol.

"I don't know. This is crazy. Mind erasure? Twenty million dollars? Child abuse?" replied Irv.

"It's not abuse. Fishel was very clear about that," said Grandpa Moshe.

"But why is Fishel even here? Is he friends with this goy?" asked Grandma Mimi.

"Maybe the goy's got something on him and is forcing him to lie to us?" wondered Aunt Gerry.

"But if he's telling the truth, we'll never feel bad about any of it," said Uncle Jerry.

"If it's real, it is a lot of money," added step-Grandpa Leonard. "I could reopen my deli."

Aunt Felicia leaned in. "I could get a full body lift every two years at least."

"We could buy the whole condo, Moshe. We could finally kick out Ida Roth," said Grandma Golda.

"No more having to listen to her brag about how much she won at the greyhound track that day. No more having to lie about liking the pictures of her ugly grandchildren," said Grandpa Moshe.

Dustin, Justin, Sid Jr., Lily, Jenny, Jorie, and Nikki were all salivating, coming up with every moronic purchase idea from a roller coaster in the backyard to a dog that's trained to put your makeup on.

Uncle Richard was torn. He cared deeply for his nephew. But twenty million dollars was twenty million dollars, and with twenty million dollars he could travel far away from this godforsaken family.

"Also, don't forget, we're helping Abraham achieve his dreams. I think if he was here and he knew about this deal, he'd tell us to say yes," said Uncle Jerry.

"That's right. You don't think Abraham would choose for us to do whatever it takes so that he can be a famous comedian and so his family could be millionaires? Of course he would. He wouldn't give it a second thought," said Grandma Mimi.

"All it is is just ignoring him and calling him stupid now and then," said Irv.

"Yeah, and Mr. Braverman was clear there would be no need for molestation. Which is a relief," said Uncle Sid.

"So . . . what do we think? Do we do this? Do we say yes?" asked Aunt Gerry.

"I don't want to hurt him. He's my only son," cried Carol.

"But honey, we won't be hurting him. We'll be making his dreams come true. Look at it this way: the worse we treat him, the better life will treat him," said Irv as he again tried the foreign act of comforting his wife.

The Amsterdams engaged in what seemed like days of neurotic negotiations. The family all worried in their various ways that something bad would eventually develop as a result of the "pushing." That they would go too far as they did with everything else. For if there was one thing that every member of the Amsterdam family had in common it was that they all excelled in the art of "going too far and ruining everything." But money was money.

And no matter how much one could lie to themselves and say that money didn't fix almost everything, this was not a lie that any Amsterdam ever told themselves or anybody else.

As they argued, Harry placed his hand on Fishel's perfect shoulder. Fishel looked into Harry's blue eyes, and Harry glared into his. There was something in Harry's glare, and if the Amsterdams were not fully immersed in their own discussion they would have seen this glare turn Mr. Braverman's face completely chalk white. Mr. Braverman must have felt the change in his color, because he then promptly pinched his cheeks and lightly patted his face to get them back to their normal rosier hue. He then cleared his throat to get his favorite family's attention, as Harry hid his face to giggle to himself.

"Well, folks, are we close to a verdict here? Don't mean to rush you, but Abraham will be waking up soon, and we should get you all home so he's not there alone."

And with that, the Amsterdams agreed. It was best for everyone involved. Best for Abraham. Best for the family. Best even for Mr. Braverman. The last thing they'd ever want to do is make the great Fishel Braverman feel like he'd failed. So *yes* it was. They would push Abraham into greatness. They would help him carve his own face into the Mount Rushmore of Comedy. And in so doing they would become richer than all of their wildest dreams combined. As their boy made millions laugh, they'd spend millions and laugh, and they would all finally best the subtle misery that flowed through the tiny blood vessels of their Jewish brains. The worry that had buried itself in their bones since the fleeing of their ancestors would be exorcised. And the real estate!!! A house in every country. A condo in every city. And these would be investments. Investments that would grow as Abraham grew more and more cherished and beloved.

With that, Harry pulled a piece of paper out of his pocket. A contract.

"Congratulations, ladies and gentlemen." He then smiled one last smile. "You've made the right decision."

Two hours later everyone returned home, with no memory of what had transpired. Abraham was still asleep in his bed. An hour later he awoke to his parents screaming at each other, in the middle of a fight about what was better: Saran wrap or tinfoil.

Soon after their forgotten encounter, Fishel Braverman, manager of the Goldenwide First National Bank, mysteriously disappeared.

Two years later the Amsterdams won the lottery.

Fifteen years after that Abraham became a famous comedian.

Mendel
Freudenberger

7.

The Legends of Mordecai Freudenberger

t was a terrible Sunday in the fall. Many Sundays are terrible in the fall in Chicago.

You'd think the colorful leaves bouncing off the gray sky would make you feel something quite the opposite. But they don't. Those leaves are dead. And the sky is, again, gray. I was currently in the middle of transitioning from all the friends I had just stopped being friends with to the new friends I would acquire, and that I would soon end friendships with soon after becoming friends with them. The Freudenbergers have always been loners. Who would want to be anything but? So it was probably this state of solitude that clouded my judgment much like the gray sky I was living under, that, in turn, led me into the living room to act as audience as my father, Mordecai Freudenberger, called me to attendance.

"Mendel! Come here! Get your ass in here. I want to tell you something!"

I crept into the living room. Hoping this "Get your ass in here" had the slight chance of being what I hoped it to be. That he'd be handing me the keys to my very own penthouse apartment in the city, and would inform me that school was now optional, and the only time I was obligated to communicate with him for now on was if he or my mother were in the hospital.

But there were no keys. Just a pair of depressed eyes and a forceful hand commanding me to sit for what was sure to be an audible living hell for the next thirty to ninety minutes.

"Did I ever tell you how I was in a gang?"

Did he know that he had told me this several thousand times? Did it matter to him if I knew?

"Yeah, Dad."

My father leaned his brown leather La-Z-Boy forward. The nightly news was playing in the background. An interview with Saddam Hussein. "Oh boy, was I in a gang. I mean there's being in a gang and then there's *being in a gang*. And I was in one, boy. You bet your goddamn ass I was in a gang."

My father's gaze sharpened, eyes smirking like the ghosts of his former enemies were in the room. Stroking me. Caressing me to taunt him. His look reminded the ghosts how pathetic their feeble efforts were to unbalance him. He knew the man he was and always would be. Mordecai got up and poured himself a vodka. He farted. My leg started to restlessly bounce. Saddam laughed.

"We were called the Rockets! Don't totally remember who named us that, but it was probably me. 'Cause along with being the fucking killer of the bunch I was also the brains. Ideas, see?! Like for instance, you probably didn't know this, but we were the first gang to use switchblade combs. All the other greasers had regular combs, but I got us switchblade combs at the novelty store. See, we'd be having a conversation, right? Let's say with a rival gang member, who we wanted to scare shitless, or a little tuna we wanted to shtup, and we'd take out those switchblade combs mid-conversation and whoever we was talking to would think we was about to cut into our own goddamn heads, but then it wouldn't be knives that would come out of the handle! It would be friggin' combs. Then we'd comb our hair all goddamn smooth and sexy-like and whoever we was talking to would know that we meant business. So if it was an enemy they'd run away, and if it was a hot chick, she'd pull her poodle skirt up and tell us to go to town."

Saddam laughed again.

"You see, son, this is what I keep trying to tell you but you don't listen. The same thing that'll scare the shit out of a guy will make a woman want to screw your brains out. Anyway, you know why I named us the Rockets? Well, I loved *West Side Story*, see? And the gang in that friggin' musical is called the Jets. And they were the coolest in the musical, but, the thing is, they were also all goys. So even though me and every other guy I knew thought the Jets were the coolest in that musical, in real life they still weren't that cool because they were all goys. I mean, how can you be that cool if you believe in Santa, am I right? So we knew we were cooler, because we was all Jews, so that meant our gang name had to be cooler, just like we was cooler. And what's cooler than a jet? What's cooler than a jet, Mendel? Come on! Don't make me wait all goddamn day! What's cooler than a jet?"

My leg was now bouncing so anxiously that I couldn't think straight enough to answer correctly even though I already knew the answer.

"Two jets?"

The old man spit out his vodka. "NO, not two jets, you fucking idiot! A rocket! A rocket is cooler than a jet. So I named us the Rockets! And guess what my nickname was. Go ahead, guess!"

"Mr. Ideas?"

"No, you fucking moron! Bird Man! Wanna know why?"

"I guess so."

The old man spit out his vodka again. More vodka had definitely been spit than swallowed. The rug was shit-faced. "What do you mean, you guess so? Why don't you know so? See, the trouble with you, Mendel, is you wouldn't know a good story if it knocked on your door, delivered you a package, had you sign for it, and asked you for a goddamn tip. But of course you wouldn't give a tip, would you? You know why? Because you got no respect for people who actually work for a goddamn living. Anyway, my nickname was Bird Man because of the Birdman from Alcatraz. He was this killer that was in Alcatraz. You know what Alcatraz is?"

"No."

"Jesus. You don't know nothin', do you? Well, Alcatraz only happens to be the most famous prison in the world. The place where every major criminal got sent back in the day. It'd be the prison you'd be put in if being a fucking idiot were against the law. Anyway, there was this killer in prison there named the Bird-man of Alcatraz. And he was called that because he lived in Alcatraz and he was so crazy his only friends were birds, and that's why my nickname was Bird Man."

"Because you were only friends with birds?"

More vodka spitting. Good thing the rug didn't have to drive that day. "No, you moron! Because I was a violent person who people feared. And during rumbles, when everyone was fighting on the ground like a schmuck, your old man would climb to the tops of trees and jump onto their goddamn shoulders, just like a bird, but I'm also a man. So I'm a Bird Man!"

"Don't birds fly?"

My father paused. Had I stumped him? "Yeah . . . birds fly. That's true. But not birdmen. Birdmen jump onto shoulders."

Saddam, for some reason, was now crying.

I rested my weary head in my underworked hands. "Seems like that could really hurt someone."

"You're goddamn right! And that's why when your father was around, people did one of two things: bow or run! Now how about the dragon. Did I tell you the story about the time I defeated the dragon?"

"The dragon?"

Saddam was now wailing. Tears splashing on the camera lens. He tore at his uniform as the interviewer and camera crew restrained him.

"The dragon! There was a dragon in Chicago and your father slayed it. What? You didn't know this? How can you know yourself if you don't know your family history? If you don't know what your family's done, how can you know what you're doing? But I guess that makes sense 'cause you wouldn't know what you were doing if God read you the instruction booklet on how to live your stupid fucking life. Anyway, where was I? Oh yeah! The dragon! So this dragon had been sleeping for three hundred years and then some asshole was poking around its cave looking for coal to turn into diamonds and poked the dragon awake. This pissed off the dragon to no end, and after the dragon ate the putz he looked at his license to see where the guy was from. So the dragon sees that this poking prick was from Chicago, so, naturally, the dragon says, 'Chicago can go fuck itself. I'm gonna fry that shit!' So next thing we all knew a dragon was here in Chicago lighting everything in sight on goddamn fire. I don't remember what I was doing at the time . . . probably shtupping a beauty queen or a model or a famous movie starlet or someone even prettier. Anyway, I see this dragon out my bedroom window and I'm pissed off because (A) this dragon was burning down the city I love, and (B) it had interrupted my world-class shtup session. So after I put my shmeckle back in my jeans, I grabbed my sword that I had pulled from a rock in the middle of Lake Michigan a couple months earlier. Funny, 'cause the day I pulled out the sword, I was like, 'Too bad there's no dragons that I can kill with this, because this sword is just gonna sit in the goddamn garage and go to waste.' For once I was wrong 'cause here I was now: face-to-face with this friggin' dragon. I raise up my sword, about to shove it into this dragon's fat friggin' chest, and what does this dragon do? He eats it. Grabs it with its long snaky tongue and swallows it whole! So, naturally, now I'm extra pissed. But not pissed enough to lose my strategic thinking. I get a genius idea! I say, 'Hey, dragon, have you ever tried deep-dish pizza?'

"Then the dragon says, 'Deep-dish pizza? Hey, asshole, I've been asleep for three hundred years. I've never tried thin-crust pizza, let alone deep-dish pizza.' So I call Giorgino's and I tells them to cook me up a thousand sausage-and-pepperoni pizzas with extra cheese. I talk the dragon into taking a break from lighting the city on fire until the pizzas arrive. He agrees, 'cause he's really curious about what they taste like. The pizzas get there. He gobbles 'em down. One pizza. Two pizzas. Three pizzas. One after the other. Just lovin' 'em. Now, my plan was that while he was distracted with eating the pizzas I'd sneak to one of my neighbors' houses, see if they had a sword, borrow it, and kill the dragon that way. But it turned out the dragon was allergic to cheese. And I don't mean just lactose intolerance. I mean like cheese is poison to a dragon like chocolate is poison to a goddamn dog. So the dragon puffed up real bad. Its face turned into a big green friggin' marshmallow. And then, BOOM, the dragon drops dead. And not only did the city throw your father a parade, Giorgino's didn't make me pay for the deep-dish pizzas on account that I used them to kill the dragon. And that's how your father saved the Windy City. Which, if it wasn't for him, would have had to change its name to the friggin' Burnt-the-Fuck-Up City."

Shortly after this terrible Sunday my father was committed. I think it was the following terrible Sunday. He was released soon after. The breakdown turned out to be the reaction to a kidney infection due to his fatty diet. His kidneys recovered, but my mother never let him eat a deep-dish pizza ever again. Some years later, Saddam Hussein was executed.

8.
Mendel's One-Man Show

ct I.

*The Studio Theatre at Highland Park High School.
A typical high school black box theatre. Not
that a black box theatre is typical in normal
high schools. Really just typical in those very
privileged high schools that support and nurture
"the arts."*

*The audience files in and gets comfortable in
their uncomfortable seats. They face an almost-
bare stage, with a minimal set consisting of a
metal chair, a wooden table, and a cot.*

*Two of the audience members are Mendel's mother
and Mendel's father. They speak as they squirm
nervously in their chairs.*

MENDEL'S FATHER: How long is it?

MENDEL'S MOTHER: Oh, I don't know. I didn't
ask.

MENDEL'S FATHER: Why didn't you ask? You
know I like to know the length.

MENDEL'S MOTHER: Why do you need to know?

MENDEL'S FATHER: I need to prep myself for
what I'm in for.

MENDEL'S MOTHER: I'll tell you what you're
going to be in for: divorce!

MENDEL'S FATHER: Oh, there she goes with
divorce again. If you're gonna do it, then do
it already!

*The house music gets louder as the lights start
to fade to black. Mendel's mother lightly claps.*

MENDEL'S MOTHER: I can't wait to see how
handsome he looks. He always looks so handsome
onstage!

*The lights come up. Mendel is dressed in a black
T-shirt and black jeans. He sits in the chair.
He stands up. He lies down on the bed. He lies
still for a moment, then starts thrashing around
like he can't get comfortable. He jumps out of
the bed, screams, and flips the bed over. He then
picks up the chair and throws it across the
room. He drops his body to the floor, breathing
heavily.*

*He lifts his head. Noticing the audience for the
first time. Like he didn't know they were in the
room with him. Like they had snuck in when he
wasn't looking. He stands and faces them.*

MENDEL: Here I am. I said, here I am. Here
I am. I am here. Here I am. Am I here? Am?
I wonder what my father would say. Probably
nothing. He'd look at me, looking at you,
and just shake his head. A headshake worth an
infinity of shame. A shame galaxy as silent as
forever death. Why? Why would my father feel
such shame? Have I killed someone? No. I killed
an idea. And some say the killing of an idea is
far more violent than killing a life. I have
killed my father's idea of me. My father being
my creator, I have in effect killed the idea
he has of himself. I have ravaged my father's
sense of normalcy. His sense of decency. His
sense of what he saw for me. I have emerged

from the closet of his expectations and my big
fat gay rampage has begun. So sorry, Daddy.
Your boy is not like the other boys. Your boy
is much, much, much more . . . fabulous! But
I can't say this to Daddy. Daddy's not here.
Daddy is not alive. He left, thinking that he
knew me when he didn't know me at all. He left
without me proving to him that I am what I see,
rather than what he imagined. Daddy probably
wouldn't like it too much. Witnessing me bring
Tommy Rosenberg to homecoming. My first real
kiss with Justin Gelbfarb. He'd be absolutely
horrified as a pastor, as a father, and as a
Black man. Oh yes, that's right. I'm Black.
What? You thought I was white? Wow, what an
ignorant assumption to make. That's probably
all you all do all day. Assume. You assume I'm
straight. You assume I'm white just because the
person who is playing me is straight and white.
Uh-oh, there I go breaking your precious fourth
wall. Is what I'm saying so hard to swallow?
Seems to me you swallow a lot. Fox News. The
meat industry. White Jesus. You swallow the
lie that you're a good person. Well, I got
news for you, no one is a good person! No.
One. Not me. Not the person playing me. Not
the person who wrote this. We are all poisoned
with trauma. Well, not really me, I guess. I'm
speaking as the writer/performer here. Not
the character. I am definitely traumatized. Now
I'm speaking as the character. But not me: the
writer/performer. I am not Black, and I am
definitely not queer. I am a white, straight
man. Very straight. So why? Why would a white
straight guy write a queer and Black character
for himself to play? Because sometimes walls

need to be put up around your fortress of
self-acceptance. And sometimes I do that by
creating a character who is everything like me
and nothing like me at the same time. My real
father's in the audience tonight. And though
I'm definitely not queer—and there's no question
about that, there's nothing I love more than a
woman's body—though I'm straight my dad still
hasn't necessarily been the most accepting and
supportive. He's been absent. So absent that
you might as well be dead, Dad. You might as
well be dead. Like my character's dad, you
might as well be dead, Dad. Who am I? I'm my
father's son. Or am I?

The lights go black. They then fade up slightly.
We can barely make out Mendel's silhouette. He
stares directly at his parents. We hear him
whisper.

MENDEL: Daddy, I am not yours. Daddy, I am
not yours. Daddy, I am not yours.

The lights then come back on full blast. Mendel
is screaming. Heavy-metal guitar blasts from
the speakers. The light then turns to a strobe.
Mendel drops to the floor and has a seizure. The
lights go dark.

The lights come back up. Mendel stands there,
breathing heavy. He bows. Everyone claps except
his father. Mendel notices. His smile disappears
as he gives his final bow and exits the stage.

MENDEL'S MOTHER: I can't believe you. I
just can't believe you.

MENDEL'S FATHER: What'd I do this time?

MENDEL'S MOTHER: You didn't clap. How could you not clap for your son?

MENDEL'S FATHER: Did you hear the things he said?

MENDEL'S MOTHER: It was a performance. It's not real.

MENDEL'S FATHER: What, do you think I don't know that?! To be honest, the real reason I didn't clap . . .

MENDEL'S MOTHER: Why?! Why?!

MENDEL'S FATHER: Well, I can't even believe that I'm saying this but . . . it was a little short.

Curtain.

The Selected Poems of Mendel Freudenberger

hat Is Who Am

I lie in bed,
My body turning to sand as I wait for something better,
From the heavens,
As I hear those who ripped me from the heavens duel below.
Wondering if one day I will have such duels.
Praying I don't.
Praying I won't place my feet in the same footprints of my
     jailers.
Praying that there is something more,
And if there is, that I know there is.
More can be more and you think it's less.
Less can be less and you think it's more.
Is there an all-knowing.
Can I know everything?
Is this the last step for the human being?
Is this the last chance for me?
Will I be remembered?
Will I want to be remembered . . .
I ask myself as I steal drops from my jailers' cabinet of
     spirits.
The only type of spirit I know is real.
I don't even know if I'm real.
And if I'm real I don't know for how long.
Life should be a song.
Instead it's a mess.
And there's no broom.
No mop.
No all-purpose cleaner to wipe missteps.
If I could know the meaning, would I?
Or would I close my eyes,
And make it up myself.

Suicide

An old friend whispers to me again.

Again an old friend whispers.

She wants me to join her.

Where there are no "nos."

Where gardens grow French fries.

And love is forever.

An old friend whispers to me again.

Again an old friend whispers.

She said it's enough.

I have nothing left to prove.

Nothing left for me to leave.

All will be rewarded.

An old friend whispers to me again.

Again an old friend whispers.

She puts a razor in one hand.

A noose in the other.

These are my paintbrushes.

Time for a final masterpiece.

An old friend whispers to me again.

Again an old friend whispers.

She wants me to hear her.

But I can't today.

She always forgives.

I know she'll whisper again.

Virginity

Our time has come to an end.

You must leave.

Pack your bags and go.

You served your purpose.

I won't say I never needed you.

Pack your bags and go.

You really just can't take a hint.

There's no way you love me that much.

Pack your bags and go.

I am ready for a new kind of friend.

The kind of friend who makes me whole.

Pack your bags and go.

Whole as a man.

You keep me a boy.

Pack your bags and go.

As you leave I'll cheer.

I'll lock the door behind you.

Pack your bags and go.

I'll laugh as you walk away.

I'll remember you fondly.

Pack your bags and go.

I'll be glad you're gone.

I'll wonder why you stayed.

Pack your bags and go.

Wouldn't you rather be loved.

Wouldn't you rather make another feel safe.

Pack your bags and go.

I don't want to be safe anymore.

I want all of the danger.

Pack your bags and go.

You'll forget me.
You'll love the new boy more.
Pack your bags and go.
Don't make me tell you how much I hate you.
But I hate you.
I hate you so much.
Go stall another life.
But before you do that.
Before you hop to the next host.
Pack your bags and go.

10.

Mendel Loves Liz/ Liz Loves Mendel

Dear Liz,

How do I say this? I'm in love with you. There. I guess that's
how I say that. Right there. The first moment I saw you I
knew. That first moment where you looked at me. I think you
felt it, too, no? If you didn't, then, wow, I'm really surprised.
You looked at me, right? You wanted me like I wanted you? I
mean, again, if you didn't, well, then I guess I just don't know
how to read people at all. Have I ever told you how much I love
your smell? It's the best smell I've ever smelled in my entire
life. Before that smell I always thought the best smell was the
mixture of my mother's perfume coupled with the booze she
had been drinking those nights she was out with my father.
The perfect mixture would fill my half-sleeping nostrils when
she'd come in to check on me and kiss me a belated good night.
That was my favorite smell until I smelled you. I think that
smell is just natural, though, right? 'Cause I don't think you
wear perfume and I'm pretty sure you're not drinking before
acting class. Or are you? If you are, I don't care. Nothing you
can do is wrong in my eyes. To be honest, if you told me that
you murdered someone I wouldn't care. Is this too intense? I
figure it's not because you're so intense. To the point where
I often worry about you. You make me feel every emotion at
once, including really negative emotions. I remember when I
used to see you with Phil in the *Grapes of Wrath* rehearsal. You
two would be rolling around on the stage. Lightly wrestling
and giggling. You probably had sex with him, didn't you? I
should have let you know how I feel sooner. But that's on me, I
know. I kept my feelings inside. I didn't say anything. I didn't
do anything. Well, that's what this letter is. From now on all I
am is a doer. You make my skin ache. I'm so in love with you.
I can't stand it. I almost wish I wasn't. It's all so tragic. But the
tragedy is so right. You feel it's right, right?

Love forever,
Mendel

Mendel!

You are fucking crazy, man! It's hot, though. I can also tell
that you hate yourself, which is also hot. Yes, I did think you
were hot that first day in class. Not just you, though. There
were three guys and one girl I thought were hot that first day
in class. Mike, Phil, Lauren, and you. Weird that you're the
only one I haven't had sex with yet. But somehow I imagine
the sex is going to be the best with you. That is if we ever have
it. I don't know. Sex might soon become a thing of the past for
me. At least for a little while. Ever since my mother called me
a whore it's the only thing I can think about when I'm being
sexual in any way. Even when I kiss someone I see that bitch's
face calling me that. Maybe she's right. Maybe I am a whore.
I don't know. I might be in love with you, too. But then again
I don't know if I'm in love with anyone. I don't know if that's
something I'm even capable of or want in my life. But when I'm
lying in my bed at night and I think of you, something warm
comes over me. Perhaps warm enough to drown my mother
out. I told you she's an alcoholic, right? Last night she passed
out naked on the front porch. I just let the bitch sleep there.
You know, you don't really look like a Mendel. You're more like
a Ron. I think I'll call you Ron from now on. If you let me call
you Ron there's definitely a much bigger chance that we fuck.
You know how damaged I am, right? You should know what
you're getting yourself into. I want to kiss you right now. That's
weird, huh? Also, I want your dick in my mouth . . . I think?
Maybe I don't. I might ask you to never talk to me again.

Love?
Liz

Liz,

Please don't ever talk like that ever again. You are not damaged in the slightest. Trust me. I'm damaged as fuck. The other day I thought of you maybe not loving me and I almost stabbed myself in the stomach with my Swiss Army knife. I went to do it and then stopped myself right before the blade reached my stomach. Just one more centimeter and I would have gutted myself. See? That's damaged. You? You're not damaged. Sure, you might be incredibly manipulative, but you are in no way damaged. And fuck your mom. Sorry, is that not okay to say that? You're not a whore. Women have a right to have sex with as many people as they want. I don't even believe there is any such thing as a whore. Just women doing the world a great service. Women who should be thought of in the same light as teachers or doctors. I gotta say that I'm confused, though. To be honest I feel a bit of a push and pull here. And I don't do well with that. That push-and-pull game makes me feel like an ugly fucking troll. And don't worry. I know what I'm getting into here. The question is, do you know what you're getting into here? I don't think you've ever been loved in the way that I would love you. And yes, please call me Ron. If I have to change my name to Ron for you to let me in, I'll gladly do it. Can I tell you a secret? No one's ever told me they wanted to kiss me before, let alone told me that they wanted my dick in their mouth. Can I be honest? I came right after I read that. I didn't even touch myself. I just exploded. I want to be absorbed into you. I want you to be absorbed into me. I want you planted in my flesh. Feeding off me like a parasite. Every little bit of me. Please, Liz. I beg you. Devour me.

Love,
Ron

Dearest Ron,

Wow. I didn't think you could top your first letter with hotness, but here you've gone and done did it. I'm still wet from reading it. You want to be my daddy, don't you? Ooooooooh, that's hot. Actually my real dad is pretty cool. Very caring. He's the better parent for sure. But I could always have two daddies, couldn't I? I mean that whole part of us "absorbing" and "devouring" each other. So fucking hot. It also actually gave me a great idea. What do you say we write to each other like we are the other person? You be Liz, and I'll be Ron. Wouldn't that be fucking cool? I love role-playing. One time I role-played with Phil. I was Sylvia Plath and he was my cable guy. I know cable wasn't invented during Sylvia Plath's lifetime, but that was part of the fantasy. Sylvia Plath (me) time-traveled during her (my) first suicide attempt. Her (my) oven, it turns out, was also a time machine that transported her (me) to the '90s. Once there, one of the first things she (I) did was watch *Sex and the City*. Which she (I) absolutely loved. Then, as I'm sure you can guess, her (my) cable broke, so she called the cable guy (Phil). He then came over and they (meaning we) had the best fuck of Sylvia Plath's (my) life. Totally wiped out her (my) depression. She (I) came like eight times. Then on my (Sylvia's) eighth orgasm, she's (I'm) transported back to the past, and everything goes back to normal and she (I) writes *The Bell Jar*. So what do you say we try it? I'll write to you as you and you write to me as me. I'll be you and you'll be me. What do you say, Liz?

Love,
Ron

Dearest "Ron,"

Hi, it's me, "Liz." That's right. I'm Liz and you're Ron. That's how it's always been and how it will always be. I've never been Ron or even Mendel, and you have never been Liz. And boy, am I glad that's the case, 'cause if it were the other way around I'd be in love with Liz and that would make me a narcissist. Which I am. But that doesn't mean I don't have passionate love for you. Well, love and lust, of course. Deep lust. Lust so deep you'd have to dig a hole to find it. Not that it's hidden. It's not. It's just deep. It's not hidden at all. It is out in the open. An open field of lust, and I'm Julie Andrews twirling and singing about it. "The hills are alive with the sounds of fucking." Beautiful, right? I tell yuh, I just can't wait till I'm eating chocolate cake out of your ass crack. Okay. No more foolin' around. No more games. I know I've been playing a lot of them. One minute I say one thing. The next minute I do the opposite. I write you about how much I want to make sweet love to you, but then I ignore you at school. That's not cool, and I'm so sorry. I'm sorry I've been so mysterious. Well, the mystery has been solved. I love you. Isn't that wonderful? What do you say we celebrate by spending the rest of our lives together? I know that might be a little fast, but I'm compensating for all the agony I've put you through leading up to this moment. What do you say? Never leave my side?

Love,
"Liz"

Hey Mendel,

On second thought, let's not do the switch thing. To be honest
it feels a little tepid. I mean if we're gonna get crazy, why half-
ass it, right? Why not just go for it? Let's turn it the fuck up. I
got an idea! How about you write me as my stalker. Wouldn't
that be fun? And yes. The answer is yes. I in fact do have a
stalker fantasy. GUILTY AS CHARGED. How does that sound?

**Loving you in this moment (even though I don't
know what the next moment will bring),**
Liz

Dear Liz,

You really think you're so fucking smart, don't you? You got
a smart mouth, don't you? The smartest mouth in the whole
school. A straight-A mouth. It graduated first in its smarty-
pants class, didn't it? DIDN'T IT, SMART STUFF!!!!!! You're
ignoring me, Liz. I talk and you don't listen. It's like you don't
hear me. But I know you hear me, Liz. You hear my whispers
in your head. I know everything about you, Liz. I know what
you think. I know where you live. I know how tight your panties
are. That's right. I broke into your house and tried on every
single pair. How could I not? I would be crazy not to. First of all,
they're panties. Second of all, they're your panties. And when I
put on your panties, I pretend I'm you, Liz, as I prance around
your bedroom. I do my panty-prancy all around your room with
a smart mouth just like your smart mouth. Here's the deal—
you better get with the program. My program. 'Cause if you
don't get with my program you're gonna get with the DEAD
program. That's right. I'll kill you. I'd rather see you dead than
see you kiss anyone else with that smart mouth of yours. How
does it feel to feel like you're better than me? Well, the thing is,

you are. I agree with you. You're superior to me in every way, and I can't have that. That's why you gotta date me, because if you date me then you'll be lowering yourself, and once you do that we'll be equals. I can't stand how much better you are than me. But then again, you're better than everybody, aren't you? Queen Liz. Queen of everything. Aren't you, smart mouth?

Be mine or die!

Love,
Mr. Fun

Dear Mendel,

This is Glen Rottman. Liz's father. My daughter just showed me the letter you sent her. Or should I say, that Mr. Fun sent her. I'll keep this short and sweet. If I ever see you near my daughter. If she ever receives a letter or a phone call from you. If I hear about anything involving you in the slightest, I will grab you by the back of the head and take your wisdom teeth out on my fucking curb. Do you hear me? I don't know what kind of sickness you suffer from, but you better find some kind of medicine, 'cause if not I got my own medicine for you. And this medicine's not in my medicine closet . . . it's in my gun closet. Time for you to SMARTEN up, Mr. Fun. Or else the fun is going to be over for you forever.

Fuck you.
Mr. Glen Rottman, Esq.

Dear Mr. Rottman,

Mendel Freudenberger here. How can I begin to say how sorry I am. I am truly mortified. Not sure you're aware of this, but Liz and I have been something of pen pals as of late. In these letters we've shared quite a bit, and have really gotten to know each other. In fact, honestly speaking, I feel like I know your daughter better than I know members of my own family. I can honestly say the last thing I would ever want to do would be to make her feel in danger in any way. Actually, the exact opposite is true. I don't want to throw Liz under the bus here. I tell you this next thing purely to ease your anxiety. I'm not sure what Liz told you, but she actually asked me to write her like I was some sort of stalker. I swear on the life of my mother, it was all her idea. I had never written a stalker letter before. The simple reason for that being that I have never stalked anyone before. In rethinking about what I wrote I definitely see how it might have been a little "too much." I most certainly could have eased up on the insults, and violent threats. Not to mention the profanity. Anyway, sir, I hope you can find it in your heart to forgive me. I truly respect you. Most of all because you raised someone as brilliant and amazing as your daughter. My deepest apologies. As much as it breaks my heart, I give my word I will never contact your daughter ever again. Have a nice life. I won't.

Truly sorry,
Mendel Freudenberger

Ron!

Hahahaha. You are so cute. Such a cute fucking idiot. Dude!
That wasn't my dad! I haven't seen my dad in four years since
he left my mother after finding her fucking my ex-boyfriend
Ron on the kitchen floor. You remember Ron Miller, right?
He was a senior when we were freshmen. He's in jail for
committing armed robbery at a McDonald's. Anyway . . . April
fools', dumb ass! I can't believe you fell for that. You think I'd
tell you to write me something like that and then rat you out?!!!
I mean, I'm fucked up but I'm not that fucked up. You should
have stood up for yourself more. If that was my dad, what
fucking business is it of his what we write to one another? Also
speaking of ratting out. I can't believe you threw me under
the bus like that. Really can't stand any sort of heat, can you?
I gotta be honest, that is a major turnoff. You're really not who
I thought you were at all, are you? I thought you had strength.
You really don't, though, do you? I really need to think here.
I thought I loved you. I thought that I wanted you more than
anyone I'd ever wanted in my life, but to be honest I'm not so
sure now.

Give me a minute,
Liz

Liz,

I can't take it. I can't take not knowing if you still love me or
not. I don't think I can live with this nightmarish wondering
anymore. So, guess what? I'm not going to. Instead, I'm taking
it all into my own hands. And by "it all" I mean a bottle of
pills, and by "my own hands" I mean my own mouth. If you've
guessed that this is a suicide note, Liz, then you've guessed
right. After your last letter I realized that I would never be
safe from losing you. You're a self-sabotager, Liz. I know that's
really hypocritical coming from someone who is about to kill
himself, but it's true. I don't think you want to be loved. Not
loved in the right way. Not loved the way I would love you. And
I know you'll just push me away for good someday. I'm not sure
how final your last letter was, but let me assure you this letter
is very final. The most final. I mean it's a suicide note. It's time
for me to finally be free from my love for you. And now you're
free from your love for me. Or at least free from wondering
about whether or not you love me. I hope there's such a thing as
ghosts. So I can haunt you. But then I guess I wouldn't be free,
would I? So I guess I hope that I won't become a ghost. Because
ghosts really are never free, are they? Are they? Are . . . pajama
pants washer board. Oh no, I'm feeling the pills take jarba jooba
booba. I'm gong. I'm tahnahnahtahlashtahtah . . .

Luvre,
Meinzjk

Mendel,

I just cannot believe you killed yourself. I gotta say it's really selfish, but I guess I've been selfish, too. I wish you would have waited a little longer to do this, because after I gave it all a good think I realized that I did want to be with you. That I couldn't see my life without you by my side. And now . . . now you're gone and that will never happen and I just can't forgive myself for that. Not just for how I treated you, but for how I treated myself. For being so reckless and depriving myself of your deep love for me and my oh-so-deep love for you. You're right. I'm my own worst enemy, and I'll always be. I'll always look for a way to just knock the whole thing down. So if that's the case, if that's my mode, there's really only one thing to do. And that's finish the job once and for all. And be a copycat. A copycat of you, my love. Meow meow. You know what that means in cat? It means "I'm going to kill myself." Good-bye, my love. Or should I say hello, because you're already dead and I'm coming to join you. Unless they don't let me in heaven, which is actually a distinct possibility. But I don't really believe in hell. I wonder if you did. We really didn't cover that wide a range of subjects, did we? Anyway, here I go. Down the hatch. Mmmm, these pills taste like nothing. I guess that's what it all is, isn't it? It's all a whole lotta nothing.

See you in a minute, Mendel . . .

My dearest Liz,

Okay, hahahaha. Joke's over. I didn't kill myself. And I know you didn't kill yourself, either. I guess we were trying to prove a point, right? Well, point proven. We really love each other and we shouldn't kill ourselves. Love is life, Liz. Love is life. But I'm not dead and neither are you, so let's take this love and this life to the next level. When can I see you?

Love,
Mendel

Mendel,

I really wish you would not have joked about killing yourself.
Because I wasn't joking and I really did. That's right, I killed
myself. I'm dead, and I'm writing you this letter from hell.
Yep, that's where they sent me. Apparently I was too much of a
sinner. Not a hot take, to be honest. Mendel, I probably should
just come out and say it—I am seeing someone. And you'll
never guess who it is. It's Satan! That's right. He's really nice. It
happened so out of nowhere. I was just strolling along when all
of a sudden I felt this tap on my shoulder. I then turned around
and there he was. And that was pretty much it. What can I say?
The guy's got red-hot charisma. He actually reminds me of you.
I'm not exactly sure why. I'm also not exactly sure if that's true
or not. It might have to do with how he makes love. How he
makes love I imagine is the way that you make love. Obviously
I can only imagine because we never did. But he's amazing in
bed. And I imagine you are, too. Guess I'll never know. Well,
maybe I will if you end up down here, and things go south with
me and Old Scratch. I'm sure they will. I definitely think you
were onto something when you called me a self-sabotager.
Well, I guess that's it. That's it for this letter and that's also
it for us. What a weird thing to know that I'm never going to
see you again. But that's probably a relief for you, isn't it? No
more crazy bullshit to deal with. I'm sorry I made you want me
so much. I should have cut you off months ago. But I'm glad I
didn't. Take care, Mendel. I hope you can find someone who
loves you all the way. Who isn't confused. And most of all, who
isn't in hell.

Love for all eternity,
Liz

11.

The Time Mendel Freudenberger Sold Weed

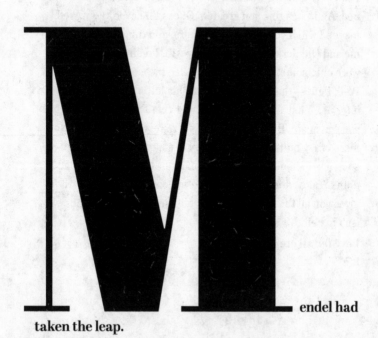

taken the leap.

endel had

He was the last in his current group of friends to do so. It was about time. It had been far too long. Up until this point he had only been a partaker of the smokable sacrament, the fruity nuggets. Up until this point he had only been a customer. But now both feet were in. He had walked through the door and fully joined the party. Mendel was now an official marijuana dealer.

The opportunity had fallen in his lap, which Mendel took to be a sign from Jah. Vickie, the resident mother hippie of Highland Park, had gotten her hands on a half pound. She was willing to give Mendel half of that on credit, and whatever profit he made after she was paid back was his. Vickie loved Mendel. He was her favorite from his generation of youngsters. Ironically, this favoritism was due to the fact that Mendel was the least like a criminal. Mendel seemed the most likely to have a future, to be destined for something. Now Vickie was giving him his first push into criminality.

But it wasn't really that criminal. It was just weed dealing. Ganja wasn't a drug. It was a way of life. It was a daily activity. No different than a cup of coffee in the morning or a drink at night. No worse than any psychotropic medication everyone and their brother and sister seemed to be juiced up with nowadays.

The first day Mendel got the bag from Vickie he assumed he would immediately feel a sort of freedom. The freedom of the new him. He had been repeating to himself that he was up for the task, even though his inner thoughts were screaming quite the opposite. Every cell of his body thought this was a bad idea. He didn't have the constitution for it. It was bad enough to lie to his parents about getting high; Mendel's parents knew he got high. And even though his mother grounded him when it was too obvious, or when it aided in his mistakes, she mostly just let it go. She felt like a hypocrite coming down too hard on him. She and his father had done more than their fair share of weed smoking when they were hippies. She once even smuggled two pounds in from Jamaica. It had been taped to her body. She thought nothing wrong of it, and still wore the memory with pride.

Mendel drove down Sheridan Road with an ounce of his new product in his glove compartment. That's all he would travel with at once for fear of being pulled over. Plus if he sold an ounce in a day that was quite enough. He had a deal that if someone bought the whole ounce, he'd give it to them at a discount for $300. That made him a whole profit of $200 that he would split with Vickie. Leaving him with a whole $100.

Mendel was on his way to Brian Tullenfeld's, and he was sweating profusely. He had smoked a little too much. Make no mistake, at this point, he was quite good at driving baked but this time he had smoked just a couple hits too much, causing his heart to beat just a little too fast. It also didn't help that every car that passed by looked just a little too much like a cop car.

Cops are like bees, he thought. *Never know when they might sting.* Mendel always thought it was ridiculous advice to stay still when a bee was on you. Even if staying still would keep them from stinging you, how was one supposed to stay still when they felt the tickling of little legs on their skin? A tickle that could, at any second, be followed by a sharp stab. Cops were no different. At any moment he could see those red and blue lights start to flash. That was their sting. Or maybe the sting was being arrested, and the lights were the leg tickle? Whatever the case, cops fucking sucked. And Mendel wondered that if cops sucked for him, what were those city cops like? What if Mendel were Black? Oooooh, then cops wouldn't be bees. Cops would be like wasps, or those killer bees that were in Asia that every once in a while found their way into Seattle, or something like that, and then killed the regular bees. Mendel then thought how unfair it was to bees to compare them to cops. Just as it was an insult to pigs to call cops pigs. Mendel liked bees and pigs. He certainly liked them more than human beings, let alone cops.

Whoa, I'm stoned, Mendel thought to himself. *Good thing, though. Wouldn't want to have to deal with Brian Tullenfeld sober.*

Brian Tullenfeld was one of these JAP putzes who, their whole childhood, thought they were going to grow up to be Michael Jordan. He really thought that. That just because he could beat a bunch of Jews in basketball he'd grow up to be not just a basketball player in the NBA, which was totally fucking impossible, but the best basketball player of all time. However, this was purely a second-grade-through-junior-year-in-high-school dream. And now that they were both seniors, the grim reality had started to set in, for Brian Tullenfeld, that that dream was dead and he would, most likely, just end up working for his father in the kosher hot dog business. In the meantime, he, like so many idiots like him, decided to start numbing this dread out with the help of Ms. Mary Jane.

Slinging nugs to Brian Tullenfeld had sort of a sweet existential vengeance for Mendel. Mendel's dreams were still quite possible. He most certainly could be the next comedy superstar. It was all ahead of him, and for Brian Tullenfeld it was all behind him. And now Brian needed him. All those years he had not given two shits about whether Mendel lived or died, and now he needed him to help reduce his inner fear of his stupid future of punching a clock and having an all-too-normal life. They'd probably both smoke weed for the rest of their lives, but Brian would continue to use it as an escape, whereas Mendel would use it as the cherry on the delicious hot-fudge sundae of his rich and famous life.

Mendel arrived at the Tullenfeld house, which was, by most people's standards, a mansion. However, by the standards of most Highland Park residents, it was merely . . . a house. A characterless, run-of-the-mill stone house.

That was Highland Park. Middle-class effort with upper-class money. The Tullenfeld house was no exception. Mendel knew to park on the street. He also knew to walk around to the back. He then knew to enter into the little guesthouse next to the pool. This wasn't so much a guesthouse as it was Brian Tullenfeld's pathetic boy cave.

Mendel entered the boy cave, and there, sitting on a strawberry-red beanbag, was Brian Tullenfeld with his big beautiful eyes, messy light brown hair, and thin physique. He still had that basketball body. He hadn't been getting high long enough to lose that. He also hadn't been getting high long enough to avoid getting way too excited about doing a drug deal. As Mendel entered, Brian Tullenfeld jumped to his feet.

"Freudenberger! Whattup, dog! I thought you'd never come."

Mendel kept his cool.

"Sit down, dude," Mendel commanded, using a deeper voice than his normal register. Brian did his bidding, apologizing for being overzealous. Admitting that he still didn't totally know how this kind of thing went.

"That's all right," said Mendel. "I used to be the same way . . . like . . . five years ago. It takes learning. Unfortunately, sometimes you learn the hard way. I got a lot of friends who have gotten shot doing this shit wrong on both sides of the deal. Brains domed the fuck out." Brian's already huge eyes widened even more.

"Wow. You know people who've been shot?"

"Of course I do, dude. What do you think the game is? Just high-fives and nice-to-see-yous? It's fucking dangerous out there. It's fucking grimy and scary as fuck. And it's the realest game there is. Now how much you want, Brian?"

"I was thinking an eighth."

Mendel scoffed. And boy, did that scoff feel good. If you would have told him even three years ago that he would be scoffing at Brian Tullenfeld and not getting his ass kicked right after said scoff, he wouldn't have believed you for a second. But here he was. Scoffing away. Damn, it felt good. Every scoff erased each humiliation he had received at the hands of jocks like Brian Tullenfeld. It almost felt as good as jacking off.

"An eighth?!" scoffed Mendel. "I mean, I guess you can get an eighth if you don't want it to last you long? Me and the bros went through an eighth in like five minutes yesterday, no joke."

Brian Tullenfeld scratched his sandy mane. "Hmmmmm. How much do you think I should get, then?"

"At least a half ounce, if you really want it to last you. But maybe you have a different tolerance than me. See, I'm high all fucking day, so it takes a lot to get me properly irie."

"Irie?" asked Brian Tullenfeld. "What's irie?"

Mendel scoffed again. "Of course you don't know what *irie* means. *Irie* means stoned, and also happy, and also like cool and relaxed. But in this case I'm using it to mean stoned. It's a term we Rastas use. You know I'm Rastafarian, right?"

"I didn't. Does that mean you're not a Jew anymore?"

Mendel gave yet another scoff. "Yep. I mean I guess I'll always kind of be a Jew. I got the nose. I got the forehead. And yeah, I'll admit it, I love money. But no, that's not my religion anymore. I'm a Rasta now. I believe mighty God is a living man." With that, Mendel looked to the sky as if he could see Jah staring back at him.

The next thing Brian Tullenfeld did was take a deep breath. His eyes got softer. He nodded like he was experiencing a profound memory. "Wow. You got really cool, Mendel. To be honest, I used to think you were a loser."

Though Mendel knew this was meant to be a compliment, it was still a shank to his side. It brought up a deep anger. An anger and a shame. And it seemed like a move. A move for Tullenfeld to cut him down so he could swallow more easily the fact that he was in a position of needing something from him. Luckily, this anger and shame was trumped by the sense of power Mendel felt in the present moment. It would be easy to keep his cool no matter what was said to him, because he held all the cards. Mendel had the upper hand. He knew it and so did Brian fucking Tullenfeld.

"Well, I ain't no loser no more, Tullenfeld. Now do you want to do a fucking drug deal or do you want to keep talking ancient history? 'Cause I got a hippie chick I gotta go bone in an hour. She's been begging me for it all day." This was a lie. Mendel was still very much a virgin and still very much uncomfortable around the opposite sex.

Then something happened that Mendel didn't expect at all. Brian Tullenfeld got silent. Dead silent. His eyes got even softer. He closed them and breathed even deeper. Like he was trying to conjure something in himself that was gone. Like he was looking for something inside that was no longer there. He grabbed his hair and gave it a yank. Then moved his hands down to his temples and gave them a short massage. Then another deep breath, but this deep breath was to help him open his eyes. To help him rejoin the outside of his damaged inner self. This time he shook his head. Shook his head in amazement that this was what he had become. Was it so hard to stomach? Being in this position? Having to be so in need of something from someone that he always thought he was better than? With this he looked into Mendel's eyes.

"Sorry, sorry. I just meant, you know . . . it's funny how things change. How people change." This was a tone Mendel had never heard from someone like Brian before. A tone that was . . . well . . . full of thought. Make no mistake, Tullenfeld knew what was in front of him. Nothing. He knew how boring his future was. This cliché observation almost seemed like he was asking for forgiveness. Not just forgiveness for his mistreatment of Mendel, but forgiveness for believing the lies he had told himself. This wasn't just Brian Tullenfeld buying weed. He was buying the potential to return to what was. Return to a time where he thought he could actually be something. A time to where life wasn't just waiting for death. But Brian Tullenfeld was already dead.

"Yeah, Brian, it is funny, I guess? Life is funny, and praise Jah for that."

Brian's eyes now started to shed the tears they had only moments ago potentially promised. He grabbed Mendel's hand. Gripped it with an athletic grip. With all his emotional weakness, Brian Tullenfeld still was quite strong. Mendel was horrified. Jesus Christ, this was a pathetic sight. It felt like the first time he had seen his father cry. It felt like something he wasn't supposed to see. Funny, though, years ago he imagined he would have enjoyed watching this. Watching such an idiot like Brian Tullenfeld cry, but there was nothing enjoyable about this. Brian Tullenfeld squeezed Mendel's hand harder to the point that one would think the next words out of his mouth would be some kind of begging. In a way they were. "Mendel. You're not really a Rasta, are you?"

Mendel pulled his hand away. Again a rage started to build. *Not a Rasta?!* Mendel thought to himself. *How dare this fuck. What won't he do to serve himself with the illusion that his existence means a fucking turd anymore.* But that rage passed through him, and then he just got sad. Sad for Brian Tullenfeld. Sad for himself that he ever let Brian Tullenfeld have any type of power over him that would now cause him to be so defensive against someone so defenseless. So pathetic. So done.

Mendel's breathing slowed. "I'm sorry, Brian. What was the question?"

Brian pleaded again, "I asked if you really were a Rastafarian."

Mendel looked back into Brian's wet eyes. His sadness grew. Not just because he had let Brian get to him, but because of what Brian's annoying question had revealed to him all too easily. A fact that he could no longer avoid, no matter how loudly he tried to drown it out in his head with contrary thoughts. The truth that he had barely been repressing. Mendel was no better than Brian Tullenfeld. He was actually worse, because in this moment he was in greater denial. Mendel looked away and then hung his head.

"Who am I kidding, Brian. I'm not a Rasta. Of course I'm not. It's just something I say. I don't know why. It's pretty fucking stupid, huh? To live here and have the lives we have and say I'm Rastafarian . . . well . . . that's idiotic, isn't it?" Mendel meant every word he said. He wasn't a Rasta. And what's more, he didn't want to be a Rasta. He wasn't even really sure of how to be a Rasta to begin with. This wasn't a dream of his. And thank Jah for that, because being Mendel and being a Rasta was no less out of reach than being Brian Tullenfeld and being the next Michael Jordan. It was a path that led to absolutely nowhere. Then Mendel felt that hope. He felt hopeful because he was reminded that his actual dreams were not out of reach at all. Mendel's dreams were lofty, but achievable. Mendel felt lucky, and he knew in that moment how foolish it would be for him not to feel grateful for such luck. He knew how foolish he was to test that luck in the reckless way he had been. He knew how foolish he had been to pretend to want something different from who he really was. He had been just like Brian Tullenfeld, but unlike Brian Tullenfeld he could stop being like Brian Tullenfeld.

Mendel looked back at Brian. He was in a bit of shock, to say the least. In as little time as it had taken Mendel to come to his senses, it had taken Brian Tullenfeld just as little time to completely fucking lose it. As he watched Brian look around the room for some sort of answer to anything, Mendel took out the ounce of weed. He put it in Brian Tullenfeld's lap. Brian Tullenfeld looked up. His despair now coupled with confusion.

"What are you doing, Mendel?"

Mendel put his hand on Brian Tullenfeld's shoulder. "Take it, man. Just take it. You're gonna need it."

Mendel walked to the door and turned around. He and Brian Tullenfeld locked eyes. Brian Tullenfeld's had dried. He smiled at Mendel in a way that he hadn't smiled since before the fall. Since he was still in line to make basketball history. This would be the last time either of them looked each other in the eyes. From that day on neither spoke a word to the other.

Mendel drove home. He was back in time for dinner. His high had worn off, so his mother was pleased that she was going to get to have dinner with a relatively sober son. He wanted to tell his parents that he had been dealing weed. Wanted to tell them that he had been dealing and now he had stopped. Wanted to see the relief in their faces to mirror his own. But he didn't tell them. He knew there wouldn't be any relief. They'd just be upset and concerned, and possibly threaten him if he ever even thought about doing it again. The next day he went to Vickie's, his "hippie mom," smoked a joint with her, and told her that he wouldn't be dealing anymore. She laughed.

"I knew you wouldn't be doing it for very long, Mendel. You got too much future in you for that." She kissed him on the cheek. Normally this would have made Mendel feel warm. But it didn't. The kiss left him cold.

"You're right, Vickie. I guess you're right about that." With that Mendel stood up and walked to the door. He and Vickie locked eyes, and in that moment they both knew, as clear as any clear thing they had ever known, that they'd never see each other ever again.

Mendel drove home, listening to "Box of Rain" ring out from the glorious speakers of his VW van. He smiled. How could he not? His future was too glorious. Too somewhere anywhere anything else.

Jackie Cohen

Jackie's Death Trip

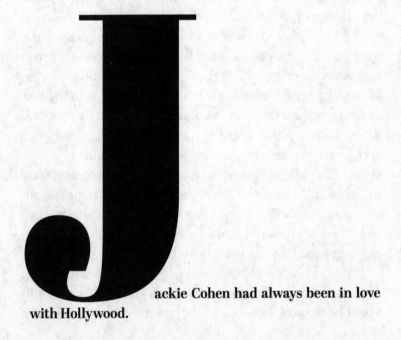

Jackie Cohen had always been in love with Hollywood.

And Hollywood had always been in love with death. Dying young. Dying tragically. Dying publicly. There is nothing more romantic. Nothing sexier. Nothing more profitable. Death has a seductive aura. After you die, they'll love you even more. Savoring what you gave them. Making every step you took and place you visited a landmark. Death: the real cash-in. The real promise of eternal love.

Jackie Cohen lay next to his pool, going over all the ways he could die. What would be the most splendid? But even more so, what would be the most "him"? Would it be drugs? Jackie liked drugs. Or perhaps a nice old-fashioned murder. No doubt there were plenty of women who had wanted to kill him while they were together. Some of them he even recognized as being justified in their desire. This gave Jackie a chuckle. A chuckle that sent his eyes to his pulsating gut. Say . . . there's always obesity. Certainly a solid option for Jackie. Not that Jackie was anywhere near being dangerously fat. He was barely overweight. But if he did get fat, it'd be a glamorous way to go. For Jackie was funny, and if you were funny, you could get as fat as you want and still have a sexy edge. Food: the heroin of comedy. Get that blubber growing so America rushed even faster to the theatre not knowing how many more years they had left to laugh with you. He imagined the gobbling of pizzas, cheeseburgers. Pouring melted butter all over his moobs, and shotgunning whipped cream till it shot out his ass. Watching his stomach bloat to gargantuan proportions. His closet filled only with linen. Consistently mistaking his curtains for a T-shirt. Women covering him in oil and trying to climb up him like a greased mountain, never reaching the peak. Sliding, giggling all the way down to his chafed thighs.

Why was Jackie going here? Well, it was the morning, and Jackie's mornings were always filled with terror. Terror that this would be the day. The day no one remembered him anymore.

The day calls would stop. This was the worst kind of death. The death while living. Hollywood death. He also felt old. He couldn't believe how many women he fucked who didn't know who John Candy was. Who didn't know who N.W.A. was until the movie came out. Who didn't know about Jackie's early work.

Any way out but that way. Any way out other than just disappearing to everyone but yourself. Better to grow in size. To grow so big that at least you'd get some sort of world record. That your way out would be remembered as something you worked quite hard at. To stuff oneself is no easy feat.

Or maybe it would just be drugs. Maybe he'd decide to never sleep again unless he was nodding off. Maybe he'd start using payphones again, too paranoid to pick up his cell phone. Everyone would be listening in. Everyone would be waiting. Waiting on that last wrong dose or that shotgun in the mouth to end the dark dependence. And skinny. Skinny and pale. A Jewish Edgar Allan Poe in black denim. And the women, how'd they worry about him. How'd they try and fix him. One after the other standing in his doorway, suitcase packed, face wet with tears because they hated themselves so much for abandoning him when he needed them most, but also knowing that there was nothing more that could be done. Then coming back to check in on him after not hearing from him for a week, finding him in his final paparazzi pose underneath his toilet. Or they'd be driving him to rehab. Or picking him up from rehab after he escaped. Forcing themselves to believe him when he told them he was fine now and all of the "recovery bullshit" wasn't for him. He could do it himself. Especially relapse. Especially overdose. Especially die.

He thought again about the ladies of his past. All of the exquisitely unstable exes. The multitudes of wives, girlfriends, and lovers who everyone knew were the last people he should be with from the get-go. Women with only themselves in their eyes and his end in their hearts. He would die by their hands or, even better, by their persuasion of his own hands. He loved crazy. Crazy kept you young. Crazy didn't care how much older he got. Crazy would drive to Vegas with Jackie and marry him after only knowing him for three days and divorce him two weeks later. Crazy would refuse to get an abortion. Crazy would raise his kids to hate him. No matter. They'd all forgive him after he was gone. After their mother domed their father with a Glock in their living room. Maybe it would be a knife, though. A stabbing after what was supposed to be make-up sex. Him too blinded by lust to see that this last time was really going to be the last time. Or maybe it'd be a glamorous oceanic disaster. On his yacht. Just like Wagner and Natalie. They'd have drunk everything on board. The booze would have brought a clarity to her. A clarity that she'd never be happy. That they'd never actually be together. That he was just another dark repetition of her abusive father. She'd break a whiskey bottle over his head as the waves crashed. So rainy. They should have never been on the boat in the first place. Not the weather for it. She'd fall back and become one with the Pacific, and he'd have too much blood in his eyes to be able to reach out and save her. Then, in a fit of remorse, he would find the flare gun and shoot it at the engine and give himself his very own Viking funeral.

So many possibilities.

Jackie's chest hurt. He probably shouldn't have lain down so soon after eating. Somehow he always made this mistake with his reflux. For some reason he didn't think lying down would aggravate his reflux as long as he was awake. To him it only registered as a consequence when he went to sleep. *I guess that would be another way to go*, he thought. *Esophageal cancer.* Or any kind of cancer. But what was romantic about that? Cancer's just sad. Sure, death by disease can bring a sort of heroism. People sitting around, praising you for being so strong in the face of your own demise. Praise you for keeping it from everyone so as not to burden them. Praise you in your final days for responding to people asking you how you were by immediately asking them how they were. But this wouldn't be Jackie. This disease shit wasn't him at all. No, this was not a way to go for Jackie. Jackie had the amount of self-awareness to acknowledge that there'd be far much more complaining, and crying, and listing off to family and friends endlessly the things he would never get to do or see and everything he'd miss. Begging for forgiveness rather than taking responsibility. Fucking those in his life twice. First for hurting them and second for making them help him erase his guilt. Yeah, disease was not the way to go.

Jackie sat up. Covered in sweat. He was starting to burn in the sun. *OH NO, MELANOMA.* He dipped in his pool, and as he dunked his head he could hear his heart thump inside his ears. *Too much death-tripping. What's wrong with me? I've got everything anyone could ask for. I have so much life left in me. Why not stick around and die an old legend? A pillar of the industry that will leave a void in my departure. Leaving the world to feel like they've lost a family member. Yes, that's what I'll do. And I'll never see it coming. I'll be asleep on the beach. Or even maybe walking on the beach. That'd be fine. A graceful collapse. Everything around me getting so soft. The sand of the beach embracing my body and the whisper of the ocean being the last sounds that glided into my ears. A stranger finding me. Everyone will be sad, but also be grateful that I went peacefully at such an old age. Amazed that till the very last day I could still walk and fuck with ease.*

Jackie came up for air. He breathed like it was his first and last. *I feel much better,* he thought. And he did feel better, but not 100 percent. He poured himself some Prosecco. As the tiny bubbles popped inside his mouth, he pictured them as if they were tiny bubbles of his own panic, bursting into nothing. That still wasn't enough, though. So Jackie picked up the phone and called his lawyer, Herb Rosenblatt. Herb pretended to be happy to hear from Jackie, even though he wasn't. Not many people were ever too happy to get a call from Jackie.

"Herb, how you doing, buddy? I hope well. Look, I'm just calling because I've had a lot of epiphanies this afternoon. A lot of future thinking. A lot of realization. I'm not as young as I used to be, Herb. Not that I'm old. But I'm not as happy as I could be. Or really I'm not as happy as I should be. And I'm making a vow, Herb. I'm making a vow to live life on my own terms. I'm not talking about being selfish. What I'm talking about is joy, Herb. Finding joy. I'm sailing to Joy Island, Herb. But here's the thing. I've realized there's deadweight on board my ship. Make no mistake, you can love deadweight. And besides, most deadweight has not always been deadweight. A lot of deadweight once had a place on board. Nevertheless, the past is the past and the present is the present. I guess what I'm trying to say here, Herb, is that . . . you're fired."

Jackie hung up the phone before he could hear Herb's reaction. Best not to burden Herb with the obligation to react, or, even more so, best to spare Herb the humiliating impulse to beg. Jackie sat down. He took another breath, which calmed him even more because the breath felt like most breaths. There was a lack of high stakes. Things had leveled out. Jackie felt better. Jackie felt hopeful. Jackie felt alive. Jackie jacked off. Jackie fell asleep, in full comfort with the full knowledge that he would wake up to many, many more days.

13.

Jackie's Love Memoirs: An Excerpt

I've had many lovers in my life. This is not me bragging. This is a simple fact.

No one could or would ever call me a model. But there is no doubt about it, I am a handsome man. More importantly, I possess a raw, nearly overwhelming sexuality that penetrates the psyche of anyone I direct it toward. Even in its dormant state, it exudes a sexual power the likes of which most people have never seen. It is an insidious power. One that often goes unnoticed until it's too late and they are in my bed, or their bed, or a hotel bed, or somewhere else, maybe not even a bed. Any type of residence. A subway platform, a wheat field, or, I don't know, the middle of the street. Usually it's a woman, but I've been known to take a male lover or two. I like to broaden my experience as much as I can. First off, I have the taste for it. Secondly, it's good for my art. Don't let anyone tell you different. Sex fuels art. You know how some artists get really bad all of a sudden? Their work goes from genius to shit? There's one simple reason for that. They stopped fucking.

I've enjoyed every single one of my lovers. Right now I'm thinking of Natasha. Polish royalty. I met her at Santa Anita of all places. She was wearing all white. She had a parasol of all things. I walked up to her and asked if I could climb under the parasol with her to avoid the sun. "You see, darling, I run hot." She liked that. She told me she likes an aggressive man. So aggressive is what she got. I took her by the arm and pulled her to the back seat of my Phantom. From that moment on we made love all hours of the day, anytime, and anywhere. At one point I thought I might fall in love with her. But then, boy oh boy, did the tide turn. She would drink and then all of a sudden her mood would become as gray as her homeland's sky. Her eyes would glaze over in a depression. She could go days in bed, just lying there. Like she was willing herself to death. But she was beautiful and I was a lot younger, so I thought that it was maybe her brilliance coming through. We would eat and she'd talk about killing herself one day. I'd get furious and tell her to stop it and her only reply would be, "Jackie, I always knew that I would die by my own hand." I asked her why. She said she was afraid that nothing happened to you after you died and she couldn't live with the terror. I'd say to her that that sounded a bit off, because if she killed herself just because she couldn't take not knowing what happens after death, and she was afraid that there was nothing after, she'd just be racing straight toward that nothingness. Why not just give it a go for just a little while longer, and see what happens. She would wake up in the middle of the night and try to bust out of the house to sprint down the street. She said running was the only way she could get the fear out of her body. I thought I'd be her savior. I forbid her from saying such suicidal things, but she couldn't keep her depressing trap shut. So one night, after we had made love all day for what I knew would be the last time, I tiptoed out of her semipermanent bungalow at the Chateau.

Another was Bianca. The famous Spanish actress. She was the most jealous person I'd ever met. I remember we went on an "ironic" date to McDonald's and she went nuts thinking that I was hitting on the fry girl. The fry girl incidentally looked like my father. Not that my father wasn't an attractive man, but he's not really my type. I told her that, and then she accused me of having sexual relations with my father. I remember she stole my phone from me one night and sent a barrage of angry texts to him telling him to stay away from me. I tried to calm her by showering her with gifts. This one time I bought her a snake. I think it was a python, because she told me that as a child snakes were her favorite animal. At first she was thrilled, and then one night the python got out and slithered to our bed. It then wrapped itself around my waist and almost killed me. She accused me of enticing the python to suck my dick. The next time I saw her it was gone and she had a new pair of boots. I was furious. I was beside myself that she had chosen to murder an animal that I had given her on my watch. That she would leave me to live with the guilt of that. At least if she was going to do that, she could have had the boots made in my size.

Another was a barista at my local coffee shop, which I won't divulge because, no offense, I don't want to be bothered there. That's the one place I don't like to engage with fans. But there was this beautiful barista who used to work there. I don't really remember what she was working toward in her life, but she had a tattoo that said "Art Is a Hammer." Single worst tattoo I've ever seen. But boy oh boy, did she have a whole lotta ass. I guess I'm not really allowed to say that these days. And I get it. But an ass is an ass is an ass, am I right? And this barista was one of the single greatest sexual partners I ever had. She smelled like coffee. Which you think might be disgusting but I found it the exact opposite. It was absolutely hypnotizing. Aromatic hypnosis to the umpteenth degree. When we made love she'd call me Karl Marx. After about the sixth time I asked her why. She said, "Communism turns me on." I asked her, "Don't you mean socialism?" Then she asked me, "What's the difference?" And much to my own shame I couldn't give her an answer. One night we were in bed. Postcoital. She's rubbing my belly, and I asked her why communism turned her on so much. She said that it was an oil-based philosophy. I still don't know what the hell she meant. That was enough for me. I had sex with her for only two more months and then I called it quits.

I could go on and on and on, but I won't. I have to freshen up. My cleaning lady is going to be here soon. She's going to clean . . . my pipes. Yes, that's right, my cleaning lady is not just my cleaning lady. She's also my lover AND my plumber.

14.
Auschwitz Antebellum: The Oral History

n 2015 Jackie Cohen wrote a script for what he intended to be his masterpiece.

The film, *Auschwitz Antebellum*, was, supposedly, a magical realist romantic comedy about a Jewish prisoner in a Nazi concentration camp and an enslaved Black woman on a plantation in the antebellum South magically switching places, then, after switching places, learning the similarities of their two situations, then after learning these similarities magically finding themselves together, first in the concentration camp, and then the plantation. In the process of trying to help each other, despite their clashing personalities, they fall in love. Their love rescues them from their oppression. They then marry and go on to form the most successful jazz label of all time.

Yes, this film was actually made. Jackie Cohen directed his own script and played the male lead of the Jewish prisoner, while the legendary star Alicia Davis played the female lead of the enslaved woman. The film was completed but was immediately shelved. Jackie was never able to get a film financed ever again, and barely anyone returned his calls for a year and a half. Since the making of *Auschwitz Antebellum*, no one has seen the film or read the script. Only a select, resourceful few have been able to get their hands on a pirated copy.

Below is the first and only incredibly brief oral history on the making of this so-called film.

JACKIE COHEN (Director, Writer, Star):
I don't care what anyone says, I've never been prouder of anything I've ever made in my life. This film was going to bring Jews and Blacks together like nothing ever had since all the Jews were EP'ing all the fucking jazz records and all those Jews were writing for Redd Foxx and Jimmie Walker. This was gonna show how much

we are all the same and how we can serve each
other in our hearts and our pocketbooks. I was
replacing a frown with a smile. I was replacing
tears with happy tears. It's a brilliant film.
But the suits got scared. Really everyone got
scared, because that's what everyone does. No
one ever wants anything that's actually going
to fucking do something. You gotta fight for
that, and in this case I lost the fight, and,
yes, it was devastating.

ALICIA DAVIS (Actress): I don't really
want to talk about that movie. It's one of the
great regrets of my life.

JACKIE COHEN: Alicia felt uncomfortable
around the material. Embarrassingly, I think
part of the problem was that she wasn't
attracted to me. I had lost a ton of weight
for the role (obviously I'm in a concentration
camp). And then I've seen who she's dated and
been with—they're usually meatier guys. When we
met to do the movie before I got on my crazy
diet I definitely felt that there were sparks,
because I was my usual meaty self. But no doing
on set. I lost my meat, and we lost our spark.
That made things hard, but luckily my desire
for her was enough for the both of us to sell
the acting. I don't know why she won't talk
about the film. You agreed to do it, didn't you?
The script didn't really change after I gave it
to her. Okay, sure, maybe I added like three
more sex scenes. But they had to be in there.
We needed to give it a little more levity, and
you can only put in so many jokes in a movie

about slavery and the Holocaust. So next to laughter, what makes people feel the best? Sex! And again, she agreed to everything. Basically what I think happened with Alicia is that everyone started getting fucking chickenshit, and she followed the pack. Just like a fucking actress. Not an original thought in her goddamn head.

STUART SILVERMAN (Producer): I'm not quite sure what any of us were thinking. But whatever it was, it wasn't clear. That's really all I'll say.

JACKIE COHEN: The fact that anyone at all could say that they were a producer on this is unbelievable. Sure, there were useless assholes around that had the title of "producer." But I produced this alone. These assholes just hid in the shadows the whole time to see what was going to happen. To see what "other" people thought before they decided to give a fuck about helping me make the movie in the right way. This was the ultimate film about anti-Semitism and racism and not being able to see the deep similarities between the Holocaust and slavery. Why would you not do everything you possibly could to make sure something this important be made in the right way and be seen by everyone? Why? 'Cause money is the only thing you think about. But the irony is this would have made money. This was *Schindler's List* meets *The Color Purple*. With a whole lotta humor and a bunch of hot sex. What person wouldn't rush to see that? Who wouldn't want to see some positive imagery in their brains to associate with those traumatic

periods of history? Humor and sex are power,
and I was handing power back to the victims.
Showing the oppressors of then, and especially
of now, that they no longer had us in their
grips. Because what are the two biggest weapons
against oppression? Funny and fucking. The fact
that no one could see that fact is the biggest
tragedy of all. Almost as big of a tragedy as
slavery or the Holocaust. I mean maybe that's a
bit of an exaggeration, but I ask you this: How
do we change the narrative if we don't change
the narrative?

TOM WOLFMAN (Studio Head): I don't know
what you're talking about. I've never heard of
that movie. Please leave me alone.

JACKIE COHEN: One of the things I'm proudest
of with this picture is the humor. No one
had ever really done that before. Okay, yeah,
Roberto Benigni with *Life Is Beautiful*, but his
character was so corny and "sweet." So weak. My
character was tough as shit. He was a fucking
badass and he was a FUNNY fucking badass. He'd
make fun of the Nazi guards and then kick their
asses. And then he meets this woman from a
completely different world and he sweeps her
off her feet, even though he's skinny as fuck
and stinks like shit, but he's still able to
get this super-hot woman. 'Cause even though
she's a slave, she still has great taste in
men. That was one of the important things in
the script. It was just as important to show
that in addition to being super oppressed these
two characters were also super hot and even
more importantly: super hot for each other. And

she was a real quick wit, too. She wasn't an idiot. You don't need a formal education to be smart. I mean, I never paid attention to one single thing in school, and my IQ is through the roof. I wanted to show all oppressed people that even if you were oppressed you could still be super fucking smart and super fucking hot. I mean, these people are weak. Physically, I mean. They've been starved and beaten, but they can still match wits with the best of 'em, and fuck like gods. And that's really what gets them through. Other than the true love that they have for each other, of course.

JERRY YURMAN (Executive Producer): That was a dark time for me. I was in a complete blackout state, so I can't really comment on anything I or anyone else did or allowed, because I just don't remember.

JACKIE COHEN: I had to pick up the slack for everyone on the movie because there was a lot of pills going on. Mostly Xanax. It was a fucking CVS on set. And every time I confronted any of these amateurs, they claimed they were being prescribed it due to panic attacks caused by the movie and by working with me, because I was supposedly "off my rocker" and "very abusive." Fucking junkies. They'll make up anything to justify their using. They also love to band together to make up one story to give the rationalization even more validity. Fuckin' drugs, man. Believe me, I've been there. But NEVER when I was working. And that's something they all still need to apologize to ME for, rather than demanding that I apologize

to THEM for "creating a toxic environment"
that triggered their "addictions." Pathetic.
Take some accountability, for Christ's sake.
Stop lookin' for fall guys for your fuckups.
Isn't that the first thing they teach you in AA
or NA or whatever the fuck? I remember they'd
all just be staring at me. Zonked out of their
gourds. I'd look in their eyes and it was like
I was looking at a bunch of fucking zombies.
They could have come to me for help. We could
have all been there for each other. But instead
they just went through the looking glass, and
didn't look back until the film was finished and
they realized all of these fingers were being
pointed. Cowards through and through.

LESLIE ACKERMAN (Co-Producer): Not sure
what you're talking about. I think you have the
wrong person.

JACKIE COHEN: I thought this was really
going to be my most major achievement. I'm not
just talking awards. I'm talking about much
more than that. I've always been loved. But
this movie was going to make me a cultural hero.
And I was ready to take that role on. More than
ready. I know this might sound arrogant, maybe
even delusional, but the world needed me in
that role. 'Cause I was gonna come at it with
no frills. Most so-called activists make you
feel guilty. Guilty that you're not like them.
Not me. I was going to make everyone excited to
be a better person. I was going to make people
be better people without them even realizing
that that's what they were doing. But what I'm

realizing now is that everyone else had to be ready to take on that role, too. But no one was. Instead of standing, they all sat down and covered their eyes and ears. Ostrich people.

EMMA SWANSON (Cinematographer): This was my last job. I quit the business after this. I realized that nothing could ever be good again. That I would never get the things I had seen out of my head. It's strange. As we were filming all of these scenes at a death camp and a plantation, I almost felt as if I was a Nazi or an overseer. I felt like the deepest form of subhuman. And I truly didn't see what any of this was for. I hit a wall. Why make anything? Why do anything that isn't directly helping people, and if you don't have the capacity for that, which I don't, better to just do nothing. I guess you could call me a recluse now. I go months without talking or seeing anyone, but I think that's a good thing. Better that than infecting anyone with the sickness that is in me. And there is a sickness or I would have never agreed to do that movie, or shoot any of the things that I was paid to shoot. I'm so grateful it was shelved, so I was able to make this decision to drop out more of my own volition rather than be forced to live this way, which would definitely have happened if the movie was released. I can't wait till I die. And when I do, I hope I'm alone and no one cares.

JACKIE COHEN: One of my greatest gifts is always being able to see when I'm clearly right and when I'm clearly wrong. And when the movie

got shelved and all these fucks tried to sue me
for emotional distress I really took some time
to reflect on the whole thing and what I could
have done differently. I'm being totally honest
when I say this without any denial whatsoever:
I did nothing wrong. I made a special movie
from a special place in my heart and I stand by
that more than I've ever stood by anything.

15.

Mamamorphosis

 ackie woke up to discover he had transformed into his mother.

He immediately knew that something was "off." First of all, unlike most mornings, he didn't feel the remnants of what he had drank, smoked, or popped the night before. All he felt was a sense of panic. Yes, in addition to the hangover, he usually woke up with a sense of panic, but this panic was different. Different, yet not foreign. He knew this panic from somewhere. He had spent time with this panic. He had grown up witnessing this panic. This panic . . . this was someone else's.

Jackie's body felt different. As he ran his hands down his chest he felt a pair of giant breasts. In addition, all of his chest hair was gone, as was his armpit hair. Then, as his hands continued to explore, he discovered the most horrific thing of all. He had no penis. He had a vagina. A vagina that was surrounded by so much gray pubic hair he wondered if his penis had just gotten lost in it.

He jumped up and ran into the bathroom. Upon gazing at his reflection he screamed so loud it set off a car alarm outside. For it was not his reflection. It was HERS!!!

How could this be? What would he do? Did his mother put a spell on him? Maybe that was it. Maybe her quest to keep him near her at all times was so obsessive that she had taken up the dark arts and found that the most surefire way to keep him close would be to change him into her.

Jackie had to eat. He figured if he ate, it might make him a little more centered, so he could figure out what to do. He went to Eggsellent for brunch and was going to order his usual egg-and-cheese sandwich with a side of hash browns and a small salad, when all of a sudden he got the penetrating thought that eating such a meal would be just too unhealthy, and, on top of that, it would make him bloated beyond belief. He decided to get a spinach and mushroom egg-white omelet with some bread and a side salad instead. His mother's favorite. The only breakfast dish she ever ordered. The waiter walked up and as Jackie placed the order, he asked the waiter to make sure that the eggs used in his omelet were not too eggy tasting. The waiter didn't quite know what Jackie meant. Jackie tried to explain:

"Just sometimes eggs taste too eggy. You know that eggy taste. It's like a smell but in a taste. So tell the chef to make sure my eggs are not on the eggy side. Otherwise I'll have to send it back."

The waiter looked back at him with hatred. It was a foreign but familiar glare to Jackie. Foreign in that no member of the service industry had ever looked at him like that (or at least not that he had noticed). Familiar that he had seen his mother get looked at by waiters like that almost every time they went out to eat. And he tried to stop the annoying words from coming out of his mouth but he couldn't.

Sure enough, Jackie did send the eggs back. Three times. He also sent back the bread six times because it wasn't the "perfect brown." He sent back the green salad, too, on account of when he ordered the vinaigrette dressing he had no idea it would have vinegar in it. Jackie also made the waiter prove the orange juice was fresh squeezed by forcing them to bring the juicer out to the table and then juicing it in front of him. He then sent the juice back, because it had some pulp in it. "Even a tiny piece of pulp is too much pulp."

Jackie tried to gain some sort of self-control. But he just couldn't stop, and when he tried to explain himself all he did was make things worse, as he held the waiter hostage.

"I don't feel well. I can't really get into it because you'll think I'm crazy, but I do not feel good at all. I woke up this morning and I'm just not myself. Literally. But I can't tell you what I mean by that, because the minute I do you'll get right on the phone with the nearest mental institution. Trust me. I usually don't do this.

Share my problems like this, but if you knew what was happening to me, it would all make perfect sense to you. But, again, I can't tell you. You will really think I'm crazy. That's if you don't think so already, which I wouldn't be surprised if you did. Would you believe that if I really was myself today you'd recognize me as one of your favorite customers? You'd probably realize you were a fan of mine. But, again, I just can't explain what I mean by that. I really can't. Is the heat on?"

After stiffing the waiter, Jackie left the restaurant and started walking. Maybe he could walk this off. He hadn't been exercising enough lately. Maybe this "condition" had something to do with that. Maybe if he put a certain amount of steps in, he'd all of a sudden take a step and with that step it'd all go back to how it was. He'd be himself again.

Jackie walked and walked. People smiled at him. *Well, that's nice at least*, thought Jackie. *At least people still respect their elders.* Though he had not gone on many walks with his mother as of late, he imagined this was how people looked at her. One would have assumed this thought would have made him feel better, but it didn't. His walking slowed. He felt out of breath. Not from the walking, but the worrying. Worrying that penetrated past and future lives. He couldn't take it. What was he going to do? He had to do something.

He drove to Tarzana and rang the doorbell of his childhood home. Her voice, that was now also his voice, answered from behind the door.

"Who is it?"

"Mom, it's me," said Jackie.

"Me who?" asked his mom.

"It's Jackie."

"Jackie? You don't sound like Jackie."

"I know."

143.

"You sound like someone I know, though. Who are you really?"

Jackie started to grasp at his chest. "I'm telling you, Mom, it's Jackie, now please open the door before I have a heart attack."

Jackie's mother gave a sigh. "God forbid. Okay, hold on. You better not be a killer."

With that, Jackie's mother opened the door, and within one second of looking into her own face she was unconscious. Jackie panicked. It wasn't his kind of panic. It was hers. A panic that he had never felt to such a severe degree, as severe as his own panics were. He thought, *My mom has to have the strongest constitution in the world. If I experienced this much stress every day, I'd be dead.* Was she dead? He lightly tapped his mother's face with the palm of his hand. It didn't take long before she came to, and as soon as she got her bearings she started screaming.

"What the hell is going on? Who the hell are you? Why do you look like me?"

Jackie gently restrained her. "Mom! It's me, Jackie. Something happened. I'm not sure what but I woke up this morning like this."

Now she was really upset. "Why didn't you call me before you came? You could have at least given me a warning."

"I don't know. I was confused."

She threw her hands in the air. "So you come to my house looking like me without a warning?"

With this, Jackie started to cry. "Why are you talking to me like this right now? This is no way for a mother to talk to her son."

Now Jackie's mother was crying, too. "This is no way to treat a mother with a potential heart condition."

"You don't have a heart condition."

"I said *potential*. When you get to be my age everything is potential."

Jackie started begging. "Well, help me. Please help me."

Jackie's mother mirrored his begging. "Me help you? You help me!"

"I can't believe you."

"I can't believe YOU!"

They went on and on like this for about forty-five minutes until they both calmed down enough to talk some of it through.

His mother handed Jackie a glass of cream soda. "So you woke up like this?"

Jackie sipped with some relief. "Yes," he said.

"Did you do drugs last night? I know some of the drugs you do. Maybe this is some sort of reaction."

"I didn't do drugs last night. And if I did, none of the drugs I do have side effects that involve me turning into my mother."

"Well, I don't know, then. Maybe something bit you?"

"What kind of a bug does this?"

"There's all kinds of spiders. Who knows what they do."

Jackie then shuddered in fear. "Don't talk to me about spiders."

"Since when are you afraid of spiders?"

"Well, you're afraid of spiders."

"Of course I am. They're disgusting."

With this Jackie and his mother started to cry. Jackie's head dropped between his knees.

"I can't believe that after all I've been through I have to go through something like this. I'm cursed, I know it. Someone put a curse on me."

"This is my fault. We've got bad luck in our blood. We're cursed."

"Don't say that! We're not cursed."

"Okay, what are we?"

"What are we?"

"What are we if not cursed?"

"I don't know."

"I don't know, either."

"I don't know what I know?"

"Wait, who are you? Are you Jackie or am I Jackie?"

"Oh no. You know what? I don't remember."

They'd really done it this time. Jackie and his mother were both so completely panic-stricken and disoriented that they'd completely lost track of who was who.

They started to trace back their steps from the last few minutes in a feverishly obsessive way. Maybe if they did this they'd be able to track who was who. But there was no doing. They were both too messed up. Then one of them got very quiet. Their eyes widened. They were clearly having an earth-shaking realization.

"Maybe there is no Jackie anymore. Maybe there's just two of us now. Maybe Jackie is dead."

"Don't say that! God forbid! Jackie's not dead. Jackie can't be dead. How could he be dead? What? Like we killed him? We couldn't do something like that! Oh my God, do you think we killed Jackie?"

"I don't know, but . . . I think . . . yeah. . . . yeah, I think we did. We killed our Jackie."

With this the ladies started to sob. The kind of sobbing that seemed like it would never end. An eternal sobbing. The ladies lay on the floor. They stared at the ceiling as they wailed like dying cats. They couldn't bear to look in the other's direction. They lay there for what must have been three hours, after which the weeping still had not stopped. When it finally did, they turned their heads to the side to look at each other.

"There's no way to go on, is there?" asked Jackie or Jackie's mom.

"How can we? Our son is gone and it's our doing."

"There's only one thing that we can do to end this, and that's . . . end it."

"I couldn't agree more."

With that the two moms went into their garage and climbed aboard their Mercedes SUV. They then kissed each other on the lips and joined hands as they pushed the button to start the ignition. As the carbon dioxide lullabied them to sleep, they sang one of Jackie's favorite songs, "Human Nature" by Michael Jackson, choosing to ignore the problematic nature of singing one of his songs. They didn't care what the King of Pop had done. It couldn't have been worse than what they had done. But now all would be right. All would be balanced. An eye for an eye. And as they sang the fallen icon's song, they smiled. They would be back with their Jackie soon, and he hopefully wouldn't be angry at them for killing him, after he found out that they'd rushed so fast to his side. They would die as they had lived: great goddamn mothers.

Jackie or his mom looked toward the roof of the car. "Sorry we're not bringing anything for you to eat, Jackie. But I'm sure they got plenty of nash in heaven." Their eyelids slid down over their eyes. And that was it.

Jackie woke up screaming. His bedsheets soaked from his sweat, no doubt from the nightmare, but probably also partially from the burrito he'd had just before bed.

His phone was ringing.

He'd forgotten to put it on airplane mode.

It was his mother.

He declined the call.

16

Canceled Dinner

ackie was eating by himself in a very popular Los Angeles restaurant.

It was the type of restaurant that wouldn't want this story written about it. The type of restaurant that bestowed extreme loyalty upon its patrons, its "family." One had to admire the loyalty. If you reached a certain status, you retained that status in the restaurant's eyes no matter if you retained your fame and influence or had fallen from grace years ago. The only thing that would instigate a regular being shunned is if they shot one of the waiters, and even that wasn't a given.

Jackie ate at this restaurant several days a week. He liked the idea of only eating at a few places regularly. It had an older-world quality to it. Not like these assholes who needed to eat at the newest hot spot so they could seem "in the know." Jackie liked to have a place or two to hold regular court. It was a powerful look. You were assured a good table. Most of all, it was in no way lonely or sad if you ate alone. If you held a regular table you were never really eating alone. You were eating with the whole restaurant. You were eating with family.

Jackie was enjoying a delicious plate of shrimp and linguine, one of his go-to dishes. To Jackie, there was never so elegant a combination of olive oil, garlic, and white wine. To Jackie, there was no one who understood al dente in Los Angeles the way his home away from home did. Maurice the waiter, a vaguely European man, maybe from France, maybe from Eastern Europe, checked on Jackie often, but not too much. Maurice knew the exact line not to cross in order to avoid being characterized as high maintenance.

"How is the linguine tasting tonight, Mr. Cohen?"

The same question every time, and Jackie loved giving the same answer. Upon being asked, he'd orgasmically roll his eyes, pucker his lips, and gently kiss his fingertips.

"Why, Maurice, it gets better with every bite."

Most nights he was able to enjoy the dish without guilt, but this wasn't one of those nights. Jackie knew he should not be eating pasta. His doctor had told him to stay away from carbs altogether. He had to lose weight. Not that he was massively overweight, but he was maybe the fattest he'd ever been despite the fact that he was lifting weights somewhat regularly. However, this was mostly being done for his upper body (chest, arms, shoulders, etc.) and did very little to attack his gut. And the gut is where all the disease is held. That's where the impending heart disease, diabetes, and fatty liver disease were waiting to get to work at killing his fat ass early.

However, it wasn't like there was cheese or red meat involved in a plate of linguine and shrimp. Or even fried food, for that matter. He couldn't remember if shellfish was still thought to have high cholesterol or not, but he had specifically asked Dr. Silvershein if shrimp was okay, and gotten a completely straightforward yes.

One thing was for sure. The pasta was not a good choice. Not a good choice at all. But what was done was done. He had had a stressful week. Three deals had fallen through and he'd had a terrible meeting with a director wherein the director thought it was a good idea to critique some of Jackie's actor habits. This was a commentary Jackie in no way asked for, and anyone who knew Jackie in the slightest knew he'd rather be vomited on than critiqued.

He'd thought the comfort of the pasta would make him feel better, but, of course, it didn't. It made him feel even more like shit. It would have been better to just get some branzino and their arugula salad (hold the pecorino, of course). But he didn't. He didn't, so now the only answer was to begin tomorrow with gusto. With a true dietary focus on living longer. He was actually not even in the danger zone. Not yet. Dr. Silvershein was all about preventative medicine. This was a matter of making sure the light did not go from yellow to orange, but instead went back down to green, where it would hopefully stay for the rest of Jackie Cohen's especially long, happy, and healthy life.

Jackie was tired. Very tired. The stress and overeating wiped him out. And the fact that he was wiped out just from some pasta and some good old neurosis only increased his spiral. He was not at his best. He needed to go home. Sit on his Bellini sofa. Smoke a joint. Forget about the linguine. But first he needed to piss. So Jackie Cohen made his way to the men's room.

As he walked past the tables, he felt eyes on him. He always liked that. He was grateful for it. He wondered how many of the stares belonged to beautiful women. He thought that maybe his evening was about to change. Instead of smoking a joint and falling asleep to an old episode of *Miami Vice*, maybe Jackie might be smoking a joint and shtupping a twenty-five-year-old model/actress/singer/songwriter/activist.

Jackie entered the bathroom. It was empty. He'd half hoped someone would be in there who would help him distract himself from his linguine shame so that he'd be able to reenter the dining room in confidence and seal the deal on whatever vixen was hopefully about to throw herself at him. But an empty bathroom was probably better. Any sort of social interaction could have thrown him into an even deeper spiral even more than his current thoughts, especially if that interaction was being had with someone who knew him. Even worse if they were a fan. Fans in bathrooms have no sense of boundaries. But he was alone. He pissed in solitude. His piss made him feel better. One of those pisses that pisses out the day.

He then washed his hands, forgetting, just as he forgot every time he washed his hands at this restaurant, that the hot water was scalding. He yanked his hands away with a muffled yell.

Jackie now was keyed up even more. He was worried that something was wrong with his memory. *How the fuck do I forget every time that the goddamn water here burns the shit out of my hands???!!!* Was this "lack of memory" because of his past hard-drinking days? Was this because of his current weed-smoking regimen? Was it from cracking his head open on the bottom of his cousin's pool when he was twelve? It didn't make sense that he'd forget when his memory functioned on such a high level with so many other things. Jackie could still memorize a multi-page monologue as quickly as reciting the alphabet. But why, then? Had something happened in this bathroom in the past that he had blocked out, that was now causing him to disassociate? Was the monotonous repetition of coming to this same restaurant making him go into some kind of shut-down mode? Regardless of the answers to any of these questions, Jackie was now in the midst of an even greater panic.

He walked hurriedly back toward his table, looking to flag down Maurice on the way so he could pay the check and get the fuck out of there. Jackie had started to almost reach a jog, when a hand reached out and grabbed him.

"Where you going, Jackie?"

Jackie looked down, and he couldn't believe his eyes. He didn't want to believe his eyes. His eyes were looking at the last person he wanted to see. The hand that was gripping Jackie's arm was the last hand he wanted grabbing him. The hand belonged to one of the three most hated men in all of Hollywood, and sitting at the table with him were the other two.

Jackie was amazed—he knew that the restaurant was loyal to its customers, but how could it still let these three men in? It had to be the only restaurant that was still doing so. Why these three men would be willing to be in public also dumbfounded Jackie.

They were ignoring the very real possibility of other patrons physically attacking them. These men were the garbage of the garbage. Despised. Not just bad guys. The REALLY BAD guys. Jackie had thought that two of them were in prison. These men had had more power over the industry than anyone could ever have imagined. These men broke boundaries in entertainment most people didn't even know existed. These men changed how movies and TV were made. These men were rapists.

Harry Weingarten, Calvin Steinberg, and Max Laberten all sat in their seats with wide, menacing grins. The hand gripping Jackie was Harry's. A large meat mitt.

"Where you going, Jackie?" asked Harry. "You gonna just pass our table like we don't exist?"

Jackie didn't know what to say. He couldn't believe his eyes, plus his burned hands were pulsating.

"I didn't see you guys."

If these men had the capacity to laugh they would have done so. Instead they just looked at each other with suspicion. Harry then released his paw from Jackie's arm and used it to indicate the open chair at their table.

"Have a seat with your old friends, huh?"

If Jackie had had more of his wits about him, he would have continued walking. Brushed them off with a smile. He would have gotten the hell out of there as fast as he could. There was nothing these guys could do to him now. It didn't matter if he offended them. Offending them was like offending a corpse, and these men would have no ghosts to haunt anyone. Even their ghosts had been killed. But Jackie was caught too much by surprise, and before he knew it, he had sat himself down in the chair.

Harry, Calvin, and Max all stared at him. Jackie had no idea what to say. There was a part of him that just wanted to tear them apart for thinking they had the right to talk to him. That they would be so careless and selfish as to drag him into their filthy spotlight, and make him look like a conspirator, or a sympathizer, or, worse, a fellow sexual predator. Then again, one couldn't really expect rapists to be skilled at thinking of others before themselves.

He now had a closer look at the three guys. They all looked way worse than when he had last seen them. They all seemed to have aged by fifteen years. You've seen the degradation of a president's looks before and after they leave office. These guys were certainly at the end of their second term. Their skin was gray with yellow patches. The circles under their eyes were darker than the restaurant's lighting. They could all take their leftover food to go in the bags under their eyes. There also seemed to be a smell. Jackie couldn't tell if his nose was maybe making this smell up, if the horrific sight of these monsters was telling his brain that there had to also be a smell. But Jackie smelled the faint scent of rot. Bad breath. Extreme dehydration.

Calvin Steinberg leaned forward. "How are you, Jackie?"

Jackie put on the fakest grin he could muster. "Oh, me? I'm good. I'm doing just fine . . . How are you guys?"

The disgraced three all looked at each other again. Max Laberten rubbed his temples. "How do you think we are, Jackie? We're terrible."

Harry slammed the table with his palm. "Everyone's turned against us. People whose calls I used to not take are now not taking my calls."

Calvin Steinberg wiped the crust out of his eyes. "We're facing jail time, Jackie. Prison. And not fucking Martha Stewart prison. Real prison."

Jackie shook his head as his stomach started to really turn. "Surreal. It must just be surreal."

Max took a sip of his martini. "Where is the fucking fairness here?"

Harry shifted in his chair. "These women. They all saw their chance and they took it. You almost have to admire the hustle. They jumped on the victim bandwagon, and twisted some meaningless messing around into something sinister."

Calvin mopped the sweat on his forehead. "You know the other day I was kicked out of a grocery store? A grocery store! I don't even think that's legal. Isn't that illegal?"

Harry played with his fork. "All of these bitches should be the ones behind bars, not us. You work your life for something, then some jealous woman decides to destroy you, just 'cause after you shtupped her you didn't fall in love."

Jackie again shook his head. "I know. I know . . . it's the times we live in. The Supreme Court of public opinion."

What the fuck am I saying? Why am I still here? thought Jackie. He started to really panic. He started to really go inward. He thought about how his hands were not necessarily the cleanest. That there were definitely bad things he had done in his life, too. Nowhere near the level that these scumbags had, but he was by no means any type of angel. He then started to wonder how many things he had done that were unforgivable and disgusting that he wasn't even aware of. Maybe he was just like these guys. Maybe these guys really didn't have any sort of sense of what they did wrong. Maybe to them the ninety-six women who had accused them were just liars. Maybe these pricks really believed that they were the victims after all. Fuck, how crazy is that? But maybe he was also that crazy. He started racing through his past. Every encounter. Every word said. Every gesture. Every fuck. What was the nature? What were their feelings the minute they left his sight? Pretty much all of them still talked to him, unless he was the one who cut off communication. Those were just the crazy ones. Of course the crazy ones could lie, but he had his truth. He would fight tooth and nail for his side, and he'd win, because his conscience would be clear. He'd blaze a trail of integrity and responsibility. He wasn't like these guys. They weren't even the same species. These were dirt people. Not even dirt. Something far filthier. Too filthy to be described. And Jackie would not be lumped with them. And if he was going to be seen with them as he was most certainly being seen in this very moment, it would be on his terms. Not theirs.

With this Jackie shot up from the table. Harry, Calvin, and Max looked at each other. Jackie slammed his newly burned fist on the table and pointed his finger from the other burnt hand right at their disgusting mugs. With the next words he said, Jackie made sure to raise his volume to its maximum level. And Jackie at his quietest was louder than anyone else at their loudest. It sounded as if he was sitting next to every single person in the restaurant.

"All right, let's get something straight. I stopped here to talk to you people for one reason and one reason only. And that's to tell you that you have no business being here. Here as in this restaurant. Here as in this city. Here as in public at all. You only deserve the deepest darkest hole in the earth in which you hopefully will experience even just a fraction of the pain you've inflicted on the women you've heartlessly abused. And in that pain I hope you will see how you could have been different. How you could have been a different person your whole life who would have avoided becoming the person that you are. No one will mourn you when you die. So good luck. God forgive you, and GodDAMN YOU!!!!"

Jackie walked away. As he strolled back to his table, again looking for Maurice to get his check, he was met with an eruption of huge applause and cheers. Jackie stopped, faced his army of dining fans, and raised a charred fist of solidarity in the air.

In the midst of the applause, Maurice discreetly made his way to the table of the disgraced three.

"Gentlemen, my deepest apologies. But you are to vacate the premises immediately."

Harry Weingarten gave the last smile he would ever smile again in public. "Really, Maurice? What a fucking surprise."

17.

The Apology

"I wish everyone would just shut the fuck up.

When did everyone decide to start acting like their mommies just stopped breastfeeding them? News flash: you're an adult and the first thing you learn about being an adult is that life is hard for everybody. And yes, it's hard even if you're white. Even if you're straight. Even if you were born a man and stay a man. Even if you're rich! Life is hard. So do me a favor, all you supposed 'victims,' stop flooding my eyes and ears with your whiny crybaby bullshit. Suck it up. We're all gonna die someday."

These were the words. These were the words that had been playing, on repeat, in Jackie's mind for days. These were the words that he had used publicly to a paparazzo as he was coming out of the Chateau Marmont, when he was asked how he, as a comedian and actor, feels about "cancel culture."

Jackie was already agitated. A model he'd been hitting on all night, and who was very much reciprocating his flirtations, had failed to mention she had a serious boyfriend who also happened to be a seriously famous basketball player, who, of course, also happened to be seriously tall. Upon walking in on Jackie flirting with his girlfriend, the basketball player promptly threatened Jackie that if he didn't stop such flirtation, good and fast, he'd promptly find himself watching his own head be dunked in his very own ass.

Jackie did not bother to question the physics of this. Besides being scared and offended, he was pretty unimpressed. Unimpressed that a basketball player would make a basketball analogy to threaten him. Pretty lazy, if he said so himself. Which of course he did not say so out loud, because he did very much believe his own head being dunked in his own ass, despite his critique of the comment, was a distinct possibility.

So Jackie left. And Jackie was furious. And Jackie was embarrassed. And when the paparazzo asked Jackie that annoying question, he channeled that fury and that embarrassment toward the unoriginal basketball player and his Venus flytrap model girl-friend into his answer to that very cliché and all-too-often-asked question, which, after it was seen on millions of different web-sites and posts and memes, achieved doing to Jackie, metaphori-cally, what the basketball player did not have the chance to do. Jackie had, essentially, dunked his own head in his own ass.

Funny—at the time when he said it, it all seemed to make perfect sense. Now? Well, now was a different story. As Jackie ran the words through his head, they certainly no longer made per-fect sense. At best, they made a solid half sense. And these words were running their loop. And now, at this moment, this loop was at its loudest. Screaming in his head as he waited behind the cur-tain. The curtain that was the only thing standing between him and redemption.

On the other side of the curtain Jackie could hear the voice of his old friend Dianne Blum. Host of *The Daily Dianne*, the most popular daytime talk show on the air. Jackie and Dianne had come up in the clubs together, and it comforted Jackie to see that loyalty was not completely dead in this day and age. Anyway, she owed him. He was right by her side when her husband, Raymond Blum, had taken his own life, and had sent a very damning sui-cide note to the press that stated it was all because of Dianne, and her tireless dishing out of mental and emotional abuse. Shortly after the suicide, several of her employees also stepped forward, issuing reports of Dianne demanding an "I Say Whatever I Want Day" every Thursday. Which would encompass her walking up and down the office screaming at everyone from her writers to the janitors, attacking everything about them that was not like her.

Luckily for Dianne, she was America's morning deity. Amer-ica's trust of her ran deeper than her hatred of them. America believed her when she blamed the whole thing on a complete mental breakdown. America bought it, because they had to buy it. There was no one to replace her yet.

But Jackie was replaceable. He was all too replaceable. And as much as he repeated to himself throughout the day that he wasn't, down deep he knew that at any moment he could be erased and forgotten. He'd be one of those disgraced people who someone, doing much much better than him, would invite to a birthday party. The birthday person would post a picture of him. And even though he had caused so many problems, when the general public looked at this birthday-party picture, there would be no anger. Only sadness. Sadness for the people who knew who he was. But most of them probably wouldn't know. And, what's more, they probably wouldn't try to find out. He'd just be old, and fat, and dying.

But it would soon all be all right. As soon as he got out there, Dianne would handsomely repay him in star-studded support. She'd give him the lift he needed. He'd take the ball and run it all the way to the goal line. Was it a goal line? Jackie couldn't re-member. He wasn't the biggest sports fan. Something he wore as a badge of honor these days to prove he wasn't the toxic male all these social media kvetches claimed he was. As he waited for his name to be called he could feel the legs of his pants brushing his leg hair ever so slightly against the grain. This gave him goose bumps along his back. And the goose bumps made his scalp start to sweat. And as his scalp oiled, Dianne started the ball rolling.

"Ladies and gentlemen. I have a friend waiting to come out here. A very old friend. A friend who, like all of us, has made some mistakes in his life. Remember that word? 'Mistake'? It's that thing we used to do that we apologized for and when we made one it didn't always mean that our lives and careers were completely over. It's that thing that's expected of us, because, why? Because we are human beings. And last time I checked, most human beings are not saints. Hey, even most of the saints made their fair share of mistakes, am I right? Even though it's not the latest fashion, because I care about this man, because he is my friend, I am going to bring him out here because ultimately, I know he is a good person. I am going to bring him out to apologize. People, let's welcome my great friend: Jackie Cohen."

The curtain separated. The lights blinded him. It was like he had forgotten how bright the lights would be. Like all of this was new to him. The lights were shining on him in a way they never had before. They were exposing him. He momentarily wondered if anyone watching could see through his clothes to his body. Through his skin to his bones. He felt a small nervous fart sneak out. Luckily he was far away from Dianne. The last thing Jackie needed was to be smelling like shit as he hugged his savior on national television.

As they hugged she whispered in his ear, "Make them remember how much they love you." This sent shivers through Jackie's body. Both making him a little more nervous than he already was and also, ever so slightly, turned on. They sat down.

"Jackie! My old dear friend. How are you?"

Jackie didn't waste any time. "How am I, Dianne? Well, looks like I'm pretty stupid."

The crowd laughed. Things were off to a great start. It'd all be gravy from here on out. Jackie had them, and once he had them he knew how to not let them go. The tension in his chest lightened as he casually crossed his legs.

Dianne echoed the crowd's laughter, then looked at the camera. "Well, I know how that feels."

The crowd erupted into even more laughter and some applause. Jackie was overjoyed. Only thirty seconds in and it seemed like he had already been vindicated. All thanks to Dianne. It felt like they were back at the Comedy Hut bar after the show. One-upping each other into the wee hours of the morning. This was no longer a plea for innocence. This would be a routine. A moment of comedy that would be remembered for the ages. Jackie could now safely sharpen his knives and cut into the jokes. He raised his *Daily Dianne* mug.

"Well, in your defense, Dianne, you weren't stupid, you were crazy."

The room stopped. The audience's energy stuttered. Dianne paused. Jackie started to sweat. Why did he say that? Why did he think that would be a thing to say to the woman who was currently saving his life? He thought it would be funny. That he could speak freely like he always had. That he could throw a jab at her and they could joyfully relate to each other's imperfections. It clearly wasn't funny, though. No. But Dianne took mercy on him. As she came out of the momentary deep pondering of what actually had just been said to her on her very own show. She decided to just shake it off. "I mean . . . you're not wrong, Jackie. Is he, folks?"

Jackie didn't know how to proceed. It was not in his nature to retreat from discomfort. If he backed down now, it'd surely look weak. The only way out would be to actually, just for now, lean into it.

"I mean, you had a nervous breakdown."

At this the audience went even more silent than before. Dianne's eyes squinted. "Yes, that's true, Jackie." Okay, so leaning into it obviously didn't work. He should have gone the other way, and that's what he would do now. Hopefully it wasn't too late.

"But who wouldn't." Jackie gave a wide, nervous smile.

Dianne cocked her head. She looked into his soul as if she was asking it why it had been born in the first place. Jackie kept retreating.

"Well, now I'm feeling even stupider."

At this the audience gave a light chuckle. Dianne's face loosened. She then playfully slapped his knee. "Well, who wouldn't." The audience roared. Jackie started breathing again. The queen had shown him mercy.

"It's true, Dianne. You know, like any of us, I'm not always the best at thinking before I speak."

"Especially in front of the camera," said Dianne. The audience laughed even harder.

Well, now that was a bit uncalled-for? Jackie thought. I'm supposed to be the one taking the piss out of me, not her. I get her doing it before 'cause I went too far, but hey, I backtracked and made myself look like the putz, and that should have been it. It's clearly time to start building me up again, and instead she gives me another knock? I'm not perfect, but I'm also not a schmuck, either. And I'm definitely not anyone else's schmuck. Jackie reminded his friend just who she was talking to.

"Well, I did pretty good when I spoke out on your behalf, didn't I?"

Dianne's smile vanished. Her eyes squinted almost to a close. Jackie knew he had started something. But he didn't care. She had made her bed and she had to lie in it. Mad at him or not, he was her guest, and it was time to treat him like that. Dianne started to laugh. It was not a laugh Jackie had seen her laugh before. In fact, to call it a laugh wasn't quite accurate. It looked like a laugh. It sounded like a laugh. But it wasn't a laugh. Whatever it was, it overcame her, and took her off her chair and onto the studio's cherrywood floor.

She kneeled mockingly to him. "And I'm so grateful to you for that, Jackie. As I'm sure America is so grateful that you've decided to take the time out from golfing to come here and beg for their forgiveness."

In the meantime, Irving Liebling, *The Daily Dianne*'s producer, was panicking behind the camera. He knew his star all too well. He had seen this many times before in the hallways, and offices, and bathroom. But never in front of the camera. It had been a while, ever since Dianne had agreed to be on her "best behavior." But no one had challenged her up to this point. No one had tried to make her look bad. No one had brought up what almost destroyed her on the actual show. And Irving knew his star. He knew his star well enough to see that she was about to have a full-on break.

Dianne extended her hand toward the audience. "Start the begging, Jackie. That's what you're here for."

Begging? Who the fuck did she think she was? And what did she think she was doing? She had just as much to lose acting this way as he did. Maybe she needed further memory jogging. With this he stood up and took a couple steps toward the audience. "Hey, all I meant was that people gotta stop whining all the time. I'm sure you can relate to that frustration, Dianne. All those pesky workers of yours, not to mention your kvetch of a late husband. After all, there's nothing more 'complainy' than a suicide note."

This was it. Dianne joined her moronic guest in the standing position. This moment was in fact a gift to Dianne. She had been gifted with freedom. The freedom of not giving one single fuck of what anyone thought about who she really was and what she was about to do.

As loud as the audience's cacophony of boos exploded, they still couldn't drown out Dianne Blum's ferocious roar as she picked up her water-filled coffee cup and smashed it over Jackie's head. Jackie fell flat as two stagehands rushed onto set to hold Dianne back, failing to grab her before she managed to sink her

Chanel flat into Jackie's stomach. Jackie rolled on the floor, gasping for breath as Dianne kicked and screamed violently into the air.

Irving Liebling ordered the cameras to stop taping and the lights to go dark on set. He had the idea that darkness would maybe help the situation. It most certainly did not. Dianne had incredible night vision. Her days of doing theatre paid off, when a director had told her a trick for entering and exiting a pitch-black stage was to close your eyes for a moment to quicken their adjustment to the dark. She broke away from the stagehands, who had not, as of yet, received any such tip. Jackie was still gasping for breath as her legs pinned his arms to the floor and she beat on his face, her wedding ring from her late husband lodging itself in Jackie's forehead and cheeks.

She would have killed him had one of her fans, on their sprint to try and help her, managed to avoid tripping over a cable and flying headfirst into Dianne's left temple, thus knocking both women out.

Jackie caught what little he could of his breath and used every last bit of it to run! Run! Run! As he ran, tears mixed with the blood on his face as he wondered how this could have gotten to where it had so fast. There really were no friends in this business. One could only pretend to be friends. And that would only be if their damage matched yours. In this case, though, Dianne and Jackie's damage was perhaps much too much the same.

As Jackie ran he felt a real sense of loss. Not only from what was absolutely going to be his last time on television, at least for a while. But the loss of Dianne. She was gone. She would never speak to him or, most likely, America ever again. And he had done that. He had made that happen.

As his body smashed into the exit door, audience members were waiting for him. Those who had at first fled from the madness, but then decided to wait for the man who had sinned against their god.

Jackie stopped in his tracks, and through many heaves and gasps muttered the words he wished would have been the only two words he said mere minutes ago.

"I'm sorry."

Iris Below

18.
Condolences

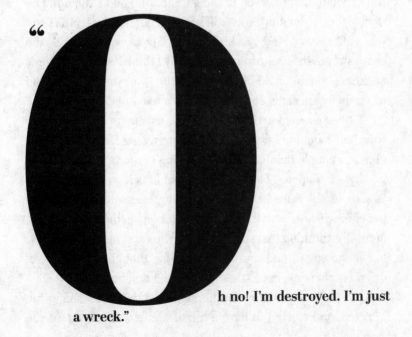

"Oh no! I'm destroyed. I'm just a wreck."

Iris Below sighed to her friend Esther Leiberman over the phone. Only minutes ago, Iris had received the news that her favorite neighbor, Felicia Fingerhut's, daughter, Danielle Fingerhut, had died.

"Esther! She was only thirty-eight. So young. A baby." Iris couldn't believe it. It didn't matter how many times the reality of death was mercilessly shoved in her face. It didn't shake the incomprehensibility of this tragic incident. How could someone so young be taken? It wasn't just that she was taken. It was how she was taken. Suicide. That's right. Iris Below's favorite neighbor, Felicia Fingerhut's, daughter, Danielle Fingerhut, had taken her own life. It had been a long while (but not long enough. It could never be long enough) since Iris had to face a suicide.

In truth, Danielle Fingerhut didn't actually kill herself, "but she meant to and that's the same thing!" Iris Below screeched. "She tried to hang herself in the garage. But, and I shouldn't be saying this, I shouldn't speak ill of the dead, but the truth is she was a little heavy. And by a little heavy, I mean very heavy. So the beam she put the rope around—actually I think it was her father's necktie—couldn't hold her body and the whole beam broke and when the beam came down it gave her a real knock on the head."

Esther listened to the grisly details as she sat on her favorite sofa, half watching her favorite soap opera *Love Hospital* and tugging at a cuticle that had been bothering her for a week now.

Iris continued. "That's right. A real knock on the head. And as soon as she came to her senses—whatever senses there were to begin with—she walked into the kitchen, feeling lightheaded, naturally, thinking that she should maybe eat something to boost her blood sugar, and grabbing what she thought was a bag of dried cranberries, but Esther . . . it wasn't cranberries . . ."

Esther realized her "bothersome" cuticle was somewhat infected, and started to have a minor anxiety attack that if she fussed with it too much it might become a bad infection. Her second cousin Carol once had a strange blood infection from an infected cuticle, and almost died from sepsis, which was the last thing Esther needed right now. However, Esther couldn't just hop off the phone in the middle of her friend's remorseful hysterics. That wouldn't be the right thing to do. And Esther prided herself on always doing the right thing.

Iris pressed on. "Yes, it wasn't a bag of cranberries at all. Danielle couldn't see on account of her head was bleeding into her eyes and grabbed a bag of peanuts, and guess who's deathly allergic to peanuts? She was, that's who!"

Esther's cuticle pain was making her eyes water almost to the point that she couldn't see. But she didn't want to reveal it to Iris. The last thing she'd want is to be high maintenance and make the moment about herself in the midst of her friend's time of grief.

Iris sighed. "That's right. DEATHLY ALLERGIC. Doesn't matter how fat she was. No one could ever call her an elephant. And you know why that is? Because elephants love peanuts, and maybe Danielle would have loved peanuts, too, who knows? But no one will ever know because she was so allergic. She couldn't even have one. And here she put a whole handful in her mouth. Before she even tasted that these peanuts weren't cranberries her throat had closed. That's when Felicia walked in and saw her daughter collapse on the floor, and Felicia, well, I like Felicia very much, I don't know her too well but I like her, but even though I don't really know her, what I do know about her is that she's never been one to deal well with pressure. Those are her words. She sat there as her daughter lay dying, all puffy, in her arms as Danielle used her last breaths to tell Felicia the whole story of what had just happened. As soon as Felicia realized she probably should stop listening to the story and call an ambulance, it was too late.

Again, Felicia doesn't respond well under pressure. Those are her words. To be fair, though, she always said her daughter was an exceptional storyteller. So, I guess, it makes a little bit of sense that Felicia would get sucked into listening to the story, rather than seek medical attention."

Esther didn't even know what she was listening to anymore. The pain from the cuticle was unbearable and had shot up her arm, down the side of her body, and straight into her abdomen. Pins, needles, knives, and the occasional swordlike stabbing. Esther wanted to be a good audience. She valued that quality in herself. Especially (at least up until this point) with Iris, for she knew that her friend did not have a lot of . . . well . . . friends. Iris was alone, and so was Esther, but Esther was more at peace with her solitude. She certainly didn't have the need to start half-assed relationships with neighbors. She was content to be by herself if that's the way it had to be. But in this moment she admitted it would have been nice to have someone there. Someone to help her deal with this godforsaken cuticle. Her body was sweating worse than on her walks, and on her walks Esther sweated buckets.

"I mean Danielle could have waited to tell Felicia the whole story, at least till after Felicia had called an ambulance. At the same time, Felicia could have told her to wait and not just sat there and listened to it."

At this Esther shot out a question. More to test her own ability to still speak, despite the pain, than out of a place of interest. "Iris, how well did you know Danielle Fingerhut? Is this a person that was in your life?"

"Well, let me see . . . I was never officially introduced— something, truth be told, I always thought was strange—but I'd see her in Felicia's driveway, and we'd make eye contact—I think—but I wouldn't wave to her because I don't like to put that on people I've never officially met—you never know if some-

one is in the mood to meet you or not. But, come to think of it,
I did smile, and she didn't really smile back but her eyes kind
of smiled, I think. She certainly didn't have mean eyes. Who
knows . . . maybe if I said something we could have become
friends. I could have shown her a little light no one else in her
life could. Maybe there was nothing to be done, though. Felicia
is certainly a nice lady. Again, I don't know her very well, but we
talk and sometimes she'll come over and have a glass of water.
Not that I don't offer other things, but that's all Felicia ever wants.
She apparently has problems with dehydration."

"What does Felicia do for a living?" Esther asked, as she felt
a deep nausea wash over her.

Iris then took the longest pause she had since she had called
Esther. But it wasn't a long pause. Iris wasn't capable of not talking for very long. It was just the longest pause, compared to the
total lack of pauses that had not occurred leading up to this
pause. "She's a pretty busy lady. I think she's some kind of busi-
nessperson. She's always on the phone. I mean people are always
on their phones, but she is really always on her phone. And it's
not social calls because I can hear her telling people to do things.
She's obviously some kind of boss. Who knows, maybe with how
hard she works she wasn't really there for her daughter. That's
a horrible thing to say, maybe, but how can I not think it? And
really, and I shouldn't be saying this, either, but really what was
Felicia doing with peanuts in the cabinet, to begin with. Even if I
loved peanuts. Even if I couldn't be without them. Even if not having them might kill me, if I knew that they might kill my child.
OUT THEY GO! But Felicia is Felicia. She's hard to figure out.
She's hot and cold. I've been trying to have dinner with her for
months. She only ever wants to have lunch. I want dinner so we
can have some wine. I'm not French. I don't have wine with lunch.
But lunch is all she'll do. Maybe she didn't want dinner because

she wanted to stay home to keep an eye on her daughter. Maybe she thought her daughter was more likely to hurt herself during dinnertime than lunchtime. Maybe she saw this coming. But if she saw it coming I would think she would have hidden the peanuts. That bag of peanuts was the same thing as having a loaded gun in the house."

Esther plucked the cuticle and, in so doing, accidentally ripped off a sizable chunk of skin. The pain should have dissipated with this. There would still be pain due to the loss of skin, but it wouldn't be so great, and would be more concentrated. What was going on? Her body was on fire and on top of that there was blood everywhere.

"Esther, I'm so sad. This has really wrecked me. And wow, you know what I just realized? Oh my God, guess what I just realized, Esther."

Esther's vision began to blur. "What, Iris? What did you just realize?"

"I just realized I don't even know what Danielle's voice sounds like. That makes everything even more upsetting, doesn't it? To not know someone's voice, but know their face and now they're dead? I'll be honest: it was not a nice face, not that she was ugly. No. She wasn't pretty but she wasn't ugly, either. But the face wasn't nice. Poor Felicia. I picture myself in Felicia's situation. I always like to put myself in other people's shoes. It's a little thing I like to do. When I was younger and we learned about the American Revolution, I would think about what it would be like to be Paul Revere. Riding from house to house. Warning everyone. I bet that made him feel good about himself. Not only that he warned everyone but how he warned everyone. 'The British are coming! The British are coming!' Simple, yet poetic, and so true, because the British were coming. He must have been so nervous but also brave. And I think of Paul Revere, and I can put myself in his shoes. I just think, *I'm Paul Revere.* And I feel nervous, and I also feel brave. Why am I talking about this? What's wrong with me, Esther? My neighbor's daughter killed herself by almost hanging and peanut poisoning, and I'm talking about the American Revolution. There's so much death. I know eighteen people who died this year. Well, not personally, but last year I only knew sixteen. Or was it nineteen? Maybe it was more last year. Regardless, that's a lot. Why so much? Maybe it's just getting older and knowing more people? When am I gonna go? Oy, why am I even asking that question? I guess that question's always in the air, isn't it? Death can come any sort of way, at any time. Kind of like gas. Ha. That's funny. That would be a funny condolence card. 'Death is always in the air. Kind of like gas.' I should have been a greeting-card writer. I should have been a lot of things. Not that I'm unhappy with what I am. I love who I am. Plus my son is alive, and that's a big relief. And doing so well. Anyway, since it happened I've been lying to Felicia, and pretending that things are going really badly for me. I don't want her to feel that my life is so much better than hers, even though it is. I want everyone to have a great life. Especially you, Esther. You are just the greatest. By the way, how are you? How are you? Esther? Esther, you still there?"

Esther was there, but also wasn't there. In the midst of Iris's endless story about her favorite neighbor Felicia Fingerhut's daughter Danielle Fingerhut's suicide, one of Iris's only remaining friends Esther Leiberman had a heart attack while on her favorite sofa, with her favorite soap opera *Love Hospital* softly playing in the background.

Esther Leiberman was dead, just like Danielle Fingerhut, and so many more.

19.

My Husband, the Bird

The cardinal was back today. That was the third day in a row.

I don't think I've ever seen any type of bird three straight days in a row before, Iris Below thought. *Maybe a robin or a sparrow. But not a cardinal. Definitely not a cardinal.*

What did a cardinal want with her house? There were plenty of other houses in her neighborhood more suited to birds. Houses with bird feeders and fruit trees. Iris had stopped putting out a bird feeder years ago. There were no seeds or fruit trees to be found. But then again, the cardinal didn't seem to be that interested in eating. All the bird would do was perch on the branch outside Iris's kitchen window. Iris sat at her kitchen table a lot. Not just for eating. She'd drink her coffee there in the morning. And a lot of times, Iris just liked to sit there. There were lots of other windows in her house. Windows she could easily stare out of. Windows she could easily sit at. But she didn't. She was committed to sitting at the kitchen table and looking out of the kitchen window. That's just how it had always been. It was the best view of the yard, really. A very peaceful view. And it was outside this very window this cardinal had been choosing to sit.

The cardinal was the most beautiful one she had ever seen. And what's more, Iris swore the cardinal was looking right at her. She could feel his gaze. He looked upon her in a way she'd never been looked at by a bird before. As he puffed his feathers it seemed like a show for her. Iris looked up the meaning of this feather puffing, and, sure enough, found it was a sign of mating. She felt an all-too-intense energy coming from him. An energy that Iris knew only too well.

Iris then had a thought. Not just a thought. Also a feeling. A thought and feeling that she probably wouldn't tell anyone about. Especially her son, Sam. If she told Sam he'd say she was crazy. She wouldn't tell Sam. She wouldn't tell anyone, but Iris thought and felt that this bird, this beautiful cardinal, was actually her late husband, Menachem. She was certain. I mean, if anyone could tell, she could tell. The cardinal looked at her the very way Menachem had looked at her from the first day to the last. The look he had given her before he said his first hello, to the last look he gave Iris right before the light left his eyes forever. Right before her honey boy left her for good. When he left to end his suffering. To end his pain. To end her pain.

She knew Menachem knew how much she hated seeing him like that. He probably would have stuck around longer if it didn't hurt her seeing him like that so much. Sometimes she wondered if she should have put on more of a face.

"I definitely shouldn't have cried so much around him. That was a dead giveaway."

It made her so mad at herself. She could have smiled more for him. She could have hidden it all. But then again, Menachem could see through anything. That was the thing about him. No fooling Menachem. So he left. In his mind (what was left of it) he probably thought he was giving Iris a break. And maybe he did. It was hard caring for him. Even harder knowing things hadn't always been perfect with them and certain wrongs could never be made right. But maybe that was better. Maybe making wrongs right was too complicated and it was just better to blindly forgive. What was forgiveness but a moving on? Maybe all forgiveness was just an exhaustion. And Iris was tired. So tired.

But these visits from the cardinal had awakened her. Had rejuvenated her. Iris could feel the cardinal wanting her. Not sexually, but something much deeper. A deep need to be with her, to hold her in the warmth of his gaze. Was it really Menachem? Coming to check on her. Making sure she was all right. Making sure that Iris still loved him.

"Well, I do, my honey boy. I do and I always will. How could I not? You were the best. Or maybe you are the best."

Iris giggled. If this cardinal was Menachem, it was quite funny. Funny that he turned into his favorite bird. *Oh yeah. That's right.* Iris had forgotten. Forgotten that until now. The cardinal was Menachem's favorite bird. Made sense. Made sense as he lay on his deathbed, his mind disappearing in front of his wife's very own eyes. Iris crying and making it all even worse. And Menachem, the protector he was, having to do something. He saw all of this, and then maybe an angel came to him. Or a ghost. Maybe his mother, even. And whoever it was told him that he didn't need to worry. He didn't need to hang on anymore. Iris would be fine. Iris would be fine and he'd still be able to see his beloved every day, and to make the whole death deal even sweeter, he'd get to come back as his favorite bird.

That's what Iris hoped had happened. Then again, she didn't know. If he was this cardinal, he probably didn't know that he was going to be a cardinal before he went. If Iris really thought truthfully about Menachem's last moment, she would admit that his face was filled with nothing but fear. Eyes wide. So wide. But then again, his face didn't really move much toward the end. He couldn't really smile or anything. So maybe his eyes all wide like that weren't fearful eyes but the wide eyes of laughter. Maybe he found it funny. So funny. How funny it would be when he would turn into his favorite bird and visit Iris every day.

One day Iris saw the cardinal masturbating. She had seen a bird masturbate before. She knew what it looked like. When he was young, her son had a cockatiel, and it would put one of its feet higher than the other on the bar of its cage and then it would squat on its perch and move its pelvis back and forth. And the cardinal was doing the same exact motion as that cockatiel, and the whole time he didn't stop looking at her. Well, every time the cardinal visited it would never stop looking at Iris. But this time he really didn't stop looking at Iris. And Iris could have sworn the cardinal had the same exact expression that Menachem got when they made love. Like the eyes of a satyr.

She knew that look from anywhere. She wanted to kiss him. But she wouldn't. Even if it was him, what if looking was all he was allowed to do? What if Iris kissed him and he was punished for it? Maybe the pact he had made with God was to just look. And if that pact was broken he'd be taken away. Brought back to heaven. Never allowed to see her ever again.

And if he didn't change. That would surely destroy her. The knowing that he might be nowhere. The knowing he just might be totally gone. Just a memory. The knowing that her loss of him had driven her insane.

But maybe it was worth a try. And as she walked into her backyard, she prayed that if she was able to kiss him and he didn't change, it wouldn't mean that it wasn't him. That it would just mean that's what he was now. Just like she was what she was. And one day maybe she'd be a bird, too.

20.
Iris's
Birthday Lunch

ris Below needed to feel sad.

Sadness got her blood moving, got the synapses in her brain twitching. Sadness was something to talk about, particularly useful since she had no idea what was happening in the world around her. She would even forget who the president was from time to time. It's not that her memory was bad, even though she thought it was. It's just that she was closed off to anything besides her own thoughts. And these thoughts were often very, very sad.

Iris Below was standing in front of her mirror while she practiced her taglines. Taglines that could be used in any conversation at any moment. She loved her taglines. Had she practiced her taglines more regularly she probably would have quoted them more correctly more consistently. Iris knew she should practice her taglines every day, but she didn't and, consequently, often got them wrong. This would then become another thing to be sad about. But there was one tagline that she never forgot no matter how long she went without practicing. This tagline glowed in her mind like the burning sun. Crystal clear like her own name.

"I'm not what I used to be."

She always got that one perfect. But others like:

"You can't teach a dog new tricks."

Or:

"You can't take me anywhere."

Or:

"I wish God would just take me already."

These were often quoted imperfectly and came out in the form of:

"You can't trick a young dog to be an old dog."

Or:

"You can take me somewhere but not here."

Or:

"I wish God took me on a vacation."

These taglines would make her son Sam's head steam. And the forgetting of the tagline would make his head steam even steamier. He couldn't understand how a person could not only repeat such cliché bullshit over and over again, but even more how she could forget that cliché bullshit when she had already repeated it over and over again. Sam worried about his mother. He worried that this forgetting was some form of letting go of life. That it was some slow surrender to death. It worried Sam for his mother, and it also worried him for himself.

Maybe in thirty years I'll do the same bullshit, he thought. That thought kept him up at night.

This was a special day. It was Iris's seventy-fifth birthday and Sam was taking her out to lunch. He had made a reservation at a great new place. A place Iris couldn't remember the name of, even though Sam had repeated it to her at least ten times. Nevertheless, Iris had given up remembering the names to restaurants a long time ago. If it didn't stick, it didn't stick. This also frustrated Sam. Why not know? Why be okay with not knowing? Why welcome a lack of knowing? It drove him crazy. Sometimes he would start to have fantasies of smacking her in the face. Which of course would then make him feel guilty. Which of course would then make him even angrier at her.

Iris waited for her son to pick her up for her birthday lunch. He couldn't have dinner with her because he had a meeting. She didn't really like eating dinner with Sam anymore anyway. He ate too late. And when Iris ate too late she couldn't sleep. So she preferred the lunch. But she would have really preferred a lunch and something extra. A lunch and some shopping maybe. Then she would have gotten some real time with her boy. She was aware that he avoided spending time with her, but she tried not to think those kinds of thoughts because those kinds of thoughts would just lead to more sadness, and that sadness would just make her wish for her own death, and as much as she wished for it, Iris was actually quite scared of death.

"Who knows what happens, and I don't need to know till I know," she uttered to Sam the last time they went to lunch. She immediately recognized after she said this that it was a great tagline. She'd have to remember that one, even though she knew she wouldn't. How could she remember that tagline when she couldn't even remember:

"You can lead a horse to water but you can't make him drink."

She had been trying to say that tagline right all morning but to no avail. She wanted an alternative to saying, "You can't teach an old dog new tricks." Just in case she said that too early in the lunch. Plus, the horse tagline had a little more poetry to it. It was more of a something. She'd try as best she could, but she wasn't confident she'd get any of her taglines right that day. The mirror practice had not gone well, and she knew she was going to drive Sam into a rage. But she'd do her best, and hopefully Sam would have some patience and understanding for once.

Iris's doorbell rang. She opened the door, and there was her son. So handsome. A movie star. He literally was. Well, not quite a movie star. Sam actually was the face of Silk Bottom Toilet Tissue. The toilet paper that was all the rage right now. It had been the rage for a minute, and not just because it was by far the softest. It was because of her Sam, who, in the Silk Bottom Toilet Tissue commercial, played Dr. Jonas Silk: the "mad scientist" who had developed the most perfect formula to create the most perfectly soft toilet paper. Sam's face was everywhere. Billboards, bus stops, and everyone Iris knew and ran into would constantly rave about how hilarious her son was. She was filled with so much pride. She wished the pride she felt meant more of something to him, but it seemed like it was just another thing that annoyed him about her. After all, Sam wasn't that proud of being the face of Silk Bottom Toilet Tissue, but the money was not something to be walked away from. Not at all. And Sam did love telling his mother how much he made. Even though she got on his nerves, it did feel good knowing that she was proud of him.

Iris stretched out her arms, ready to embrace her son.

"Aren't you the sight of my sores!"

Sam closed his eyes. That was one of the things he did when he got annoyed and Iris knew it. She knew all of his little tics. He closed his eyes, doing so with the hope that when he opened them he would be in another place and time where people didn't speak in goddamn taglines. Especially taglines they didn't remember.

"Mom, it's 'Aren't you a sight for sore eyes.' That's the saying."

Iris scratched her head. "It is?"

Sam shook his. "Yeah, Mom."

Iris continued to scratch. "Are you sure?"

Sam closed his eyes again. Iris frowned. "Well, I'm sorry I got it wrong. I'm not what I used to be."

Oh, fuck, Sam thought, *this is going to be a long lunch*.

They got in the car. The whole way there Sam could hear Iris breathing heavily.

"You okay, Mom?"

"Yeah, it's just, you're driving so fast. I mean, 'Where's the burning?'"

This confused Sam. It didn't matter how much time he spent with his mother, she still could completely confuse the shit out of him.

"Where's the burning? What does that mean?"

"You know, when you're going fast and you don't need to, you say, 'Where's the burning?'"

Sam dug his palms into the steering wheel. "Do you mean, 'Where's the fire?'"

"Do I?" asked Iris.

Sam tried to laugh through it. "Yeah, I think you do, Ma."

Iris's eyes glazed over. "Well, then I guess I do. 'There's the fire.'"

Sam started to grind his teeth. "No, not 'There's the fire,' 'Where's the fire.' 'Where's the fire!'"

Iris nodded her head. "You learn something new every day, I guess."

Sam tried to focus on the road. It was hard. He was really worried. If he was getting this annoyed with her now, what would be happening thirty minutes from now? An hour from now? He was terrified that he was going to lose it on her in the restaurant. That would be bad. She was old enough now where any type of yelling or stress he put on her could really do something bad. It was only a matter of time where him yelling at her might give her a heart attack. God forbid. He needed to keep his cool. He needed to remain calm.

They got to the restaurant and sat down. Iris loved it. It was a delightful French bistro. Just the type of place Iris would go for. Homey yet classy.

"Ooooooh, I feel French already," she announced as she sipped her water like it was a glass of wine. "I can't wait to order. And you know how good I am at ordering, don't you, Sam? Ordering is one of my specialties. You know that about me, right?"

Sam shook his head. "Did I know that you specialize in ordering? No, actually I didn't know that."

"Well, you know what they say. It is the voodoo I know that I'm swell."

"It's the voodoo you do so well."

Iris laughed, thinking Sam was joking. "That's great."

Sam's face got red. "No, Ma, that's the saying."

Iris turned up her palms. "If you say so."

Iris was getting nervous. She could see that Sam was getting annoyed. And she knew that if he got in a certain way there would be no calming him down, and her birthday present would be her own son humiliating her once again in a public place. She decided to address it right away.

"Honey, I'm not what I used to be."

This statement had the opposite effect on Sam than Iris meant it to have.

Sam tried to smile with compassion as he pushed down his angst. "I know, Mom, you keep telling me."

Iris leaned in. "No, I really mean it, though."

Sam looked at his shoes. "Mom, just because you can't remember these sayings doesn't mean you're losing your memory."

"But I am, and you have to accept it. You can't teach a dog to drink water, honey."

That was it. That was all Sam could take. And with that Sam punched the table. The café was small. Everyone saw him do this. Everyone stared. Everyone started to whisper. Both Iris and Sam could feel their stares and hear the whispers. Sam slouched down in his chair.

Iris folded her arms. "See what you do when you lose your temper. You embarrass both of us."

Sam whispered, hoping Iris would follow suit, for his mother's voice could carry like an opera singer's. "Mom, I know you're getting older, but it seems like it's the only thing we talk about."

Iris stared Sam down. "Well it's happening and it's my life and that's what's happening in my life." Tears started to well up in her eyes. "Of all people I would think my son would understand this, and be there for me. But you just can't, can you?"

Sam started to panic. "Mom, please stop crying."

Iris grabbed her heart. "Well, what else can I do? Just sit here and take this from you?"

All of a sudden, a perfectly sculpted physical trainer strutted over to their table, his chiseled face filled with angry concern. The trainer put his hand on Iris's shoulder. "You okay, beautiful?"

Sam immediately stood up. "Hey, she's fine. I'd appreciate you not touching my mother."

The physical trainer lifted his marble-like hand off Iris and pointed directly at Sam's chest. "Well, I think we'd all appreciate . . . everyone in this restaurant would appreciate you not making your mother cry. I mean, who slams a table in front of their mother. I mean, don't get me wrong, I'm a violent guy. I kick all sorts of fucking ass, but I would never slam a table that my mother was sitting at, and I'd sure as shit watch my fucking temper around her."

Sam sat back down. It was clear he was in over his head. "You're right, man. I shouldn't have behaved that way. Now can you please leave us alone and let us celebrate my mother's birthday here?"

The personal trainer smacked his own forehead. "It's her birthday. It's her birthday and you're treating her like this. You're lucky I don't drag you outta here and make you beg for death."

Iris piped up, "Young man, thank you, but I'm really fine. Please don't threaten my son. He didn't mean anything by it."

The personal trainer put his hand back on Iris's shoulder. "You sure you don't want me to kick your son's ass, ma'am?"

Iris giggled at this. She could have sworn that the personal trainer might be flirting with her. No surprise to her. Young men liked her. "No, that's fine. He's just stressed. He's a very successful actor, so you know how that is."

The personal trainer got a closer look at Sam's face. "Wait a second. Holy shit. It's you! That can't be you." He looked back to Iris. "Is your asshole son who I think he is, ma'am?"

Iris proudly nodded her head. "He sure is."

The personal trainer smacked Sam hard on the back. "You're the toilet paper scientist, right?"

Iris nodded her head again, even prouder this time. "He sure is."

The personal trainer smacked Sam on the back again, this time a little harder. "Holy shit! You're fucking hilarious, dude, and I love the toilet paper you invented."

Sam dug his fork into his wrist. "Thank you . . . I mean, I didn't invent it, but . . . thank you . . ."

The trainer's smile immediately disappeared. "Too bad you're a no-good asshole." With that the personal trainer raised his hand. "Hey, waiter. Their meal's on me. This guy don't deserve to pay for such a beautiful birthday girl. Cool, buddy?"

Sam nodded his head. His head nod was just like Iris's. Sam nodded his head again. "Yes . . . cool . . . thank you."

The personal trainer gave a mocking grin. "Don't mention it." He then leaned over and gave Iris a big kiss on the cheek. "Happy birthday, gorgeous." He walked away and squeezed back into his chair and resumed his niçoise salad. And as he chomped his greens, Iris Below blushed redder than a bleeding strawberry. Sam was also red but not for the same reason, obviously. Iris then leaned forward.

"See? It's got me still . . . It's still got me."

Sam closed his eyes again. "I think you mean to say . . . Ma . . . 'I still got it.'"

Iris took another sip of her water. "I do, don't I?"

21.
Dear Diary

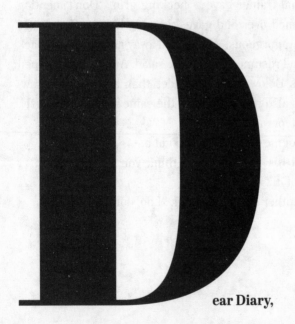

ear Diary,

I'm scared that my cleaning lady hates me. Don't get me
wrong, I'm not afraid for my safety or anything like that.
Mostly what I'm afraid of is that there's been a horrible
misunderstanding. That Sarah (that's my cleaning lady) thinks
I'm not the person I actually am. Or even worse, thinks I'm a
person that I'm actually not. Basically a bad person. A person
who likes to accuse, and point fingers. But that's not who I am.
I want Sarah to feel welcome in my home. I want her to feel that
as she cleans my home, she's cleaning her own home. That she
could almost move in if she wanted to. Not that she could, and
that's not because of her. I'm sure Sarah would be a lovely
roommate. No, it's because of me. I'm too much. I know I'd
drive her crazy to the point where she would want to murder
me. Just kill me in cold blood. Stab me in the shower so all the
mess was only in the bathtub. Or if it was a bath, she'd throw in
the plugged-in Vitamix (that I never use). Still making sure
that the only mess was in the tub. Or maybe she'd poison me.
Fill my toothpaste up with bleach or something. I guess that
wouldn't kill me, though. It'd just all stay in my mouth that way.
Very little would be swallowed. However, maybe being
absorbed through the teeth would be enough? Right? The teeth
go right to the heart. My sister died that way. She had a rotten
tooth and it gave her a rotten heart. Oy, terrible. I wish I
missed my sister more than I do. I feel so guilty I don't.
Anyway, my sister is why I try to floss as much as I can. Unless
I'm too tired, of course. And I know that's terrible but if I'm a
certain type of tired I can barely bring myself to brush, let
alone floss, my teeth. But I know I have to. When Menachem
was alive I'd floss, otherwise he'd call me disgusting and say he
didn't know which end of me he was kissing. That made me
floss, all right. But now, who do I need good breath for? I'll
never have sex again. I'm sure Sarah has sex. Lots of sex. She's
a person who I'm sure experiences pleasure on a regular basis.

She has that glow about her. And I feel awful that there is this misunderstanding that could in any way be diminishing that glow. I know it's not me, though, probably. It's what I represent. I represent that type of woman who treats her with disrespect. Who orders her around, and thinks she's stupid just because she's cleaning my house for a living. When that's of course not what I think at all. I grew up cleaning my house. I wasn't stupid. I got all of my homework done. I graduated high school and college at the top of my class. Was I the smartest one? Far from it. But I held my own. My son told me the other day (or rather he yelled at me the other day) that I speak too loudly to Sarah. "You raise your voice in volume, because you think that's going to make her understand you better, but it doesn't. It makes her think that you're talking down to her." I don't agree. First of all, I don't notice the voice raise. I know when I raise my voice. It's not that often that I do, so when I do, trust me, I notice it more than anybody else. That being said, this one day I felt like she did get noticeably annoyed with me after I did her the favor of warning her not to put the wrong type of floor cleaner in the bucket. There's cleaner for the wood floor, and cleaner for the tile. And the tile cleaner will just destroy the wood. Sure, I tell her every week, but she cleans a lot of houses and I've never seen her take any notes when I've told her what to do, and I sure have never given her any written instructions. So to me it would be easy for her to forget. If I were her I would want to be reminded. So that's what I do every week. Remind her about every little thing that she could justifiably forget because she's so busy and so very tired. Well, last week I told her and she looked at me with a rage I had never seen her look at me with before. Looked me right in the eyes. Like I was a wolf that had just eaten her child. Then she took her fist and she hit her thigh. I've never seen anyone hit their thigh so hard. And I knew in that hit that she didn't want to hit her thigh. No, not

her thigh. She wanted to hit my thigh. Or even worse, my arm.
Maybe even my head. Oy vay, if she hit my head as hard as she
hit her thigh, she would have definitely knocked me
unconscious. Then I tried to make it up to her. I asked her if
she wanted my leftover dinner from the night before. I was bad.
I got myself a burger with fries. But at least the burger had
grilled onions. I cut it in half, because I knew that I would
probably only eat half, and should only eat half, so I cut it
exactly in half to make sure I didn't have too much or too little.
Plus I had some fries. I asked her if she was hungry and
wanted the leftover half of the burger. I told her that I never
touched it. I cut it with a knife, but my hands had barely
touched it, plus I wash my hands so thoroughly before I
prepare food or eat that my hands had less germs on them than
a brand-new bar of soap. She said no at first. But I begged her.
Pleaded with her to eat the burger half, and if she was still
hungry I'd gladly order her more. She must have been more
hungry than angry because she finally agreed to eat it. I was so
happy that she was going to eat the burger half. Happy that I
could make up for anything that I might have said or done. But
then when she bit into it she got this look. Like fear and also
disgust. She spit the burger all over the place, and started dry-
heaving right in the middle of the kitchen. Turns out Sarah
hates onions on a burger. Who hates onions on a burger? And if
that's the case, maybe ask me if there's onion on it before you
take a bite? Onions are not a weird thing to have on a burger. In
fact, it would be weird if a burger didn't have onions.
McDonald's, the most famous burger restaurant there is, puts
onions on their burgers. It's not like it had cranberries on it and
I didn't tell her. Or even bacon. Not everyone eats pork. I
certainly don't. But onions? That's like someone getting mad at
you for not telling them that ketchup was on a burger. Anyway,
I think that did something. Because since the onion incident

things really haven't been the same with her. She hasn't smiled at me for two weeks. And her hellos and good-byes are almost at a whisper. And for what? Onions? I don't know. Maybe it's all in my head. Maybe she still loves me. I love her. I really see her as a part of the family, and she really is just so very good at cleaning. I'd probably let her go, if I knew of anyone else who could possibly clean as good as her. But it took so long to find someone as good as Sarah, so I'll risk it, I guess. Hopefully she gets her cheery self back again soon. And if one day my son comes in and finds me stabbed to death in my shower, at least the rest of the house will be spotless. God forbid. I've been crying a lot around her. And it's not that I need her to take care of me. That's not our relationship. She's never been one to mother me. But it's the warmth of her presence that brings me a certain comfort. Because when I get sad, things get so cold and I need warmth. My son used to give me that warmth, but I think he's mad at me, too. I don't know, I think he's maybe reached some kind of breaking point with me. There's no patience for me anymore. Really everyone seems to have lost their patience with me. Things have been so hard since Menachem died. I don't know why people can't see that. I don't know why they can't cut me a little slack. Sure, it was eleven years ago. But what is time. There's nothing like losing someone. Especially a husband. It changes everything. I always knew that I was going to die someday, but now that he's gone I really know it. Maybe that's why people have lost their patience for me. Maybe my time's up soon and everyone can feel that and maybe they're afraid of death. Or they're afraid of losing me and they can't deal with it. Sure, maybe that's it. Maybe this impatience and this coldness is all out of love, and fear of losing me. I don't know. Who's to know? What do I know. All I know is I thought things would be different by now. I thought I'd have a son who called me every day. A son I'd have to tell to leave me alone, because I have my own life and other friends and I can't just only spend time with him. I thought I would have to remind him that he can't marry me, because I'm his mother. That I'd wake up on a Sunday morning to the security alarm going off because he broke into my house to serve me breakfast in bed. I thought I'd have a cleaning lady who called me mother. Who would use a big chunk of the money I paid her to buy me a first-class ticket to Mexico, and when I refused it she'd threaten to quit if I didn't take it so that I'd go and meet her biological mother and tell her that she was my daughter now. And her mother would be fine with it because she'd know what a wonderful mother I'd make for her daughter. I wish more people would look at me. Their eyes avoid me. They know I'm sad. I wish strangers would come up to me on the street and ask me for advice because of the natural wisdom I give off. I wish I'd be walking down the street with my cleaning lady and someone would do that. And then Sarah would watch me give a total stranger amazing advice. Maybe then she'd be proud to be working for me. Maybe then she wouldn't hate me so much.

22.
Abraham Lincoln's House

ris Below had gotten in a fight with her son, Sam, and her day was ruined.

She could hardly see two inches in front of her face. Her body felt like it had given out completely. The idea of even walking to the fridge for her afternoon hard-boiled egg (a recently added daily ritual) seemed impossible. She blocked Sam's number on her phone. Then she cried. Then unblocked his number. Then cried. Blocked, cried, unblocked, wept, fell asleep, blocked, and cried . . . The process cycled for hours. Her head hurt. She feared a stroke, or just for her heart to shut down altogether from the hammer of cruelty Sam had once again taken to it. She just couldn't understand it. How could a son talk to his mother that way? How could she have raised a son who would talk to her that way? Who was he? How was he her son? Did she have any idea? Had she ever had any idea? When she had had an idea, was that idea just an idea she had made up so that she could still think she had a son? How had he gotten so angry? It couldn't have been from her. Iris had never been an angry person. She hated anger. Avoided it like pork. It wasn't her. Nor was it on her side of the family. Her side was a happy bunch. Sure, many of them had acute mental illness, but never anger. They were a positive crew. No, it wasn't her—it had to be Sam's father he had gotten the anger from. Yes, it was most likely from Menachem.

Menachem could be an angry man at times. But Menachem wasn't angry in the way that Sam was angry. Menachem was more of a miserable grouch. A sit-on-his-chair-and-brood kind of anger. A walk-into-another-room-and-slam-the-door-and-stay-in-that-room-for-hours-upon-hours kind of anger. Whereas Sam . . . Sam had rage. Just a lunatic. The way he screamed and yelled. Sam could go crazy. To the point Iris worried he might hit her. Just punch her teeth out of her head. Kick her in the shins and when she bent over to rub them, knee her in the face. These are the disturbing movies that would play in her head. Threatening her well-being and safety. But at the end of the day she knew this would never happen. Sam would never hurt her. When all was said and done he was actually a good son. But make no mistake, he had a real rage problem. And this day was one of the top prime examples.

Iris had called him that morning to tell him how excited she was. Because she was. She was very excited. But as excited as she was to tell him how excited she was it didn't stop her from noticing that the moment he picked up the phone Sam was already in a bad mood. Iris could tell that sort of thing with him. She knew her son. The first clue was that he neglected to ask his mother how she was. Sam always asked her that when he was happy to hear from her. That's what everyone asks when someone calls them, and they're happy to hear from them, and they're in a good mood, right? When one doesn't ask that usually means that they don't want to talk to them. And why wouldn't Sam want to talk to her? Iris was his mother. His last remaining parent. Who knew how long she was even going to be around for. For all Sam Below knew Iris could die tomorrow. Or later today. Or now. Or now. Or even now. So why not do the loving thing, the decent thing, the normal thing and ask his mother how she was doing. But instead, like so many other times before, all Sam greeted his mother with was a very cold "What's up?" Like she was one of his harem. After all, Sam Below was quite the ladies' man.

"What's up?" asked Sam Below, cold and distant with a put-on toughness.

Iris tried to move past it, refusing to diminish one ounce of her excitement. "Guess what, honey?"

To which Sam gave an equally icy reply of "What?" One of the other tragic aspects of him communicating with Iris in this closed-off way was that normally Sam had an amazing vocabulary. A real mastery of words. This was surely one of the qualities that got him all those women, that and his gorgeous good looks, even though he had gained a little weight in the face.

Despite all of this Iris still chose to ignore Sam's obvious aloofness and proceeded to inform him that she was the happiest she had been in quite a while, because "Guess where I went today?"

"Where, Mom?" Sam asked, deepening his detachment.

If Iris could have done an impression of a drumroll she would have, but she didn't know how to do that, so instead she just gave what is often referred to as a pregnant pause, leading to her oh-so-exciting announcement that she had paid a visit to none other than "Abraham Lincoln's house!"

Then silence. Just silence. Iris was confused.

"Did you hear me, Sam? I went to Abraham Lincoln's house in Springfield. Just on a whim. Just for fun. You always tell me I need to be more spontaneous and that I have to live my life more. And I didn't have anything scheduled today. And I opened my wallet and the first thing I saw was a five-dollar bill. And you know whose face is on a five-dollar bill? Abraham Lincoln!!! So you know what I did? I got in my car and I drove all the way down to Springfield to Abraham Lincoln's house!"

Sam's interest wasn't necessarily piqued at this, but this was the point where he consciously entered the conversation. "You drove to Springfield to Abraham Lincoln's house?"

Now that Iris finally had her son's full attention (she could tell), her excitement multiplied and she took full advantage. "Of course I did. I mean, you know how much I love Abraham Lincoln."

Then more silence, and more confusion for Iris.

Maybe the connection was bad. That could be the only reason for his lack of response. "Sam, did you hear me?"

He had heard her, and in his response it was clear that he was now more annoyed than when he originally was when he answered the phone. "You love Abraham Lincoln? Since when?"

Iris's confusion changed focus from her son's cold silence to how bad his memory was. "I've always told you how much I love him."

With this Sam Below let out a deep sigh of frustration. "You've never told me that." Followed by another sigh. "This is the first time I'm hearing this."

Iris was baffled. Beyond baffled at how her own son could not remember that Abraham Lincoln was not only her all-time favorite president, but one of her all-time favorite historical figures, next to Martin Luther King Jr. and JFK, of course. Yes, there was no question. Iris Below absolutely couldn't get enough of Abraham Lincoln. This was clear as she took her son through her magical odyssey.

"I tell you when I stepped into that house of his, it was like I was stepping into a whole different time. And it wasn't just because his house looked like it was from another time. I mean, sure, that helped. And it's a good thing they kept it that way. Kept it the way it was when he lived there. I mean, they have to keep it old like that or what would be the point of going there, right? You don't want to go to Abraham Lincoln's house and see a La-Z-Boy and a microwave, and a flat-screen TV mounted on the wall. You want it to have all that old stuff. And that's what was there, and it made me feel like I was transported. So much I started to wonder if maybe I actually was transported. That as soon as I stepped outside everything would be like it was then. I'd look around for my car, and instead of my car there'd be a horse and carriage. And my sweatpants would, all of a sudden, be a big beautiful dress. And men in top hats would all bow to me and throw their waistcoats over muddy puddles to keep my cowboy boots from sinking into the muddy road."

The whole experience had been quite spiritual for Iris Below. The moment she stepped into the former president's home she felt she could feel his presence. Like he was standing next to her, whispering in her ear: "What do you think of my house, Iris?" "Thank you for coming, Iris." "I love you, Iris." Sweet nothings that felt so real that she was compelled to respond. She looked in the direction of where she imagined he was standing and answered: "Very nice indeed, Mr. President." "Thank you for having me, Mr. President." "I love you, too, Abe." She'd responded with such volume the other people on the tour heard her. For a moment Iris feared that they'd think she was insane, but quickly discarded that worry. After all, none of her responses were that weird of a thing to say. Her fellow houseguests probably just saw her outbursts as poetic expressions for her love of this great man and his home. Everyone there surely loved Abraham Lincoln as much as she did—otherwise why would they bother to go there? Who the hell would travel all this way to Abraham Lincoln's house if they didn't love Abraham Lincoln? She wanted to press this point to her son. Assuring him that she did not embarrass herself. That the people around her did not give her strange looks, but instead smiled and nodded with her in agreement.

Iris proceeded to unfold the day's incredible events, despite the continued silence from Sam. She chose to interpret his lack of response as a deep investment, and thus continued:

"I started to imagine that we were married. That I was his Mary . . . wait, what was it . . . Mary what? Mary Joe Lincoln? No, that's not it. Mary Jane? No, that's not it, either. Hmmmm. I have to look that up, I guess. But then again I was never really a fan of hers so it makes sense I wouldn't remember her full name. To tell you the truth, I never really liked her at all. He deserved better. I mean, didn't she stay in bed all the time? She was a real depressive. Not that I don't get depressed. Sure, I can. Oy vay, can I. But I always get out of bed. At least most of the time I do. Sure, there's days I don't, but I'd say seven out of ten of my depressed days I'm out and about. Maybe not out and about outside, but out of my bed and in the house, for sure. I think Abe was depressed, too. That's too bad, isn't it? I really think I could have made him so happy. I know it's a crazy thing for me to say, but I think the two of us would have been really good together. Oh, what a wife I would have been to him. I'd stroke his hair in bed as he lay next to me and just get all of the junk of the day to melt right off him. I'd call him my skinny Santa, because he was so thin and had a beard, and he'd love it and just laugh away. Probably being with that Mary is what made him sad. A bad marriage is just a killer. Plus all that Civil War and slavery stuff. Talk about stress. But I know that if Iris Below was in the picture, I would have made all of that stress melt away just with the light touch of my tiny finger."

She heard no agreement or encouragement from her son at this. But he wasn't disagreeing, either. So that was a good sign.

She went into great detail about her encounter with a wax figure of the president outside. She spoke of running her fingers through its hair, pretending it was really him, and how it all felt so nice in her hands. She got yelled at for touching him, though. Which she, of course, understood. She knew she wasn't allowed to touch him, but she just couldn't help herself. A few of the people around her even whispered that they couldn't blame her. She assured Sam that if he ever went (which he most certainly should) he'd most certainly relate as well. The wax figures were very very real, and, just as was the case inside his house, she could feel Lincoln's soul poking through.

Anyway, it was all just a really great day for Iris Below. She left Springfield, loving Abraham Lincoln like she never had before. More than she ever thought possible to love a man she had never met. As she took the long drive back to Chicago, she hoped her imaginary beloved was resting in heaven at peace, and, at the same time, deeply hoped that John Wilkes Booth was burning in hell.

Iris finished her day recap panting with excitement. Or was it anxiety? Perhaps she was panting with anxiety. An anxiety that immediately overtook her knowing that the recounting of her glorious day would not only be dismissed but would be grounds for deep disrespect and lack of feeling. Unfortunately she was right, for as soon as she finished, all Sam Below could mutter was:

"Honestly, Mom. I don't know what the hell this story is. Just because you went to Abraham Lincoln's house doesn't mean you're happy. And I didn't really need to hear this right now."

With this Iris started to cry. A son talks to his mother like this? Abraham Lincoln would never talk to his mother like this. He wouldn't listen to his mother reveal her heart like this and then act like she was telling him a story about sweeping her floor. After all the support she had given to her son's hopes and dreams. This was how he treated hers?

"I just don't have time to listen to hours upon hours of the minute details of your life."

Minute details?! MINUTE DETAILS???????!!!!!!!

What rage. What selfishness. What absolute cruelty. Once again, Sam Below had wiped clean all traces of Iris Below's happiness, and she not-so-calmly informed him that she never wanted to speak to him ever again. Then she hung up.

Obviously Iris didn't mean what she said. She loved her boy. He was her prize of all prizes. But she hated his rage.

What is wrong with that generation? she sadly wondered. *They're all so angry. They've forgotten how to appreciate their history. To learn from people who, frankly, are better than them. Don't get me wrong. I'm proud of my son. But an Abraham Lincoln he is not.*

Iris sat on her bed. Staring at a five-dollar bill. Crying. Longing. Wishing for a love and a life that she would never have.

But maybe that's a good thing, she thought. *The assassination would have just wrecked me.*

Z

23.

Z's Mistake

 sat alone on his cloud.

He wasn't sure how long he had been sitting there. Just as he was unsure of how long he had been in heaven at all. In a way it felt like his first day. But so much had happened, and besides, was there such a thing as days anymore?

It seemed like only yesterday when he was hit by that bus. Hit by a bus . . . What a joke. After all of the worrying Z did about dying. After all of the different scenarios that played out in his head that would befall him and end his existence. The diseases, the environmental catastrophes, the random acts of violence . . . all it took was him being distracted by some sort of shiny object that redirected his gaze, which, if it had stayed its original visual course, would have seen the Greyhound number seven coming right at his head as he leaned over to get a closer look.

And what was that shiny object? He never found out. He at least could have seen it a little more clearly to make his death seem a little less stupid. Maybe it was a tiny portal poking through, signaling from the dimension that he was currently residing in. Or maybe it was just a fucking nickel. Z would never know.

Entering heaven was easy enough. Yes, many people entered at once, but no one had to wait. No one checked Z's credentials or eligibility to enter. That had already been determined. It was for all intents and purposes the type of heavenly entrance one would have thought entering heaven would be.

Z then briefly met God, and the meeting was quick but far from disappointing. Z followed his fellow newly deceased freshmen to a great clearing—a meadow that was the brightest green Z had ever seen. But much like entering heaven, though there were many there to meet their creator, there was no wait. God stood tall, a perfect blend of all genders and races. Not just of human but animal as well. To put it simply God looked like a beautifully magnificent Everything, and as Z approached, God greeted him with the most perfect and genuine warmth he had ever felt.

But it was very brief, and as Z was led to his cloud by a pair of sexless cherubs, he felt a great longing for the next time he would meet the sovereign of the universe. Not just for the thrill, but for a chance to get to know them better.

Now Z sat on his cloud alone. The light was perfect, as it shined on a much-needed solitude.

Peaceful solitude, without the pain of loneliness. This was exactly what Z had wished for in his imaginings of the afterlife. His whole life he always felt swarmed. His therapist told him this "swarmed" feeling was a result of him being easily inundated. Easily overwhelmed. Even so. Even if that was true. Even if Z was easily inundated and overwhelmed, that didn't mean that the people in his life weren't, also, inundating and overwhelming. He felt possessed by these people. His wife, his kids, his parents, his sister, even his dogs. They wanted all of him all the time.

Months before he died, Z had a recurring nightmare. He would be tied to his bed with ropes, his legs spread wide. As he lay there, splayed out, every one of his close relations marched single file into the room. One by one, everyone he knew approached the bed and crawled right up his ass. Once they were all inside, Z could hear them haggling about which parts of his mind, body, and soul belonged to them. He just lay there paralyzed as they argued, staking their claim on his organs, his personality flaws, his fashion sense.

Z was no dummy. He knew how cliché this dream was, but that didn't stop him from feeling a combination of terror and depression when he awakened. In real life, most of these "ass miners" would characterize him as selfless. And he tried to agree with them. Not only to their faces but internally. But when Z had clarity, he knew this was all bullshit. Z wasn't selfless. He just never lived as his actual self. Only as a mirage that the people closest to him had created.

And then came death. And although it was a bit embarrassing, and frustrating (just what the fuck was that shiny object), with death Z actually felt a great release. Now, as a spirit, or angel, or whatever he was, he had the chance to live, or rather not live, he had a chance to exist, or rather not exist as himself. This made him feel a happiness and ease he had never felt. The best part was, he had eternity to feel this way. To exist this way. He would never not be himself again.

Z sat on his cloud and gazed into the everlasting imitation of morning, tears flowing down his cheeks. Every tear held every wasted second of his self-erasure. Every tear rolled down, cleansing him of his invisibility. And as the last tear fell, he heard the unmistakable choir of his maker's voice.

"Hey there. How's it going today?"

Z couldn't believe it. This was unfathomable. God was taking time out of their busy schedule to give Z personal individual attention. Z was touched. However, Z being Z, he also registered the very real possibility that this special care might be just one of those "heaven things." Maybe millions, even billions, of people in heaven were simultaneously having a one-on-one with God, each feeling as flattered as Z. But even if that was the case, it didn't matter, at least not right now. Right now, it all felt pretty great. *Maybe that's really what heaven is all about*, thought Z. *Self-confidence.*

"Oh, I'm fine. Thanks so much for checking on me."

God laughed.

"Well . . . you're welcome, I guess, but I'm checking on millions of people right now, silly. Not just you. It's my job. Know what I mean?"

So Z was right. It was one of those "heaven things." Even though Z had prepared himself for this possibility, that this moment only had the illusion of individualized attention, an ego was an ego. Sure, Z had just been thinking of the possibility that God was, quite literally, "spreading the love," but it was one thing to wonder it and another thing to have God rub it in his face.

Maybe God didn't mean it like that. Maybe Z heard it wrong. Maybe God's tone was different than the tone Z was used to. It certainly wasn't the worst thing someone could say, but at the same time Z still couldn't help but feel a little miffed.

God patted Z on the back. "That doesn't mean that I'm not totally focused on you right now, you know? That might not make sense, but it's the truth. This is all of me. And the me that is checking in on someone else right now, that's all of me, too. I know it defies all logic, but that's the thing. I define logic. And that's not a brag, it's a fact."

Z felt more at ease. "No, I get it. Thank you for saying that."

God nodded their head. "Of course. And again, just to be clear, I don't know if I've told you this already, but I never brag."

Z slowly nodded his head. *What a thing to say*, he thought. *I never brag? But . . . isn't that a brag?*

God gave a nervous chuckle. "Well, I just want to make sure you know that. Because to me there's nothing worse than a bragger. I hate insecure people. Well, *hate* is a strong word. I don't hate anyone, but insecurity is a big turnoff. Me myself, I'm never insecure. I can't be. I literally can't afford to be insecure. I have a universe to run. A pretty great universe at that, right? Sure, it's not perfect. What is? But it's a universe, and I should get at least some credit for that. Now I know what you're going to say. If I'm so secure, why do I need the validation, right? Great question. It's natural that me wanting that validation might come off as insecurity, but it's not. I just deserve it. There, I said it. I deserve the credit and, sue me, I want to be acknowledged for that. That's my right, right? At least I can ask for that? After all I've done, right? I mean, I invented sex, for crying out loud. That's pretty cool. Right?"

"Right," replied Z. But obviously Z didn't want to say *right*. Obviously, Z wanted to say *wrong*. I mean, this was terrible. Just terrible. The whole conversation had quickly taken a pathetic turn. God was shaping up to be one of the most insecure people (or beings) Z had ever met. Though, honestly, it wasn't much of a surprise. Z had always suspected God of insecurity. I mean, sending people to hell just for not believing in you. What was more insecure than that? But maybe God didn't do that. After all, Z didn't know if hell actually existed. He hadn't talked about it with anyone yet. Z hadn't really talked about anything all too substantial yet. All the conversations he had had with anyone were sort of built around getting settled in. This current conversation had been one of the longest so far. But if that was the case, if God did send people to hell, who would dare talk about that up here? No one would, that's who. Including God. If God was insecure enough to send people to the worst punishment imaginable just for not believing in them, they probably wouldn't have the self-awareness that they were doing that because their insecurity ran so deep. But then again, this was God, and maybe God operated on different modes of behavior. Maybe it was only perceived as insecurity from Z's limited human perspective. Z started biting his nails. He wanted out of this whole convo. Out of this moment. But, at the same time, he really wanted to know. This was one of those "lifelong" questions of his, but the only way he'd know the answer was if he asked, and if God was sending people to hell for not believing in them, it was completely possible that God would do the same thing to someone who questioned them about it. But maybe not. Maybe God would be glad to talk about it. And even if the conversation went south, maybe God would still give the questioner a chance to change their perspective before they were sent down below. That probably was the case. God didn't seem so bad as to have a "one strike, you're out" policy. Even if God was off-the-charts insecure, God still seemed amicable. They weren't defensive in a hostile way. But then again, Z hadn't really said anything that would rub God the wrong way. He was just letting God monologue. Which was no skin off Z's nose, either. He had let people monologue his whole life, plus he wanted to hear what God had to say. Who wouldn't? Could you imagine how arrogant someone would have to be to meet God and not just listen, and think they had something to add to the conversation? Someone like that would be the biggest asshole in the universe.

Z had moved from his nails to biting off his finger skin. The desire to ask God about the whole hell thing only grew. It was like having to take a shit, and the closer you got to the toilet, the more you had to take one, to the point where when you're taking down your pants, the shit is practically falling out of your ass. That's what Z felt in his mouth. His mouth held the soon-to-be exploding shit, and God was the toilet.

God had to understand that people came to their new home with millions of questions. God was right there. God knew what being right there would mean. That it would mean many moments of mystery-solving for their children. God would have to know that everyone who met them would want to ask them every question they've ever had. How could asking a question be a damnable sin? Z was so perplexed. He didn't know what to do.

God probably would have heard a lot of these thoughts Z was having, but fortunately for them both, God was too distracted with their own body to pay attention. For no clear reason, God had begun flexing. God held up their arm in front of Z's face and made a muscle. "Look at that, huh? I made it the perfect size, right? It's really a bulge, but not too big? To me, if I made it bigger, I'd look too body obsessed, right? Here, feel it, is it too much, or not enough?"

Z was taken aback. As Z felt God's muscle, he started to get angry. Z tried to conceal it, and God still seemed too self-obsessed to notice the change in Z's temperament. As Z's anger grew, God's bicep got warmer. Then hot. Till the point that holding it made Z feel like he was palming a burning hunk of coal. Z whipped back his hand. God looked at him inquisitively.

"What's wrong?" God asked. "You seem to not be enjoying our time together. Was it my muscle? I should have warned you, it can get quite hot. That's a little thing I did to myself. The hotter I look, the hotter I am to the touch. Cool, right?"

What the hell was God talking about? Where had this come from? Hotter to the touch, the hotter God looked? Z's head was a cyclone of growing contempt. The kind of mental state you should never talk to God with, especially when they were showing off their body. Without thinking, Z snarled at God, "I don't know. I guess. Why is that cool?"

God's eyes shifted. Their voice dropped a register. "Why is it cool? Isn't it obvious?"

Z had dug himself into a hole, and he began to frantically try to dig himself out. "I'm sorry, God. I'm sure it's very cool. I'm sure I just don't get it. Honestly, I might be in a bit of shock from my burned hand."

God smiled. "Of course. Totally understandable. Let me explain. See, the hotter I look, the hotter I am to the touch. And that's because . . . because . . ." God paused. Their eyes darted back and forth, searching for an answer. God let out a frustrated sigh. "You know what, I've forgotten why. Wow, that's annoying, huh?"

Z's fear was in a head-to-head race with his anger. He was terrified, but couldn't help but wonder why his beloved solitude had been interrupted for this. He knew he couldn't just let loose with finger-pointing. If there was anyone you had to humor, it was God. And so Z did. "It's understandable. I'm sure you have a lot to remember, and even you can't be expected to remember everything."

God's eyes softened. "That's right. No one has to remember more than I have to remember. Could you imagine if you had to remember as much as I do? I mean, your head would explode!"

It was clear now to Z that all God wanted him to be was a yes-man, and so Z obliged. "Absolutely, you literally have to remember everything."

"That's right!" God bellowed. "I literally have to remember everything. I have to remember everything, everyone, and everything everyone does and says every second. And when I say *everything* I'm not just talking about earth. I'm talking planets. I'm talking asteroids and stars, and aliens! So sue me if I can't remember the reason I made myself hotter to the touch, the hotter I look! It's not nearly as important as remembering, say, oh, I don't know, making the earth revolve around the sun."

Z gave a chuckle. "Definitely not. You gotta wonder why someone would even do something like that."

God cocked their head. "Do something like what?"

Z diverted eye contact from the eyes of his maker. "Like . . . like . . . make yourself hotter to the touch, the hotter you look."

God cocked their head further. "What do you mean?"

Z stumbled. "Oh, I don't know."

God leaned in. "No. Explain. What did you mean by that?"

Z started shaking. "I don't know what I'm saying."

God leaned in some more. "You don't think that kind of thing is important. You don't think me making myself hotter to the touch, the hotter I get is of value?"

Z half laughed. "You said it wasn't important."

God coughed. "But I didn't say it was unimportant."

Z couldn't see straight. Let alone string his thoughts together in a way that could in any way help with navigating this. At this point it was as if he was on autopilot. It was like his words were not his own, which was probably why he said:

"Yeah, but if you said it was unimportant, you wouldn't be wrong."

God smiled a smile. A smile that held no joy. A smile that held the plagues.

"Is that so? Please, oh pretty please, tell me what you mean by 'unimportant.'"

Z tried to backtrack and play dumb. "I don't know what I'm saying. Just please forget it."

But God didn't shake it off. Instead, God's whole visage seemed to grow darker. Like they had stepped into the darkest shadow of shadows. "You're lying to me. You're lying to the Lord thy God. You know exactly what you meant. You think I'm a narcissist, don't you?"

Truth or lie? Which one would be worse? God was on high alert. There was no lying to God. But maybe God would appreciate a lie. Maybe a lie would be more forgiven than a harsh truth. Then again, lying to God could also be seen as a full disrespect of their intelligence. Perhaps the most offensive thing about lying to God was Z thinking that he could get away with lying to God. But then again, maybe a lie would show respect. After all, there was no proof that this was how Z felt about God down deep, even though it was. It could just be taken as a momentary lapse in speech, and the lie would almost act as an apology. Like "I'm so sorry I said that that I'm going to just pretend that I didn't." However, even if God got upset, it didn't necessarily mean punishment. Maybe Z would just get chewed out. It might be really scary, but what's a little scare? He'd get over it. Z had to make a choice. Whatever it was, some sort of choice had to be made.

So Z made a choice.

"I mean . . . can I be honest with you, God?"

God stepped even farther into the shadow that was covering

him. "Can you be honest? You must. You must be honest to your maker. Speak, mortal!!!"

"Well . . ." started Z. "Honestly, the whole muscle thing, and having me feel the muscle, it all feels a bit . . . oh, I don't know . . . a bit . . ."

"A bit what?!"

"A bit . . ."

"A bit what, mortal human?! A BIT WHAT!!!???"

Z's whole body clenched as he finally squeezed out, "A bit . . . insecure."

God's shadow-self grew darker. "Are you saying I'm insecure?"

There was no stopping now. What's done was done. It was impossible to turn back.

"A little, but all of us are. Heck, you invented insecurity, didn't you?"

God's vocal register steadily got lower. "No. As a matter of fact, I didn't. That was Satan. Satan invented insecurity. Everybody knows that."

Z desperately tried to turn it all into a philosophical discussion without seeming like he was challenging God. "Really? But insecurity's such a human thing."

"Sure, but I'm not human. I'm God. Satan likes to play in the human emotional sandbox, not me. Why would I invent insecurity? Insecurity is vile and sad."

Vile and sad? Z couldn't believe that God was using such words for such a normal human condition. And at this point, Z's frustration with God's whole perspective made him forget that this crazy perspective was coming from God at all. Z felt like he was having it with some sort of shitty right-wing family member at Thanksgiving. And whenever stupid debates like this arose, it was next to impossible for Z not to call out his opponent's inconsistencies. And in this case God was certainly no exception. So Z pressed on.

"So? You didn't invent emotions?"

God's eyes reddened. "I invented the good ones. Happiness, joy, fun. That's all me. But the rest, like sadness, and anger, and of course insecurity, that's all the devil."

"You didn't invent sadness or anger? What about sadness over the loss of a loved one? Isn't the sadness in a way the expression of that love? And what about anger when it's used to get someone to stand up for what's right?"

God grabbed their head. Almost like they were about to tear it off. "Yeah, well, that type of sadness and anger was me. Dammit! You got me all turned around here."

Z now was feeling a rush. He couldn't believe it. Was he actually about to win a debate against God? He felt a sudden sense of pride. He wondered how many people had had the guts to take God to task like this.

Z took a triumphant stand. "It's just hard for me to believe that you didn't have something to do with insecurity. Even insecurity can do good things. Look at comedy. So much comedy comes from insecurity. Also, insecurity can stop people from doing hurtful things. Sometimes—"

God cut Z off with a thunderclap.

"Enough! Listen to me. Let's get this all straight, you fucking arrogant asshole. Listen up and listen good, 'cause I'm only going to explain this once. Everything that has a good outcome, that's me. All the other bad-outcome stuff, I let Satan do."

Z knew he now had them. "So you don't think insecurity is totally bad?"

God grunted. "Of course not! I don't think in terms of bad or good. I'm not a judgmental prick like you."

Z squawked. "You think I'm judgmental?"

God shook their head in disbelief. "Do I think you're judgmental?! I know you're judgmental! I made you judgmental, bitch!"

Z could have gotten scared here, but he was now enjoying this all too much. All possibilities of consequence had left his mind. All he could do was gloat in his satisfaction of having God against the ropes. "Oh, you made me judgmental, huh? So are you saying that being judgmental is good?"

God was now fuming. Fuming in a way they had not in centuries. They pressed their fingers to their temples. "Look, you're really pushing me here. I really don't like being pushed like this."

Z started to laugh. He was on a roll. "Why is there war?"

Steam was now seeping from God's ears. "Oh, we're going to start with this now?"

"It's a simple question. Why is there war?"

God started breathing really hard. "I . . ."

Z was exhilarated. He had never felt this alive. Especially when he was alive. "Why is there war?"

God's whole body started to spasm. "I . . . I . . ."

Z threw up his hands to the great everything. "God! Creator of all things, except, of course, negative emotions, I ask you . . . why is there war? You did create war, didn't you?"

God shook a shake they hadn't shaken for a thousand years. "I . . . I . . . I don't know. I don't think so. I can't remember."

Z laughed. "Yes, I know how busy you are. But try, won't you please! Answer me why!!!"

"NONE OF YOUR MOTHERFUCKING BUSINESS! THAT'S WHY!!!"

Z smiled a smile that didn't hold the plagues, but he did his best.

"If I can be honest with you, God: you don't seem like someone who doesn't brag. You seem like someone who is quite addicted to bragging. You also are exceptionally bad at accepting accountability. On top of that, you are one of the most defensive individuals I've met. Frankly, all of this adds up to the fact that I think you're actually . . . very insecure."

With this, heaven ripped with an ear-piercing screech. The sky cracked open. God darkened once again. And God grew. Grew to the size of a thundercloud big enough to cover the whole earth.

God's eyes filled with tears, and rain fell on every inch of heaven. All was flooded with God's humiliation. God squatted down so that Z was standing right in front of their giant eyes. As God blinked, Z was splashed with more tears, and the tears were so hot they scalded Z's skin. Much worse even than God's hot bicep.

"You really make me sad," God said. "And not the good sad. The bad sad."

God's soaking-wet eyes blinked, and everything surrounding Z began to swirl in a giant vortex. The heavenly floor opened, and as Z looked down all he could see was fire, and all he could hear were screams. It wasn't hard for Z to guess what that was. God stood back up, still giant and still very, very, very upset.

God then blew a gust of hurricane wind from their mouth, lifting Z into the everlasting, and then, with no clouds to catch him, Z fell.

And God rested.

24.

Z Meets Satan

 sat in Satan's office, and to say he was impressed was a massive understatement.

It was a beautiful office. Sleek and modern, employing different rich shades of gray. A gorgeous painting stretched across the
whole wall, manifesting itself like a second version of Picasso's
Guernica. Which in fact it was. Z later found out that Picasso had
painted this specially for Satan. When Z inquired if Picasso was
in hell, Satan gently raised his eyebrows.

"Sometimes."

Satan's desk was handcrafted from a glistening cherrywood.
A golden clock displaying a multitude of numeric symbols hung
on the wall opposite *Guernica 2*. It was no surprise that time read
differently down here. Satan sat there smiling at Z. A way friend-
lier smile than God had ever given him.

"I'd love to take you on a tour of the facilities, but I'm just
swamped. I'm always swamped. Besides, what good is a tour really going to do except upset you even more?"

Z nodded. "Makes sense . . ." Z paused. He wasn't sure how
he should address his new overlord.

Satan chuckled. "You can just call me Satan. Sorry. Maybe
you were looking for a more exciting title to address me by. But
that's it. I'm Satan. I don't really like the other names. They're so
pretentious, and there's enough for everyone to wrap their heads
around down here without worrying about how to address me."

Z nodded again. "Sounds great . . . Satan." Wow, Satan was
so polite and easygoing. Way more so than God. Not to say that
Satan didn't also possess some insecurities, but he seemed at
peace with them. Satan was not afraid to let it all hang out. To
top it off, Satan was gorgeous. Sure, he had the horns and hooves
and blood-red skin, but none of those monstrous qualities took
away from his inarguable sex appeal. Despite being snakelike,
his bright emerald-green eyes conveyed a deep kindness and
a fun flirtatiousness. His skin glistened against the beautiful
Dutch antique lamps that punctuated his office. Shirt off, Satan

glowed. Normally a guy just hanging out with his shirt off would be a turnoff to Z. But in this case it was quite welcomed by him. Satan had the best body he had ever seen on a man. His muscles were like chiseled marble, but supple and soft. Unlike God, Satan didn't really call attention to it, either. Sure, his shirt was off, but it seemed more that he was casually lounging than showing off.

Z's whole body started to pulsate. He had never wanted anyone as much as he wanted Satan in this very moment. His body ached for him. But Z knew there was no way. I mean, who was he? Some new schmuck who'd pissed off God? He was the trillionth version of the same old thing. Nevertheless, Z pined and fantasized. Z wondered. Everyone in hell probably wanted to do it with Satan. Maybe the true hell was that one would never be able to taste their sweet Satanic desire. An eternity of blue balls for red balls.

Who did Satan have sex with? Did Satan have sex? Of course he did. How could he not? But with who? It had to be with someone. Serial killers were often quite hot. Maybe it was with some of them. Or maybe there were some hot demons. Or maybe the Devil had the power to replicate so that he could literally fuck himself. Questions raced through Z's mind as quickly as the mental images of what he wanted to do to Satan and what he wanted Satan to do to him.

This whole thought journey Z was on almost perfectly and coincidentally produced a coy smile from Satan. He was so fucking cute you could just eat him up.

"You want to see something I've been working on?" He giggled.

"I'd love to." Z giggled back. Who could say no to that face?

With that Satan blinked his perfect eyes and the wall behind him opened. Satan stood up, giving Z a better peek at his delicious goat legs. He then motioned with his perfect arm for Z to follow him into the room behind him.

The room was large. It was like the inside of a medium-size warehouse. And in this warehouse-size room were what seemed like a few hundred men of different shapes and ages. Z noticed that a great number of them resembled current famous corporate CEOs and congressmen, quite a few cable news hosts as well, and, of course, a whole bunch of influencers. They all stared ahead in a trance. They would have seemed dead if not for the fear in their eyes.

Satan put his arm around Z's shoulder, giving Z a direct line to the aromatic musk that was emanating from Satan's armpit. Z put his hands in front of his crotch, in the likelihood that he would get an erection.

"This is one of my new projects. I'm really excited about it."

Z was all ears. "What is it? I thought all these guys were alive? Did someone nuke Washington and Hollywood?"

Satan laughed. "If only, right?!" He squeezed Z closer, and Z could feel his penis shift to the left side and down his pant leg. Not a full erection, but definitely some movement. "No, they're all still alive. They're just sleeping. And when they sleep their souls come here. And I've made it so they can't move. But they can hear and feel everything. They think they're just dreaming. One big, crazy, horrible dream."

Z was fascinated. "So, what? You just have them sit here? Do you torture them?"

Satan smiled even wider. "Well, depends what you consider torture. See, after our meeting, what I'm going to do is I'm going to go in there and I'm going to close the wall, and I'm going to fuck the shit out of each and every one of them."

Z started to feel faint. "You are? All of them?"

Satan slapped Z's back. "Yep. I fuck them. I fuck them in

their dreams. And let me tell you, it's nasty."

Z liked the sound of this. "Can I watch?" he almost pleaded. To see the Dark Lord punish the worst people on earth and to get to see him fuck, that was a total win.

Satan gave his answer some thought. He looked long and hard at Z. He gave him another light pat. "You know, as much as I'd love you to, I think it'd be a little irresponsible of me. You just got here. As much as you feel like you want to see it now, I think it will ultimately be way too intense for you. Seeing me do that might make you go insane. Not so much the fucking, but their reactions. It's really horrible. I mean, I like it—of course I like it—but it's a lot."

Z was disappointed but he understood. Despite only knowing Satan for not more than thirty minutes, he already had complete respect and trust in his judgment. "That's fine," said Z. "You know what's best, I'm sure."

Z was getting nervous that his meeting with Satan was coming to an end. When would be the next time he could see him again? He was going to miss him so much. Too much. Was that crazy? Yes, of course it was, but he couldn't help it. Never before had his desire known such ravishing hunger. Never before had he wished he was a congressman.

But maybe he didn't need to be. Z had an idea. Maybe if this room filled with sociopaths was the main course, maybe Z could be an appetizer? Maybe he could be Satan's little warm-up for the main event. He was scared to ask. Surely many had asked before. How could they not? Especially with the amount of sexual deviants who came down here. But Z wouldn't be asking from any type of perverted place. No way. Z's lust for Satan was as pure as his childhood lust for Jessica Rabbit. Z's worry grew. Who knew if after this moment he would ever have the opportunity to ask again? Who knew if he would even see Satan ever again? Maybe it would just be this first meeting and that was it. A whole eternity without ever seeing the one person he had ever desired this much in his whole existence. He had to ask. Surely if he was rejected it would be painful, but not nearly as painful as the not knowing. Not nearly as painful as the eternal regret of being a coward.

So Z asked:

"Satan?" Z murmured as he took what was hopefully not the last strong whiff of Satan's intoxicating BO.

Z could feel Satan's eyes look at him, and when Z looked up, he could feel his penis become rock hard from the sexiest gaze he had ever gazed up at. Satan lowered his head and, with this head lowering, penetrated Z's being even more than ever before.

"Yes?"

Z reached up and gently touched Satan's forearm. "Satan, I've so enjoyed our meeting. As horrible as I know hell might be, I'm so grateful that I've gotten to meet you and spend this time with you. I hope it's not the last time . . . maybe it is . . . but whatever the case . . . I was just wondering . . ."

Z started to tremble. Satan pulled him ever so gently closer and closer. "What is it?" Satan asked.

Z opened his mouth, and out came the words he had been wanting to speak for minutes, which felt like hours, which felt like lifetimes. "Satan . . . will you make love to me?"

Satan cocked his head. He took his arm off Z's shoulder. "Make love to you?"

Z's face grew almost redder than Satan's. "Sorry, is that a lame way to ask that? Is it too soft? Should I have said 'fuck'? Okay, will you fuck me? Will you fuck me, Satan?"

With this, Satan's beautiful eyes glazed over and his face seemed almost sad. "No, it's not that. It's just . . . I don't really see you that way. And also I've gotta fuck all these guys in their dreams, and I . . . Maybe some other time, okay?"

Z's heart broke in a million pieces. He had never felt such an atomic rejection. He had never wanted to die more that he did in this very moment, and he was already dead. Maybe there was something worse than death. Actually, there was. And he was about to experience it for eternity. The thought that the Prince of Darkness, when all was said and done, just wasn't sexually attracted to him.

25.
The Dog

**.** was not in a good mood.

He had just been stretched out on a rack. His arms and legs yanked to the point of feeling like they were being torn off. To the point where Z almost wanted them torn off. At least then it would all be over with. At least the pain could no longer increase in severity. But alas, his limbs stayed attached to his body, continuously excruciatingly stretched for what seemed like ten years, which in reality was probably one hundred years. After the torture was finished, Z was allowed to take a few moments for himself. That was one of the good things about hell. In the midst of all the horror, at least Satan always let you take some personal space to try and get your head together. And Z needed it.

I gotta stop thinking about time altogether, thought Z. *It's such a waste. I'm never going to have a sense of it again. I didn't really care about it when I was alive. In fact, to tell the truth, I was very anti-time. I hated my birthday. Refused to celebrate it. Not because I was upset about getting older—it's just that age meant nothing to me. I don't even remember how old I was when I died, so why am I always thinking about time down here?*

Was time a way to escape loneliness? Was time that companion one latched on to when no one else was there and there was nothing to look forward to, in the hopes it would eventually lead to someone or something? Z had even begun to hear a ticking in his inner ear. A ticking that sounded exactly like the ticking of the golden clock in Satan's office. And as he thought about time, the ticking only got louder. *Oh, shit*, thought Z. *That's it. I'm starting to go crazy. Oh, great, this is all I need. To just go nuts in hell. Walking around here not having a sense of anything or anyone, especially myself. Just yammering on and on in my own brain about time and hearing all of this ticking. For all I know, I'm saying all this shit out loud right now. For all I know, I'm screaming all of this ramble rubble at the top of my lungs and everyone can hear it, and everyone's laughing and thanking the heavens they're not me.*

He thought more about his time on the rack. Man, was it awful. Not only was it pain beyond all measure, but to make things worse the demon that stretched him kept calling him *fat boy.*

"No amount of stretching is too much for you, fat boy."

"You might get longer but you'll never be thinner, fat boy."

"Better not stand too close to you so you don't try and eat me, fat boy."

I'm not fat, thought Z. *In fact, I'm one of the skinniest people here. If I were fat, I actually wouldn't mind so much being called* fat boy. *I get it that it would be a really effective way to emotionally torture me while they were physically torturing me. But I'm not fat, so more than offending me it's just annoying. Frankly, I think it's pretty lazy. Talk about zero creativity. A rack and fat jokes? What does it take to be a demon here?*

Then all of a sudden Z's thoughts were interrupted as he felt something licking his leg. He jumped, because who wouldn't. He looked down and staring up at him was the absolute cutest dog he had ever seen. He couldn't tell what breed it was. It was about forty-five pounds, and it looked like a combination of every dog that had ever existed.

Needless to say, this "every dog" immediately brightened Z's mood.

Z couldn't help but say hello.

"Hello there. I gotta tell you, you're the cutest dog I've ever seen."

And even though the dog couldn't get any cuter, it did. Why? Because it spoke.

"Thank you so much."

Wow, thought Z. *As cute as this dog is, its voice is even cuter.*

Much like the dog's look was a combination of every dog, so was its voice the combination of every cute voice that ever was. It was the voice of a thousand of the cutest children of all cultures.

Z couldn't handle it. He wanted to hold it, squeeze it, and never let go.

Z bent down and gave the dog a great big hug.

The dog smiled. "That was a great hug. Thank you."

"Oh, it's my pleasure," replied Z. "I could hug you all day. I could make my job hugging you."

"Oh, really?" said the dog. "Well, in that case, you're hired."

"Wow. Best job I've ever had. You better believe that now I've punched in, I'm never punching out."

This was wild. Z had never said such corny things before. But, at the same time, his corny words didn't feel corny at all. They felt like the clearest, most untainted expression of joy. The dog had unlocked something in him he had never experienced before. He felt like he would never be sad again. Everything made complete sense. Even awful things felt inspiring and beautiful.

Z started to cry. The dog licked Z's tears. "Why are you crying? Did I do something to make you sad?"

Z stroked the dog's chest. "On the contrary. You've done the opposite. I've never felt so good. These are happy tears. And I've had happy tears before, but never like this. These tears are like a joy waterfall. Does that sound dumb?"

"Of course not." The dog laughed. "A joy waterfall. I love that. I love it so much I want to play in it."

The dog then started to dance under Z's tear-flowing face. He ran in and out of the falling tears, all the while ecstatically screaming, "I'm a rain dancer! I'm a rain doggy dancer!"

Watching the dog dance like this in his happy tears only made Z cry more, and more, and even more until he was up to his knees in his own saline. Z's tears reminded him of the tears God shed before they sent to hell. But Z's tears were different from God's. God's crying had almost made crying seem evil and selfish. He still couldn't believe what an insecure mess

God was. But, again, Z's tears were different. Z's tears were an expression of something that in life he'd never allowed himself to express. Z's tears made him feel that he was connected to everything that was beautiful. And Z was grateful. Grateful that his whole association with crying was being redeemed. And this gratitude made him cry even more. The water was now up to his waist, and the dog started to swim. And not just doggy-paddle. Breaststroke! Backstroke! The whole nine yards of classic swim forms. The dog was an expert swimmer.

"Come with me! Come with me!" said the dog as he swam from Z. Z did what his new best friend commanded and followed the adorable pooch to higher ground. And from this point he and the dog watched as, from the bright blue pool of tears, the most beautiful and majestic bright blue whale emerged.

The whale towered over them. It was so enormous that at first Z was a little scared, but when he saw the look of joy on the dog's face, he knew the whale was a friend, too, and as it stood tall before them, the whale started to sing. It sang with a voice so operatically beautiful, it could end all wars. The whale sang and sang, and Z and the dog marveled as they embraced. Then as it finished its singing, the whale gave the two new best friends little kisses on the tips of their noses. And with that, it sang one final perfect note as it sank slowly back into the lake of Z's happy tears. The tears then drained and the ground that had once been black with soot now shined with gold. Gold that lit up Z and the dog's faces, turning them both into the cutest little rays of sunshine.

Z hugged the dog again. The dog gave Z a big lick on the cheek.

"Feel better?" asked the dog.

"So much better. The best better ever!" Z exclaimed.

The dog then sat down on its hind legs and gave Z the most loving look Z had ever received.

"That's good," said the dog. "I'm glad you don't feel so distraught anymore. Now, do me a favor. Can you do me a favor?"

"For you? Anything," said Z. "What is it?"

"I want you to remember this moment. I want you to remember me always. Because from this day forward, you will never see me again, and no one will ever again make you feel like I made you feel today. But at least you got this, right? Most people don't even get this. You're lucky. He likes you."

With that, the dog stood back up on all fours and walked away.

Z's whole body then crumpled down onto the hellish cold gravel. He couldn't move. He couldn't move for what felt like two years. Or was it twenty?

26

Choose Your Own Adventure

 took a walk through hell.

As he walked, he suddenly noticed that, actually, hell wasn't all that fiery. Sure, there was fire, but Z had always pictured that *everything* would be on fire in hell. Like even when you took a sip of coffee, the cup would be covered in fire, and the coffee would be liquid fire, and as you held the cup your hand would be set ablaze, and as you drank it you yourself would just become a roaring fireball. But it wasn't like that. It looked more like a desolate back-alley scene from the movies dotted with trash-can fires. The type of movie trash-can fires the homeless characters would gather around and talk about their woes, or laugh, or argue, or sing. Hell didn't have trash-can fires but it did have its "fire pits," and instead of homeless people gathered around, there was usually a demon or two, along with the occasional famous evil person (on this particular day Z had thought he spotted Mussolini). Z steered clear of these pits. He feared they might be some false facade for some sort of torture trap. A decoy of an entrance into a kind of "choose your own adventure" type of punishment. It was easy to think of hell as some big menacing game show. Behind every fire pit there could be some sort of prize. In this case, the prize was a uniquely perverse and creative type of suffering for at least a thousand years. Maybe you'd be standing around the fire pit, and you'd be talking about your favorite albums with the Son of Sam, and then the next thing you knew, you'd be hog-tied, laid across the edge of a giant razor blade, long-ways, and slowly be split in half. Or maybe you'd be comparing recipes for the perfect fried chicken with Christopher Columbus, then you'd blink and find yourself being slowly digested by a giant replica of your own penis.

So Z just walked. He wouldn't take the risk of being tricked. But the trouble with walking was it always got his mind racing. And Z's mind started to race through his life. He thought about a lot of things, but mostly he thought of where he went wrong and where he could have gone right but didn't, which was just another way of going wrong. So really all he was thinking about was where his life went wrong.

He thought about what a pig he had been to the women in his life, while simultaneously regretting not being more of a pig. He'd always thought that sex was one of the main reasons to go on living, and now that he was in hell, there didn't seem to be any possibility of that in sight. But there wasn't really any promise of fucking in heaven, either. Then on the other hand, he never really had the desire to have sex when he was in heaven. Sure, he wasn't there long, but he really never thought about it. Why was there no sex in heaven? Holy shit. Was sex actually a sin after all?

Of course, it might depend on the type of sex. Using someone for sex could be a sin. Sure, he did do that, but he was also used. Using himself for sex could be a sin. It was all about disconnection at the end of the day, right? Maybe disconnection in general was a sin. Maybe in heaven he was connected to himself. And that connection sapped him of his sexual desires, because so many of those desires were built on disconnection. Not that Z was sexually problematic, really. His sexual partners were probably not so aware of his disconnection. At the very least they didn't feel any type of insidiousness. No, Z's disconnection simply caused him to "check out" of relationships. To slowly devolve into a self-absorbed bubble of inaction. Someone thoroughly uninspiring to be around. And who wants to fuck someone like that? Lucky for Z . . . many, actually.

Or rather, unlucky for Z. He could have lived more of a life of love. He would have liked for at least one of his relationships to have a real connection. He would have liked a long stint of allowing himself to really care for someone and really be cared for. But he couldn't. He had no emotional road map. He couldn't decipher what was real or unreal inside of him. He just didn't know himself, so how could he know love?

Jesus Christ, thought Z. *I gotta stop this. This is so depressing. Was it really this bad? I mean, I was married three times. Surely there were moments of love there. Surely my marriages ending wasn't all my doing. Surely they had a part in it, too. Surely some of it was just the nature of relationships.*

But Z couldn't help but keep thinking it was all his fault. He had no love for others and he had no love for himself. He belonged in hell. As he continued this violent self-abuse he came across yet another fire pit. Standing there was a slightly overweight, slightly balding man around his age, wearing a soiled silk kimono. The kimono, despite being filthy, was very expensive. Z recognized the man. OH MY GOD. That was Jackie Cohen. At one point he had been Z's favorite comedian. Z watched everything he did. That was, until the multiple cancellations.

Surrounding Jackie was the largest group of demons Z had yet witnessed around a fire pit, and Jackie's hands gripped his chest hair, seemingly on the verge of tearing it out, as the demons laughed heartily. Z got a little closer. He assumed Jackie was performing some sort of classic routine. But he wasn't.

"There's just no way. No way none of you know who the fuck I am. I know you've been down here, and you probably don't watch too many movies, but still, I was an international treasure! I gotta be in at least two of your favorite movies of all time."

A demon shrugged its shoulders. "Sorry, never heard of you."

The response drove Jackie insane. "You gotta be kidding me! I was the funniest man alive! My movies meant something to people. I meant something to people. I mean, sure, people forgot about me. But everyone gets forgotten about at some point, right?"

The demons just continued to shrug their shoulders and laugh as Jackie finally succeeded in tearing out two enormous tufts of chest hair (plus some sizable chunks of bloody skin), which made the demons laugh even harder.

Z stood there disappointed. *Jesus, Jackie . . .* , he thought. *Why not just let it go? So the demons don't know who you are. Who cares. They're demons. They don't watch movies. And even if they did, why would you even want demons as fans? What, when you were alive did you go looking for fans at Klan rallies? Probably not. So why this now?*

Z wanted to say this thought out loud. But he didn't. Z just walked on. He didn't want to get anywhere near something so pathetic. He walked for another long while where he didn't see much except an occasional lone demon. Each of the demons waved to him. And each wave from each lone demon was exactly the same. Z wondered if the identical waves were a coincidence or if all the demons had privately agreed to wave in the same exact way. Needless to say, Z waved back. No matter how rude Z could be, he always made it a point to return a wave. But that was it. Just a wave, and then he walked away quickly.

Z then came upon a scene that really caught his eye. It was an older woman who looked very much like his mother. But it wasn't his mother, thank God. The woman was seated at a table that had been placed next to one of the pits. And sitting with her was what looked like an actor from the 1800s. He wore a woolen overcoat. In one hand he held a smoking old pistol as he and the woman ate what looked like plates of shit. The meal seemed incredibly awkward. The woman in particular did not look like she wanted to be there. And as Z passed he was able to overhear a snippet of their conversation.

"Iris, please, I know you're angry with me, but does that mean that we just have to sit in silence like this?" asked the man.

The woman's face grew purple. "You know, Mr. Booth—"

"Please, call me John," interrupted the southern gentleman.

"John, I've never said this type of thing to anyone, because I pride myself on my politeness, but can you please go fuck yourself."

As Z walked on, he wondered what the man had done to the woman. *We are all so hurtful if we let ourselves be*, thought Z. Then not before too long Z came upon a sight that made him the saddest he had been in a long time. It was surely the saddest thing he had seen since he had arrived in hell. Most things had been horrific, but not downright sad like this. There was a demon standing at the fire pit, but that wasn't the sad part. It was that next to the demon stood a child. A little boy. *How could a child be in hell?* thought Z.

Z walked up without saying hello. It was best to always let the other have the first word in hell. Didn't want your own words used against you. If he was alive he would have warmed his hands at the fire. But here, at least in this wing of hell, it was quite warm, so he didn't have to. The demon stared ahead smiling, but the boy had tears in his eyes. He looked at Z, quite relieved that he was there.

"Hi, I'm Abraham," he muttered. He was trying not to fully break down. He almost sucked in his words as he said them.

"Hi," replied Z. Z felt so bad for the boy, and he couldn't help but connect to the boy's sadness, even though it was the last thing he wanted to do. It was all too much.

The boy pointed at the demon. "This one is really driving me crazy today," said the boy.

"And why is that?" asked Z. The demon still said nothing. It simply stared with a gruesome, self-satisfied smile.

"Well, I'm usually put in another room when I'm here. And there's a lot more of them, but today this one brought me here.

Which is actually better. It's a lot less scary. But it's still terrible, because he keeps repeating the same thing and I can't get him to stop. Usually I can, but today it's hard."

With this the demon spoke. "That's right, Abey. Today I got you locked in, don't I?!" It then laughed maniacally.

Z was disgusted. "Come on. He's a kid, for Christ's sake."

Abraham put his hand up. "You're wasting your time."

"Why are you here, Abraham? How are you here? Surely you couldn't have done something so bad before you died."

Abraham wiped his nose. "See, that's the real kicker. I don't even live down here. I'm still alive."

Z was confused. "Wait. You're still alive?"

The boy nodded his head. "I come down here 'cause all day long these guys put horrible thoughts in my head that I can't shake. It's actually easier to deal with them if I'm here. I can see them. They're too much of cowards to come up there, and just hearing their voices in my head is actually more stressful."

This stopped the demon from smiling. "Cowards?!" it snarled. "We're not cowards. You know we're not allowed up there. You know we don't make the rules, you little asshole. No wonder no one loves you and no one will ever love you."

"See?!" pointed out the boy. "They've been saying that to me all day. And they've said it before. Many, many times. But today it's hitting me real hard. I got lied to yesterday. My friend Dan Hurwitz canceled our plans last minute. And when I asked him why, all he said was he didn't feel like it. So I guess he's not my friend. Anyway, these jerk demons just love it, 'cause when that stuff happens, it makes me weak."

"You are weak," replied the demon. "You get weaker every day."

Z really pitied this boy. He pitied him more than he had ever pitied anyone. Even himself. And Z was a professional at feeling sorry for himself. He wanted to help the boy. And maybe in helping him it would give his whole existence in hell more fulfillment. "Look, kid, I'm sure you're loved. I'm sure your parents love you and I'm sure you have friends that are better than that Dan Hurwitz. This guy right here is just kicking you when you're down. It's okay to be scared of being alone. I just was thinking about this exact thing before I came over here."

The boy looked at Z with hope. "You were?"

"Sure. I mean in a different way, but yeah. I was just doing to myself what this demon is doing to you."

"What were you doing?" asked the boy.

"Well, I can't get too into it, because it involves some adult stuff. But I was basically thinking that maybe I had never loved or been loved. That I had never truly been me. And if I wasn't me, then I couldn't have any real feelings. And that means I had a loveless life. But I'm dead. I'm not alive like you. You can fix all of this."

The boy looked down at the ground, contemplating this. "I am still alive, aren't I? I got time to love. I got time to know how to do that."

Z put his hand on the boy's shoulder. "You sure do."

With this, the boy looked into Z's eyes. "But you don't. It's too late for you. I'm so sorry."

Z gave the boy's shoulder another pat. "Oh, that's okay. Hey, maybe I can learn to love down here."

With this, the boy's eyes welled up with tears. "Oh, I'm sorry. I'm so sorry. But no . . . you won't. You never will."

A freezing shiver went down Z's spine as the boy looked at the demon.

"Can I go now? I did what you asked me."

Z was confused. He looked at the demon. "What's going on here?"

The demon ignored Z's question and looked at the boy. "Yes, you can go."

The boy pointed at the demon. "So it's a deal. You got him, and now you can't bother me for a week."

The demon pointed back. "I thought we said five days."

The boy got in the demon's face. "The deal was for a week."

The demon smiled. "Fine. A week it is." And with this the demon bit off a piece of its own finger. Then he held it over the boy's face. The boy then opened his mouth as the demon dripped three dark drops of blood in.

Z watched this transaction, frozen. Not just from fear. Z literally couldn't move. The boy then looked straight into his eyes again.

"I'm so sorry. I just need to give my brain a rest."

And with this the boy disappeared, and now it was clear that Z's not moving was certainly not psychosomatic. It was the demon, who then took a step toward Z as its burning breath shot up Z's nostrils.

"So nice of the boy to loan you his room for the week."

The demon leaned closer, his breath even hotter. Burning Z's whole face, as Z clenched his eyes in pain, and when he opened them he found himself in a whole other place. A gigantic room of fire that surrounded Z as he sat in an ornate chair of steel and wood. And from the fire danced what seemed like an army of demons, and from their ranks rose a demon that didn't quite look like the rest. Instead of two horns, this demon only had one very large horn, and as the demons danced and laughed, the Demon King sang in a horrific falsetto.

"You never loved, and you never were loved."

And as the demons danced, and the Demon King sang, and Z's throat bled from screaming, Satan sat in his living room watching the whole thing play on his flat-screen.

"If only he knew that everyone down here is just as insecure as God. He'd be runnin' this fuckin' place."

With this his phone rang, and Satan had to answer.

"Yes, God?" he asked.

God's voice sounded quite enraged. "What the fuck did you just say?"

Satan gave a sigh. "Nothing. Sorry about that."

27.
The Writer

 found himself in a familiar room.

Like most rooms he wound up in when he was in hell, Z had no idea how he had gotten in this room. It was one of Satan's tricks. You would almost teleport from one room or space to the next without warning. People took for granted just how important entrances and exits were. Just appearing and having no idea where you came from was one of the most unsettling things that could happen to a person. And this had happened several times to Z since he had arrived in hell. And it didn't matter how many times it had already happened, or how many times it would happen after this . . . Z knew he would never get used to it. But that made sense. If one got used to hell, then hell wouldn't be hell now, would it?

The room resembled a dark dystopian government office. Small and closed in. There was a familiarity even though it didn't look like a room that Z had ever been in before. It didn't look familiar but it had a familiar feeling. An all-too-memorable sense of deep failure. A feeling of being completely stuck. Repetitive days. A staleness.

The room's walls were lined with filing cabinets that busted at the seams. There were about ten clocks in the room. Only one of which worked, and it barely worked. The second hand barely moved, and when it did it was like it was coughing its final breaths. The last efforts of a dying organism. The room was cluttered with books and papers, but when Z looked at these closely, everything that was written on them was nonsensical. Jibber-jabber. Unrelated letters, numbers, and symbols.

Pity, thought Z. *Would have been nice to read something for a change. Even if it was terrible.*

But maybe it was Z's eyes. His eyes were still unadjusted to the room. It took a minute after these spontaneous entrances. Z rubbed them, and the dim office lamp became more of a reliable light source for him, and as Z's eyes adjusted he could make out a figure in the corner, which was accompanied by the sound of furious typing.

"Fucking shit," muttered the shadowed figure as they lowered their head to the desk and started breathing deeply. Almost as if they were trying to force themself to sleep. Z didn't know what to say. He felt awkward. It was clear this person was very much focused on what they were doing and was also deeply frustrated. Z didn't know much about the artistic process but he knew enough to know that it wasn't the best idea to interrupt someone as they were struggling to express themselves.

Well, they were most likely a writer. I mean, there was a chance they weren't. They could be some sort of office specter typing up meaningless reports on meaningless things. But the way that this person was upset there was no way they were not fully invested in what they were doing. So if they weren't engaged in some sort of artistic endeavor, they might as well be. Z didn't want to interrupt, but he didn't have to, for the "writer" raised their head and, without looking at Z, addressed him.

"Hi."

Z was thrown. Z suddenly felt as if he was expected to be there.

"Hi there," Z said, and then started to introduce himself. "I'm—"

With this, the writer raised his hand. "Yeah, save it. I know who you are."

Z was intrigued. "You do?"

With this, the writer gave a laugh. "Yeah. I'd say I know you pretty well."

Z cocked his head. "You do?"

The writer exhaled, like he had had this conversation with Z many times before. "Yeah."

Z leaned in. "Have we met before?"

With this, the writer leaned back in his chair. "In a way, yes."

Z leaned farther forward. "What do you mean, in a way?"

The writer diverted his eyes from Z in contemplation. There was a hesitancy in his face coupled with a great need to tell Z what was swimming around in his head. His hands rubbed his thighs and he closed his eyes to search for the decision he should make. Z could see the writer's eyes frantically shifting underneath his lids. There was clearly an inner push and pull going on between at least two options of what the writer wanted to say next. His closed eyes twitched faster and faster and right at the point that it seemed like his eyes were going to bust out of their sockets, they opened and the writer smiled.

"Wanna smoke some weed? I need some weed."

Z was taken aback. Did people smoke weed in hell? Was that a thing? Z hadn't seen it, but if this writer was offering him some, it must be a thing. Z hadn't smoked weed in a while. Besides how much time had passed in heaven and hell, the last time Z had had some weed was about twelve years before he died. He used to love it. But at one point it had taken a turn. What at one time had provided him with relaxed inspiration or a childlike disposition had devolved into the worst type of anxiety. Amplifying thoughts that had no business being given the importance and volume they were given. Those thoughts that were the heckling asshole in the back of the theatre, and weed gave them a microphone. But hey, why not. This would be a new experience, and maybe in hell it would have the opposite effect. Maybe it would make hell just a little bit better.

"Yeah, thanks, I'd love some," replied Z. With this, the writer picked up the phone on his desk—a landline, no less—and made a call.

Five minutes later a young man, roughly fifteen years old, walked in. He was wearing baggy patchwork corduroy pants and an extra-large green hoodie with a picture of Bob Marley's face on it. The teen seemed not affected at all with the fact that he was in hell. Z was amazed by this. Even if people weren't screaming, everyone you came across down here had some sort of energy to them that reflected the utter hugeness of the situation they were in. But this boy, he could have been anywhere. This was all old hat to him. He sat down next to Z and opened his backpack.

"This is Mendel," said the writer.

Z looked at Mendel. "Nice to meet you."

Mendel shook Z's hand. "Yeah, you, too." Mendel then looked back at the writer. "What is it this time?"

The writer leaned back in his chair. "What have you got?"

With this Mendel's face grew red. "You know what I've got."

The writer laughed uncomfortably. "Okay, okay, point taken. How about give me a half ounce of Satan's pubes." The writer looked at Z and smiled. "It's the name of the strain. Pretty great, right?"

Z did not think it was great. Not just because it was the lamest name for a marijuana strain he had ever heard, but it also made him think of Satan. And Z still could not think of Satan without deeply longing for him.

Mendel shook his head. "It's always Satan's pubes."

The writer laughed, more comfortably this time. "Why would it be anything else?"

Mendel gave Z a look. "Hope this dick doesn't want to smoke with you. Take it from me. Big mistake."

The writer snapped his fingers. "All right, Mr. I Know So Much, just give me the fucking weed."

Mendel whipped out a glass jar that held neon-green marijuana. He handed it to the writer, who then opened the jar and smelled it. The jar might as well have been opened right under Z's nose, because the skunk-like scent was so strong he felt the odor sting the inside of the back of his skull. The writer then handed Mendel a small roll of cash. But as soon as Mendel touched the money it turned into dust. Mendel shook his head. This whole sequence had obviously occurred many times before. Mendel then zipped up his backpack, stood up, and made for the door.

"I'll see you later," he said to the writer without looking at him. He did look at Z, though. Right before he walked through the door that Z may or may not have used, Mendel turned toward Z. "Nice meeting you, man." With that he walked out. His departure was immediately followed by the sounds of bloodcurdling screams. Z couldn't tell if those were Mendel's or somebody else's.

The writer then promptly rolled a joint quickly and lit it up.

"This is the best shit you'll ever smoke. Here, let me show you." The writer put the joint to his lips and when he exhaled, the cloud of smoke formed a realistic depiction of a baby's head. Before the smoke separated the baby head gave a horrifying wail. The writer laughed heartily.

"How about that, huh? I told you this is some good shit." The crying baby's head was not an incentive as far as Z was concerned, and he declined the offer. The writer shrugged as he took another hit.

"Suit yourself. But for me, this is the only thing that gets me by down here."

Z leaned back. "What did you mean before?"

"What do you mean what did I mean?" asked the writer as he coughed.

"You said that you knew me . . . in a way," Z replied.

"Oh, that. Yeah. Well, you see . . . I'm a writer," said the writer

"I figured," said Z.

"I know you figured." The writer grinned. "I know everything you figure. I know everything about you."

Z readied himself to run. He could feel there was something bad brewing.

"What are you talking about?" asked Z.

The writer then learned forward. "I created you."

Z had no patience for this. Absolutely no bandwidth for anyone's psychotic delusional ego-tripping. Z got up and made his way to the door.

"Hey, where you going?" the writer exclaimed, shooting out of his chair.

Z turned toward him. "It's just . . . Come on, man. I know where this is going. It's all a little obvious. You're a writer. You created me. I get it. I don't really exist. I'm just a figment of your imagination. You've written every experience I've ever had, including this one. You've written my whole experience including now. Huh. It's just some real low-budget lying, bro. What do you think, I just got to hell? I'm just going to believe what some random writer is telling me? Ooooooh, what's that on your laptop, huh? I bet it's everything we're saying to each other right now, right? Gimme a break."

"No, what's happening now I actually wrote last Thursday. Took me a hot minute, actually. I'm really stuck on you. To be honest I don't find you incredibly interesting. For a second I thought I might scrap you altogether."

Z nodded. "Yeah, yeah, yeah. I get it. This is all you. Me, that weed-dealing teenager. God, the devil, heaven, hell."

The writer held up his hand. "No, you got that wrong. Yes, I created you, and the teenager, and pretty much everyone else you've met, but not God or the Devil. And not heaven or hell. That's all real. I just wrote us meeting because, well, to be frank, I needed the company.

"Here." The writer handed Z his laptop. "You know what, you had a good idea. You should read my laptop. Here, check it out.

Let's nip your disbelief in the bud. I can't tell you how tired I am of doing dances for people, let alone people I created. Just read and you'll see and then maybe we can have a real discussion."

Z reluctantly took the writer's laptop and started to read. Sure enough, everything that had happened in his life and since his death was written down, to the word. He jumped and shoved the laptop back into the writer's hands.

"So I'm your creation?" Z asked, wiping a mess of new sweat from his brow.

"Yeah, yeah, you are. I've been writing you for God knows how long. Well, God does know, and so does Satan, but I sure don't. I have no fucking idea how long I've been sitting here writing this fucking thing."

Z didn't know what to do. He still wasn't completely convinced. It could all be a trick. Hell didn't adhere to the rules of logic. The "story" he just read could have magically appeared right after it happened. What if this writer was a demon, because if he was, he could have just cast a spell on the computer to make it type everything they did as they did it. But deep down Z believed what the writer was saying. And every torturing entity he had come across in hell did not have the same constitution as this writer. They did not have the type of stress that this writer did. They did not themselves seem to be tortured. This writer seemed like one of the most stressed-out people he had ever met. Z could tell that the writer not only easily gave in to anxiety and depression, but very likely thrived on it. Really, the only thing he could really do at this point was play along and see what was what.

"Well, if you're my creator, but you're not God or Satan, who are you? How does this work? Why are you here? Why are you creating me?"

"Don't you see? You're my punishment. This fucking book that you're a character in is my hell. You see, just like you, I was all geared up to go to heaven, but, just like you, God didn't like me."

"Did you tell God they were insecure, too?"

The writer laughed. "No, I'm being punished for a different kind of arrogance. There's a lot of artistic types down here, actually, and we're all being punished for thinking that all of . . . this . . ."—as he said "this," he lifted up his laptop and shook it— ". . . this . . . all of this . . . for stupidly thinking that this can do anything. I thought that what I do might make the world a better place, but God wasn't cool with that. In God's mind only they can do that, and apparently, and I wish I knew this sooner, but apparently that's a true fuck-you to all that is holy. So I'm here, and I gotta write this book for the rest of eternity."

"What's the book about, then?" asked Z.

"You know, if anyone else asked me that, I'd be so annoyed, but I wrote you asking me this, so obviously I'm not annoyed. So what's the book about? Essentially it's about you and four other characters and you're all fucking nuts. I describe the book as a comet of deep Jewish anxiety. You're the soul. Then there's a child, a teenager—that's Mendel, who you just met—a guy in his forties who's a famous comedian, and an incredibly lonely older woman. And the stories themselves basically are all these random slices of your lives. With some of the stories they're not even necessarily stories. Really, all of the characters are different extreme versions of me. There's a little autobiography in there, but it's not really about that. You're really all just different takes on the darkest parts of my personality. And a lot of it is funny. At least I hope it is."

Z had had enough. Whether this was real or not, the book sounded terrible. He also had no interest in spending any more time with this writer. Liar or not, he was clearly a narcissist. If it was true, Z was glad. Glad God would punish someone so arrogant. And in this gladness he started to understand his own punishment. He had had a real lack of understanding of things. A real know-it-all attitude about something he didn't know anything about, and instead of just taking cues and allowing himself to be the new guy in heaven, he'd exerted his false sense of superiority. Maybe what God was teaching him was that humans were just supposed to be humans. Not question so much. Be animals with just a little more know-how, and stay in your lane and not ever think you can contend with things you don't understand. Maybe art was a test. Maybe ego was a test. Maybe most humans failed, and most belonged in hell.

Who knows, thought Z. *All I know is I've had enough. I'm tired of it all.* And with that, Z disappeared. No exit, just as there was no entrance, and . . .

I sat alone. Alone with my laptop in hell. Kicking myself. Knowing the only thing interesting about me was the fact that I was in hell. Everything else was just paper thin. My hell is my only interesting quality. So, I guess, thank God for that.

About the Author.

Brett Gelman is an acclaimed actor whose signature intensity and fearlessness enable him to navigate both comedy and drama. Brett's work can be seen on television in *Stranger Things*, *Fleabag*, *Love*, *Curb Your Enthusiasm*, *Twin Peaks: The Return*, and the Adult Swim special trilogy *Dinner with Friends with Brett Gelman and Friends*, and in films including *The Other Guys*, *Lemon*, *Without Remorse*, and *Lyle, Lyle, Crocodile*. *The Terrifying Realm of the Possible* is his first book.